NOW WE ARE HERE

Now We Are Here

Family Migration, Children's Education, and Dreams for a Better Life

GABRIELLE OLIVEIRA

STANFORD UNIVERSITY PRESS
Stanford, California

Stanford University Press
Stanford, California

© 2025 by Gabrielle Oliveira. All rights reserved.

No part of this book may be reproduced or transmitted in any form or by any means, electronic or mechanical, including photocopying and recording, or in any information storage or retrieval system, without the prior written permission of Stanford University Press.

Library of Congress Cataloging-in-Publication Data
Names: Oliveira, Gabrielle, author.
Title: Now we are here : family migration, children's education, and dreams for a better life / Gabrielle Oliveira.
Description: Stanford, California : Stanford University Press, 2025. | Includes bibliographical references and index.
Identifiers: LCCN 2025010748 (print) | LCCN 2025010749 (ebook) | ISBN 9781503638297 (cloth) | ISBN 9781503644540 (paperback) | ISBN 9781503644557 (ebook)
Subjects: LCSH: Immigrant children—Education—United States. | Teenage immigrants—Education—United States. | Immigrant families—United States. | Immigrants—United States—Social conditions. | COVID-19 Pandemic, 2020-2023—Social aspects—United States. | United States—Emigration and immigration—Social aspects. | Latin America—Emigration and immigration—Social aspects.
Classification: LCC LC3731 .O44 2025 (print) | LCC LC3731 (ebook) | DDC 371.826/9120973—dc23/eng/20250410
LC record available at https://lccn.loc.gov/2025010748
LC ebook record available at https://lccn.loc.gov/2025010749

Cover design and illustrations: Jason Anscomb
Cover photograph: Unsplash/Ryan Loughlin

The authorized representative in the EU for product safety and compliance is: Mare Nostrum Group B.V. | Mauritskade 21D | 1091 GC Amsterdam | The Netherlands | Email address: gpsr@mare-nostrum.co.uk | KVK chamber of commerce number: 96249943

CONTENTS

Acknowledgments		vii
Note on Terms		xi
	Introduction	1
1	Parental Migration and the Promise of an Education	31
2	Im/migrant Children's Embodied Narratives of Immigration	57
3	Pedagogies of Silence	83
4	COVID-19 and the Breakdown of Care and Schooling	118
5	Lost and Found	157
	Conclusion	177
	Appendix: Historical Antecedents	189
	Appendix: Notes on Methods	195
	References	203
	Index	229

ACKNOWLEDGMENTS

I would like to express my deepest gratitude to every family, every parent, every child, every teacher, and every educator who allowed me into their life. I always say that what you read in books is only the result of who agreed to speak to the author. I feel a great sense of gratitude (and luck?) that, for one reason or another, parents, children, and youth talked to me. I am forever in awe of your strength, your resistance, and your care. Even in the most vulnerable times you allowed me to spend time with your families and learn from you. Thank you for allowing me the privilege of a window into your lives. To the children and youth, I learned so much from you. Listening to your words, reading your writings, and appreciating your drawings have taught me so much about agency and power. Parents, I am so grateful you trusted my presence in your homes and lives and shared so much wisdom with me. I am so profoundly grateful to the educators in this research. They are heroes that care so deeply about the children and youth. There are many people in the U.S. who also helped me meet the amazing participants in this research. I have to keep their names confidential, but I want to say that without your trust, none of this would have happened. The nongovernmental organizations, churches, after-school programs, and community organizers have worked so hard to support migrant families, and I am thankful you supported my work as well. The invisible work of care is ever present in this work. Doing this work has been my greatest honor. Gracias! Obrigada! Thank you.

This book began when I started my work in Massachusetts in 2017. I am indebted to so many students (at the time) who supported my work. Mariana Lima Becker, Chris Bacon-Chang, Eunhye Flavin, Olivia Barbieri, Ginny Alex, Marisa Segel, Haylea Hubacz, and Ahrum Jeon who were part of a dream team at Boston College that I will forever miss. Corinne Kentor at Teachers College was an incredible research assistant who provided me with endless knowledge and sources for the book. Carolina Lindquist at Harvard read the book cover to cover and supported the efforts. Ben Blanco at the Harvard Graduate School of Education helped me straighten out my numbers and tables. Maricruz Vargas always checked in and provided me with great conversations about the work. I have been very lucky.

I am thankful to the National Academy of Education/Spencer Foundation for the support they gave me in funding this research as a postdoctoral fellow. They believed in me when they funded my PhD research back in 2013 and then gave me another shot for funding for what became this book in 2019. I was also lucky to work with brilliant, generous mentors through the fellowship: Ofelia Garcia, Guadalupe Valdéz, and Sarah Dryden-Peterson. Thank you for taking a chance on me and allowing me time to work on this research. At Boston College, Marilyn Cochran-Smith, Patrick Proctor, Maureen Kenny, and Larry Ludlow reviewed my initial proposal and gave me influential feedback. At Boston College I am also so grateful to Stanton Wortham, Brinton Lykes, Rebecca Lowenhaupt, and Ana Martinez Alemán who provided letters of support and powerful inspiration for the work.

At the Harvard Graduate School of Education, I am so grateful for colleagues who listened to me present on this research or read parts of the book and gave valuable feedback. Thank you to my mentors Paola Uccelli and Nonie Lesoux for holding my hand and providing expert guidance at every step of the way. To my colleagues who supported me with kindness and wisdom Adriana Umaña-Taylor, Meredith Rowe, Ebony Bridwell-Mitchell, Paul Harris, Meira Levinson, Bridget Terry Long, Catherine Snow, Jal Mehta, Jarvis Givens, Andrew Ho, Jimmy Kim, Marty West, Nancy Hill, and Monica Higgins—thank you. At Harvard I am thankful to Marcia Castro, Mary Waters, Jesse Hoffnung-Garskof, Danny Schneider, Bruno Carvalho, and Dalia Showalter for being motivators and sounding boards at different times and challenging me to rethink my work. Heartfelt special thank you to Carola Suárez-Orozco and Sarah Dryden-Peterson's brilliant generous minds that helped me shape my argument and provided avenues and questions for me to pursue. Bianca

Baldridge—my bright role model—read through feedback and reassured me that things were going to work out. In her words, "we have to bet on ourselves." Thank you. Thank you to my fabulous faculty coordinator fairy godmother Ela Sikorska for keeping me organized. The Institutional Review Boards at both Harvard and Boston College worked with me so I could do this work, and for that I am so grateful.

Some of my favorite scholars offered their generous time to help me think through the book. Roberto Gonzales, Jason De León, and Annette Lareau provided me with powerful insights that I will be forever thankful for. Alysha Gálvez has been a constant inspiration and source of support. Thea Abu El-Haj, Denise Brennan, Marjorie Orellana, Inma Garcia Sánchez, Ariana Mangual Figueroa, Andrea Dyrness, Ameena Ghaffar-Kucher, Marcelo Suárez-Orozco and Gerald Campano probably have no idea how much their support, their words of encouragement, and their scholarship have shaped my own.

I have had the best support group in my academic/friend community. These friends guaranteed my well-being throughout this journey. I have had the greatest support from my dear friends Jon Wargo and Andrés Castro Samayoa. To the powerful women who have offered me unlimited care and strength, Sarah Gallo, Michelle Bellino, Elizabeth Bonawitz, Nadine Gaab, Dana Mccoy, Soledad Vázquez, Emily Gates, Jessica Pesce, Cassie Brownell, Betty Lai, Sarah Bruhn, Gretchen Brion-Meisels, Becca Miller, Tolani Britton, and Aaliyah El-Amin—thank you. I am so grateful for a crew of friends who always cheered me on, Travis Bristol, Scott Freeman, Doug Mosher, and Tony Jack. At the Radcliffe Institute I am grateful to Sarah Vaughn, Jessica Vaughn, Yxta Murray, Paulo Fontes, Jimena Codina, and Lisa A. Crooms Robinson for helping me get to the finish line.

I also write this book in memory of my dear friend Valentina Glockner who truly gave me a start on my research with children and will forever be an inspiration.

I am profoundly grateful to Lesley Bartlett (once an advisor, always an advisor) who always, no matter where she was, came to the rescue. She read parts of the book, she read the feedback I got from reviewers, she helped me craft responses, and coached me through. I am forever grateful.

Thank you to my developmental and line editor, Bridgette Werner, who read every word of this book, suggested cuts, edits, corrected my verbs, and believed in the work from the beginning. To Rich Furman, academic coach extraordinaire, who served as therapist and tough love enforcer when I was having doubts. To Dylan Kyung-lim White, my editor at Stanford University Press, who held my hand throughout this process with patience and kindness and believed in the work through and through. I am grateful to all the folks at Stanford University Press—including Justine Sargent and Tiffany Mok, who provided support; Catherine Mallon, who copyedited; and Jason Anscomb, who designed the art for the cover. I have profound respect and gratitude to the anonymous reviewers who helped me strengthen the work.

I could not have written this book without the support of so many women. All my mom friends who helped me by picking up my kids, driving them places, helped me work, went on walks, and cheered me on—I am so grateful and lucky to live in this community. I have also had the professional help of Renata Ferreira and Renata Dias who looked after my kids and allowed me to travel, go to conferences, and present emerging work while being away from my children.

I am grateful to Mariana Oliva, Ana Sarkovas, Marina Mansur, and Roshan Shah for talking through big decisions and choices made along the way.

My family is everything to me. It is a love and care that know no borders. My in-laws—the Thomes—have been my cheerleaders and incredibly supportive of all my milestones and achievements. My sisters—Carol and Mica—have always supported me, cheered me on, and have seen the value of what I do. They have also insistently acted as my pseudo publicists. My parents, Blenda and Newton, are the reason I am able to do what I do. From the very beginning they supported my choices, talked to me about conundrums, decisions, work, where to live, what to do. They cheered through every piece of writing, every interview I gave, every opportunity I took. Even though we are thousands of miles away, through WhatsApp I am able to pick their brains instantly for anything I need. I do this work because I think I can contribute, even if it's a little bit, to bettering the lives of children and youth. To the children in my life—my beloved nieces, nephews, and godchildren—I do this for you.

The grand finale is dedicated to my husband, Alex, and my two kids, Jack and Noah. I am privileged to share my life with you. Alex is the most supportive partner anyone could ever have. He is relentless in his love and care. Not a word could have been written without his support. Jack and Noah are my reason to try to do good in the world. They bring me joy, balance, humility, and lots of hugs. As a parent I want nothing more than to give you both a good life.

NOTE ON TERMS

I primarily use the term *migrant* to describe families who have moved from their homes to the United States. The term refers more broadly to any person who moves from one place to another, either within a country or across international borders. The United Nations defines an international migrant as "any person who changes his or her country of usual residence" (United Nations, 1998). Migrants may move temporarily for reasons such as work, education, or family, without necessarily intending to settle permanently in the destination location. They do not necessarily obtain formal immigration status in the new place.

In the social sciences and related fields, *immigrant* often carries more long-term connotations of integration and adaptation to a new country/culture, while *migrant* can refer to more temporary or seasonal forms of mobility (Castles et al., 2014). Scholars caution that the terms are sometimes used interchangeably in practice, and intentions to stay permanently can change over time for individuals. The key distinction is usually viewed as permanence of residence versus temporariness (Bakewell, 2008).

Families in this study discussed their *permanence* in the U.S. as vulnerable, thus my choice to use *migrants*. At the same time, I use *immigrant* when speaking about policies, statuses, and communities, and when quoting any literature that engages with the term. All families in this study requested asylum from the U.S. government, thus I use *asylum seekers* at times as well. Families were *in waiting* in many ways. They were waiting for their court dates to find out if they might gain status and what kind, or if removal and deportation would be the outcome. Additionally, I refer to the families as Latin American or the specific nationality they self-identified with, but I only use Latinx/Latino/Latina/Latine when the literature refers to the population as such or if participants used the term to describe themselves.

NOW WE ARE HERE

Introduction

"I THINK PEOPLE DON'T UNDERSTAND how much we want to live," Adriana, a 15-year-old migrant youth from Brazil explained to me. "When people ask me: why did you come here? I tell them that's the wrong question. The right question is: do I have the right to have a good life, to dream?" As we sat at the cafeteria of Adriana's school in the U.S., she continued:

> If we were all equal, like we should be or like we are in the eyes of God, don't you think people would understand when someone leaves their home? Sometimes I feel like only the rich get to have a purpose and me and my family we have to explain and explain ourselves... wanting a good school, good education, having a chance... is that a crime? Quase tenho que pedir desculpas por estar aqui [I almost have to apologize for being here]. Well, here I am now... now we are here.

Adriana, along with her family, made their way from Brazil to the U.S.-Mexico border in 2018. They were detained together and released after almost two weeks. Upon their release they made their way to Massachusetts in the hope of forging a better life for themselves.

This book describes the lives of 16 migrant families from Latin America who experienced detention and/or separation at the border during 2018–2019, telling a story that interweaves parental sacrifice, children's and youth's articulations of embodied migration, teachers' understandings of the trauma experienced by these families, and the consequences of a global pandemic on already vulnerable families. The instability these children and parents faced in their homelands and during detention and/or separation was compounded by exposure to housing and food insecurity, unfamiliar and (at times) seemingly menacing environments, interrupted schooling, prejudice and discrimination, anxiety about the future, and the threat of illness. This is the story of how the promise of a good life, anchored by the constructed ideal of a *good* American education, underwrites the migratory decisions, trajectories, and experiences of families traveling from Brazil, El Salvador, Guatemala, and Honduras to live in the U.S.

Migrant families who were detained and/or separated at the border hold on to the promise of an education in the U.S. as a signifier of stability and prosperity for their children. While migrant families experience rupture, violence, fear, and uncertainty before they leave and during their journeys north, the idea of U.S. schooling represents, for parents and children alike, a safe and constant environment where opportunity lives. Books and articles have documented the economic push and pull factors that cause people to move; other work has analyzed the negative impacts of draconian immigration policies on larger education trends. *Now We Are Here* examines how migrant parents and children explain their pasts and their reasons for migrating, and how they center U.S. education in their narratives of their present and future.

The book asks: How have multiple disruptions—migration journeys, harsh border policies, a global pandemic—shaped the experiences of migrant children and their families in the U.S.? How did migrant parents and children experience education and schooling once they were settled in the U.S.? It also analyzes how teachers and schools responded to the knowledges migrant children and their families brought to school before and during the pandemic.

Every day, all over the world, families make one of the most difficult decisions of their lives: to leave their homes in search of a safer, better life. For migrant parents with children, education is a key motivator of migration. Migrant families leaving Brazil, El Salvador, Guatemala, and Honduras struggle with poverty, corruption, unemployment, and a lack of hope for the future. When the fear of staying outweighs the fear of fleeing, people leave. While migration flows are not new, in the last few decades immigration policies have become increasingly consequential to how migrant children experience life, come of age, and adapt in the U.S. Intimate stories of migrant families' sacrifices, motivations, and decision-making remain untold. For migrant families, dreams of a better life are closely related to the ability to provide their children with an education in a stable school environment. Based on three years of ethnographic research with 16 families from four countries in Latin America who crossed the border between 2018 and 2019—the height of extremely restrictive immigration policies like the zero-tolerance policy, commonly known as "family separation," and the Migrant Protection Protocols, commonly known as the "remain in Mexico policy"—*Now We Are Here* shows how the idealized chance for a better education in the U.S. counterbalanced the destabilizing effects of U.S. immigration policies and a global pandemic on migrant families.

Between 2018 and 2019, migrant families faced several challenges upon their arrival in the U.S. In addition to the strain imposed by hostile immigration policies at the U.S.-Mexico border, they faced numerous social and institutional pressures that impacted their ability to build secure lives. Families left behind structural violence, domestic violence, poverty, lack of educational opportunities, and unemployment, but also their beloved homelands. After going through separation and/or detention at the border and being reunified and/or released together, families encountered yet another challenge: a global pandemic. Surviving these multiple disruptions required determination.

The idea of providing a different path for their children was a crucial motivator for families that requested asylum at the U.S.-Mexico border. Parents often invoked improved educational opportunities to justify migration to themselves and to their children, even as they faced immigration policies that threatened and separated their families. Once in the U.S., parents sought to ensure a fair shot at educational opportunities for their children to counter the compounded consequences of the multiple emergencies their families experienced. Disruptions like relocation, separation, and detention threatened parents' visions of themselves as good caregivers and stable providers. In this book I illustrate how migrant families are potent in their determination but vulnerable within a U.S. immigration system that was designed to undermine their lives. I argue that the idea of providing a better life through educational opportunities is migrant parents' currency of love for their children: to guarantee an education in the U.S. justifies the sacrifices of the immigrant journey and, most importantly, shows care. While children are the assumed beneficiaries of their parents' sacrifice, this book demonstrates that they are also agentic individuals who articulate their own understandings of migration and education, thus challenging linear assumptions of achievement and success.

The book follows families from the time they were first reunified and establishes their narratives of motivations, difficulties, perseverance, and agency as they experienced detention and separation and settled in the U.S. Migrant parents focused on their continual effort to be "good" parents and their sense of agency in providing stability for their children. However, the book also narrates parents' feelings of guilt, shame, and fear regarding their decisions to leave their home countries. As they recounted the violence and poverty they experienced back home, they also reflected on the immigration policies they faced once they requested asylum in the U.S. Parents' love for their children was unwavering: care came in the form of migration, and education was their goal for improving their children's lives. To migrate is to care.

Migration Trends

Searching for hope and improved living conditions continue to be top priorities for populations that leave their homes to migrate. Many migrate to survive. This phenomenon is especially pertinent in the case of youth and family migration: young professionals and/or caregivers of young children lose hope that opportunities at home will improve for the new generation. While each of the countries of origin in this study has a particular historical relationship with the U.S., families and children had lived experiences in common—independent of their nationality. I use the concept of methodological nationalism (Beck, 2006; Chernilo, 2006, 2011; Dyrness & Sepulveda, 2020; Levitt, 2012; Wimmer & Glick Schiller, 2002) to show how we can understand the experiences of migrant families from different nation-states in the U.S. as they relate to one another.

To begin, it would be inaccurate to assume that a common country of origin shared by a group of people would generate similar experiences within that group. Regional inequalities across each of these countries, rural and urban divides, race, ethnicity, language, class, gender, and religion all deeply influenced the experiences of children, youth, and parents in this research. Thus, while it is important to contextualize the individual migratory relationships between the U.S. and Brazil, El Salvador, Guatemala, and Honduras, respectively, following the work of many scholars (Abu El-Haj, 2015; Dyrness & Abu El-Haj, 2017), I challenge the assumption that the nation-state is the primary factor affecting similarities and differences in migratory experiences.

The four countries of origin represented in this research have experienced ebbs and flows in their migratory streams to the U.S. However, between 2018 and 2019, the families in this research found themselves in similar predicaments. Upon surrendering themselves to Border Patrol agents at the U.S.-Mexico border, all were detained and some were separated.

According to data from U.S. Customs and Border Protection (CBP, n.d.), there were 107,212 apprehensions of family units (defined as individuals, including children under 18 years old, arriving together with a family member) at the U.S.-Mexico border in fiscal year 2018 (October 1 to September 30). Apprehensions of family units at the southern border has increased significantly over the past few years, rising from 75,622 in fiscal year 2017 to 107,212 in fiscal year 2018 to a whopping 473,682 in fiscal year 2019, before declining precipitously during the COVID-19 pandemic (42,180 in 2020). The U.S. government considers apprehensions to be a proxy for unauthorized crossings and immigration at the border, though some individuals may attempt to cross multiple times.

Tables 0.1, 0.2, and 0.3 show the numbers reported by CBP and the U.S. government, but do not account for other types of crossings. I have included Mexico for comparison. Notably, between 2018 and 2021, U.S. CBP reported more contacts with Honduran nationals than with any other group, despite the fact that Honduras has a smaller population than El Salvador, Guatemala, and Brazil. While the nature of its collection makes this data both incomplete and imprecise, it is important to note that Hondurans consistently have more interactions with U.S. border officials than other Central American groups, suggesting that Honduran migration is making a noteworthy contribution to the growing Central American population in the U.S. Guatemalans and Salvadorans rank second and third, respectively, among Central Americans when it comes to the most common contacts between migrants and Border Patrol. Among Guatemalan migrants, there has been an upward trend in emigration from the Western Highlands, with rural communities keeping pace with Guatemala City, contrary to past trends. While Salvadorans still made up the larg-

TABLE 0.1 Total Apprehensions by Country and Year, 2017–2023.

Fiscal Year	Brazil	El Salvador	Guatemala	Honduras	Mexico
2017	2,621	49,760	65,871	47,260	127,938
2018	1,504	31,369	115,722	76,513	152,257
2019	18,012	89,811	264,168	25,3795	166,458
2020	6,720	10,609	32,296	23,200	102,337
2021	54,275	39,457	105,878	142,005	46,708
2022	46,335	37,058	74,305	65,415	69,889
2023	21,369	32,307	150,453	126,416	243,086

Source: Customs and Border Patrol Website.

TABLE 0.2 Total Apprehension of Family Units by Country and Year.

Fiscal Year	Brazil	El Salvador	Guatemala	Honduras	Mexico
2017	1,177	24,122	24,657	22,366	2,271
2018	136	13,669	50,401	39,439	2,261
2019	12,458	56,897	185,233	188,416	6,004
2020	5,962	3,505	9,367	8,247	5,796
2021	43,285	22,268	43,742	97,141	2,399
2022	35,312	17,009	7,006	19,630	2,793
2023	9,244	13,778	75,144	67,752	15,725

Source: Customs and Border Patrol Website.

TABLE 0.3 Total Apprehensions for Unaccompanied Alien Child (UAC).

Fiscal Year	Brazil	El Salvador	Guatemala	Honduras	Mexico
2017	41	9,143	14,827	7,784	8,877
2018	37	4,949	22,327	10,913	10,136
2019	54	12,021	30,329	20,398	10,487
2020	35	1,883	6,973	3,388	6,299
2021	188	15,291	57,806	39,501	20,682
2022	195	16,328	60,511	37,180	25,945
2023	121	10,039	49,012	33,329	4,355

Source: Customs and Border Patrol Website.

est percentage of Central American immigrants in the U.S. (37.1 percent in 2021), the Honduran population grew by 47 percent between 2010 and 2021 (Ward & Batalova, 2023). This trend is likely to continue in coming years, as working-age Hondurans report deep dissatisfaction in their home country and a desire to migrate when possible (Ward & Batalova, 2023).

Contemporary Central American migration trends are most attributed to the confluence of extreme poverty and escalating violence perpetrated by gang affiliates throughout the region since the 1980s. However, it is important to situate the origins of these trends in relation to the destabilizing effect of U.S.-backed civil wars and the deportation of gang affiliates from the U.S. to Central America that began before the 1980s (Batista Willman, 2017; Massey & Pren, 2012). Between 1898 and 1994, the U.S. government intervened to influence regime change in Latin America at least 41 times (Coatsworth, 2005). When President James Monroe implemented a type of protectorate in the 19th century, commonly known as the Monroe Doctrine, it meant that the U.S. would be constantly involved in everyday politics and policy in the Latin American region, often intervening on behalf of authoritarian and right-leaning forces. In his most recent book, *Everyone Who Is Gone Is Here: The United States, Central America, and the Making of a Crisis* (2024), the journalist Jonathan Blitzer details how U.S. intervention in Central American countries influenced migratory patterns. While media and politicians tend to call the large numbers of people escaping complicated realities in their homes a "surge" or a "flood" of migrants to the border, Blitzer argues that the Cold War mentality of the U.S. and the alleged fight against communism in the region removed options and hope for the future for many in El Salvador, Guatemala, and Honduras, among other countries. In 2024 anthropologist Jason De León published *Soldiers and Kings* which furthered the argument of needing to understand deeper histories of often overlooked human aspects of border policies.

While violence is certainly one factor, emerging data on Central American migration reinforce researchers' assertions that it is a complicated phenomenon motivated by personal, economic, political, and environmental factors. Poverty and violence doubtless contribute to migration from Honduras, Guatemala, and El Salvador alike, but it is important to note that experiences are not homogeneous across the three countries. Each government's response to the challenges posed by criminal groups, economic inequality, climate change, and COVID-19 has influenced the conditions that lead to migration. In addition, public perception of domestic and international opportunities can influence migrants' decision to leave their country of origin.

Calculations of gross domestic product (GDP) per capita place Honduras, Guatemala, and El Salvador in the bottom third of all countries in Latin America and the Caribbean, according to the World Bank (World Bank Group, 2023). As of July 2021, approximately 73 percent of the Honduran population lived below the poverty line. More than half of these citizens were classified as living in extreme poverty. A public opinion study conducted in 2019 reported that working-age Hondurans experienced deep dissatisfaction with the state of the country and a lack of confidence in their personal professional prospects, which led many to express an interest in emigration (Montalvo, 2019). This same study highlighted that a significant percentage of Hondurans felt that their own economic situation, as well as that of the country writ large, was getting worse over time. These statistics were also associated with high levels of food and housing insecurity. The survey found that young Hondurans tended to be more motivated to migrate than they were to vote in domestic elections, a statistic that highlights growing disillusionment in the country. Guatemala also has a high poverty rate with extreme disparities between urban and rural populations, though general disillusionment is not as prevalent in the reported literature (Instituto Nacional de Estadística Guatemala, 2015).

Hopelessness about the economic situation in these countries may contribute to another pressing problem: rates of juvenile violence and gang affiliation. Extortion, violent crime, and the recruitment of children and teenagers into gangs have long been concerns for Central American governments. On the whole, violent crime in the region was decreasing for several years but has recently been on the rise. Gangs are notorious for extorting small, hyper-local businesses, such as subsistence farmers and street vendors, who are already struggling to make ends meet. When families are unable to pay, they often make the decision to leave home to avoid retribution. Those who stay report that paying *cuotas* (fees/tithes) increases the economic pressure they already feel (Burnett, 2021). More Salvadoran and Honduran migrants have reported violence as a motivating factor, while migrants from Guatemala are more likely to ascribe their decisions to economic reasons and, relatedly, to indicate plans to return to Guatemala at some point in the future (Creative Associates International, 2019). Rates also vary within countries. While Guatemalan migrants on the whole are less likely to report experiences with violence, urban migrants cite more instances of violence than those from rural communities (Instituto Nacional de Estadística Guatemala, 2015).

Between 2015 and 2018 both the drought and the coffee blight had devastating effects on precarious populations that depended on farming for their daily subsistence, as well as their income (World Food Programme, 2019). These ecological events exacerbated existing economic inequalities affecting Honduras's rural population, encouraging some families to undertake internal migration to nearby cities, where they hoped to find more opportunities for employment. Others decided to leave the country altogether. As analysts at the Brookings Institute point out, climate migration cannot be disentangled from other motivating factors (Bermeo & Leblang, 2021). When poverty, violence, and corruption make internal migration unsafe, families displaced by climate events are more likely to move internationally, meaning their movements are actually attributable to a complex intersection of factors (Reichman, 2022).

The case of Brazil follows some of these trends. While the country is the largest economy in Latin America with a gross domestic product (GDP) of US$2.2 trillion—significantly higher than El Salvador (US$34 billion), Guatemala (US$104 billion), and Honduras (U$34.2 billion) (World Economic Outlook Database, 2023)—analysts have pointed to Brazil's economic crisis and political instability as key drivers of increased migration, including flows to the U.S. (Waters & Batalova, 2022). Beginning in 2012, Brazil experienced multiple periods of economic slump characterized by soaring joblessness, compounded by escalating criminal activity, widely reported corruption cases, and unstable political conditions (European Central Bank, 2016; Mantoan et al., 2021).

The number of Brazilian immigrants residing in the U.S. has grown steadily over the past four decades (Migration Policy Institute, 2024). However, the scale and destinations of migration outflows from Brazil have changed notably in recent years. Between 2010 and 2019, as Brazil's economic woes continued, the Brazilian population in the U.S. increased from approximately 340,000 to over 500,000 (Coritz et al., 2023). Other sources bring this number to 1.9 million Brazilians in the U.S. (Simon et al., 2023). This surge has been attributed to pull factors like the steep appreciation of the U.S. dollar against Brazil's currency and disillusionment with economic prospects and safety (Gombata

& Fagundes, 2022). Additionally, Brazilians have increasingly used the U.S.-Mexico border as an entry point (Barrucho, 2021; Hessom, 2020; Lupion, 2021). U.S. Border Patrol apprehensions of Brazilians jumped from around 3,100 in FY2016 to a record high of nearly 57,000 in FY2021. Similarly, Mexican immigration authorities detained approximately 300 Brazilian migrants in 2016 compared to nearly 17,000 in 2021 (Waters & Batalova, 2022). Brazilians have joined other Latin American nationals transiting through Mexico to seek entry to the U.S. (Barrucho, 2021).

During the time families in this study left Brazil (2018–2019), political instability—marked by ongoing corruption scandals and uncertainty—further eroded trust in government institutions and influenced migration choices (Barrucho, 2021; Oliveira & Segel, 2022). There was a transition in power in which President Jair Bolsonaro, a candidate on the far-right, defeated Fernando Haddad, a candidate from the Workers Party, with the majority of the votes. In 2018 the nation's homicide rate reached 30.8 per 100,000 inhabitants, rising from 29.9 recorded in 2016 (Darlington, 2018). Poverty levels increased as Brazil's economic woes deepened, limiting access to healthcare, education, and social services for many lower-income citizens (World Bank, 2020). As basic needs went unmet, socioeconomic push factors exacerbated individuals' desire to migrate abroad (Stargardter, 2021). In summary, the confluence of economic hardship, currency depreciation, political instability, rising crime, and diminished social conditions in Brazil pushed increased numbers of Brazilians to migrate between 2017 and 2019, most notably to the U.S.

All the factors recounted thus far—the history of U.S. intervention, poverty, restrictions on employment, food insecurity, gang violence, and climate crises—have presented challenges to governments already facing intense (inter)national scrutiny. Perceived changes in international politics can give people considering migration hope for a better future elsewhere. While the factors described above are not new, reporting suggests that families are more likely to make the journey to the U.S. when they believe the political environment to be more welcoming. Even though the Biden administration was consistently restrictive when it came to immigration policy, after the 2020 election rumors circulated that the president intended to reverse the worst elements of Trump-era policy, particularly when it came to families. The expectation of more open access to asylum and related pathways following the 2020 U.S. election may have encouraged more families to risk migrating. There is also some evidence that increasingly robust transnational social networks are contributing to regional migration trends (e.g., among low-income families from the Western Highlands of Guatemala), a phenomenon known in the theoretical literature as "cumulative causation" (Kaldor, 1970). While some migrants undertake the journey with specific plans to enter the U.S., others initially intend to journey to Mexico and Belize, which are slightly more accessible destinations for those who cannot afford to pay the high smuggling fees required to enter the U.S.

In Massachusetts, where this study takes place, the top country of origin for migrant populations is China, but about 40 percent of the foreign-born population or about half a million people in the state are from Latin America (Migration Policy Institute, 2023). This data may be undercounting the undocumented population. Central Americans and Brazilians each make up 9 percent of the foreign-born population. Almost 40 percent of migrants arrived in Massachusetts since 2010 (Migration Policy Institute, 2024). According to the latest available data from the American Immigration Council (2022), there were approximately 150,000 immigrant children under the age of 18 living in Massachusetts as of 2019. The Migration Policy Institute (2024) estimates that in 2019, around 55,000 immigrant children in Massachusetts had at least one parent who was unauthorized. Many of these families are likely from Latin America. A 2016 report from the Boston Foundation found that over 40 percent of children in the Boston metro area were from immigrant families (Edozie et al., 2016). While it did not break down data by specific countries or regions, Latin America continues to be a major home region of immigrant families.

Immigration Policy and the Border

The U.S. has a complex history of immigration policy that has faced criticism for its restrictive and discriminatory nature. Scholars such as Ngai (2004), Zolberg (2006), and Daniels (2004) have explored how immigration laws have historically marginalized specific groups. Ngai's work highlights how the concept of an "illegal alien" emerged through laws like the Naturalization Act of 1790, which limited citizenship to "free white persons" and excluded Native Americans and African Americans. This contributed to a racialized foundation in U.S. immigration policy. Legislation like the Page Act of 1875, the Chinese Exclusion Act of 1882, and the Immigration Act of 1917 further entrenched racial and national origins as determinants of lawful entry and status. These laws created a framework for categorizing immigrants and controlling immigration based on racial and national stereotypes, with significant impacts on Mexican migrants in the early 20th century.

Across the 20th and early 21st centuries, U.S. immigration policy saw varying degrees of restriction and reform. The Immigration Act of 1924 imposed national-origin quotas, favoring certain European immigrants, while the Immigration and Nationality Act of 1965 shifted focus toward family reunification and skilled immigrants, signaling a major demographic shift. The 1986 Immigration Reform and Control Act under Reagan offered amnesty to undocumented immigrants yet increased employer sanctions. The Illegal Immigration Reform and Immigrant Responsibility Act of 1996 emphasized border enforcement. Post-9/11 policies, like the USA Patriot Act and the formation of the Department of Homeland Security (DHS), increased surveillance and prosecution. More recently, initiatives such as Deferred Action for Childhood Arrivals (DACA) in 2012 attempted to provide temporary relief for certain undocumented migrants, although deportations remained high under the Obama administration.

One week after taking office in 2017, President Trump issued the first in a series of orders restricting entry into the U.S. of individuals from several Muslim-majority countries. Facing multiple lawsuits and losses in court, the Trump administration issued revised versions of the travel bans, and the Supreme Court ultimately upheld the third iteration in *Trump v. Hawaii* in 2018. Following the Supreme Court victory, the Trump administration continued to revise and extend the restrictions, imposing additional limitations with respect to nationals from Myanmar, Eritrea, Kyrgyzstan, Nigeria, Sudan, and Tanzania.

According to the Southern Poverty Law Center (2022), in mid-2017, prior to the implementation of the 2018 "family separation policy," the El Paso program initiated a practice where adults crossing the border without legal authorization—a misdemeanor for first-time offenders—were arrested and prosecuted. This policy applied even to parents traveling with young children. The children were removed from their parents' custody, and many families lost the ability to locate or reconnect with their children due to the absence of an organized government system for reunification. By the end of 2017, this approach expanded, with authorities separating families throughout the entire U.S.-Mexico border region, including those presenting themselves legally at official ports of entry. Official lawsuit documents explained that in July 2017, the Trump administration initiated a policy of separating migrant families at the border to discourage immigration (*Ms. L et al. v. ICE*, 2018). Started quietly by the Department of Homeland Security through Customs and Border Protection personnel at border facilities in Texas, the policy was eventually publicized on May 7, 2018, when the U.S. Attorney General announced that under the "zero-tolerance policy," all migrant parents entering unlawfully between ports of entry with their children would be criminally prosecuted and separated from their children. Any accompanying children under the age of 18 were handed over to the U.S. Department of Health and Human Services (HHS).

The policy resulted in the haphazard separation of over 5,500 children from their parents, most of whom were seeking asylum from countries in Central and South America—and many of whom entered the U.S. at official ports of entry (*Ms. L et al. v. ICE*, 2018). Most of the children were ages 12 and under; more than 200 were under 5 years old (*Ms. L et al. v. ICE*, 2018). During this time, children were sent to facilities sometimes thousands of miles away from their parents (*A.I.I.L. v. Sessions*, 2019). Separated family members were often not told when or if they would ever see each other again—and many did not see each other again for months or an entire year. In many instances separated children were detained in dreadful conditions with no way to communicate with their parents for days, weeks, or months. Parents had no idea how their children were being cared for or by whom.

In her book, *Taking Children: A History of American Terror* (2021), historian Laura Briggs states: "Separating children from parents is more than just another version of a larger mistreatment of immigrants and asylum seekers or enslaved and indigenous people. Taking people's children participates in a very brutal kind of political punishment, a symbolism—and reality—that is meant to be starkly tangible, crude, and cruel" (p. 6). As Briggs demonstrates, the U.S. government practice of separating and detaining families is older than we may care to remember. Briggs examines three episodes in recent history in which the government systematically removed children from their families.

The first is slavery and its aftermath through the decades after World War II: with the support of the federal government, Southern cities put Black children in foster care as punishment for Black adults' activism, thus pathologizing families (p. 11). Second, Briggs investigates the removal of Native children to boarding schools during the Indian Wars in the 1870s; the "schools" were effectively military-run detention centers (p. 46). These actions were meant to tame the revolt and to "civilize Indian children" (p. 53). Finally, Briggs narrates anti-communist wars in Latin America, contending: "You can't get to 2019 at the Southwest border of the United States without going through Cold War Latin America" (p. 78). During the Cold War in many countries in Latin America, children of perceived communists or leftists were taken from their parents and placed in adoption agencies.

In December 2018, the Trump administration implemented the Migration Protection Protocols (MPP), also known as the "remain in Mexico" policy. It required certain non-Mexican asylum seekers who arrived through the southern border of the U.S. to wait in Mexico until their immigration court hearings in the U.S. Bellino and Gluckman (2024) argued that the MPP undermined due process in the United States and access to asylum procedures by forcing migrants to wait in unsafe Mexican border towns. Over 68,000 people were subjected to MPP between January 2019 and February 2021, when President Biden first ended the policy; less than 1 percent successfully obtained asylum in the U.S. (American Immigration Council, 2025). The Biden administration reinstated the policy in December 2021, but it was formally ended again in 2022.

Between the Obama and Trump administrations, the cap on the number of refugees admitted to the country was drastically reduced from 85,000 in 2016 to 18,000 in 2020. Under the Biden administration the cap was 125,000 from 2022 to 2024 (Migration Policy Institute, 2024); however, the actual number of refugees admitted was lower at 25,000 in 2022 and 60,000 in 2023. The discrepancy between the number of allotted spots versus the number of refugees admitted shows the complicated process of accepting people through the so-called legal pathways (in 2022 over 239,000 people applied and in 2023 over 465,000).

During the pandemic the Trump administration invoked Title 42, which allowed for the quick expulsion of migrants arriving in the U.S (Gramlich,

2022). These removals took place under an obscure clause of U.S. health legislation: Section 265 of Title 42, which is a Public Health Service act from 1944 aimed at preventing the spread of communicable diseases in the U.S. Thus, if and when the Centers for Disease Control determines that there is a disease that could easily spread, health officials—with the support of the president—can prohibit the entry of persons from other countries.

Thus, one cannot untangle the long history of U.S. immigration policy from the present iterations of highly restrictive border enforcement. It is crucial that we understand the lives of these 16 families in a fuller historical context. Furthermore, migration policies compound over time, and presidents and administrations have more similarities than differences in terms of approaches to immigration and policy. According to a briefing by the Department of Justice's Executive Office for Immigration Review (Straut-Eppsteiner, 2024), "the number of pending cases (backlog) in immigration courts has grown each year since FY2006 and has ballooned in recent years. It exceeded 1 million for the first time in FY2019, reached nearly 2.5 million at the end of FY2023, and was approximately 3.6 million at the end of FY2024" (p. 1). The lack of will across parties to reform immigration policies will persist as long as immigration is used as a scare tactic or for inauthentic actions in elections.

Education as Currency of Love in Multiple Disruptions

As a researcher, scholar, and teacher, I am rooted in the field of anthropology of education. According to Levinson and Holland (1996), anthropology of education examines "how local forms of education both shape and are shaped by larger political and economic forces" (p. 1). Methodologically, I anchor my understandings of how people experience life in the tradition of ethnographic work. The anthropological field, long defined by the study of cultures, came under fire in the 1980s when scholars challenged the static notion of culture as a "cause" to explain and justify everything. In "Writing Against Culture" (1991), Lila Abu-Lughod argued that "culture" as a bounded, homogeneous, and coherent system tends to essentialize and oversimplify societies, reinforcing the notion of the "other." Abu-Lughod called for anthropologists to move "against culture" by focusing more on local contexts, power relations, and the agency of individuals to negotiate and resist dominant norms. It is in this tradition that my ethnographic work exists. By focusing on the lives and experiences of children, parents, teachers, and educators at the local level, I connect everyday realities to broader patterns in immigration, capitalism, and the global political economy. What does it mean to spend almost three years with a group of 16 families and teachers who have navigated the travails of the modern world? How do we push back against the idea of culture as monolithic and unchangeable when there is so much migratory movement across borders and boundaries?

When thinking about these multiple contexts of existence (home countries, transitional spaces, the border, and the U.S.), migrant parents elaborate their decisions to leave in a reciprocal stance: it is for the children, but the children also must show effort, progress, and a form of advancement in their education. When French sociologist Maurice Mauss published his work *The Gift* in 1925, he argued that gift giving is not simply an act of generosity or altruism, but rather it creates social obligations and is integral to economic and social relations. For many parents, to migrate is to care, but it is also a *gift* they give to their children: the gift to live, survive, and thrive. However, this gift is not without the setbacks, traumas, and complications that larger macro structures subject families and individuals to during migratory processes, including violence, detention, and in some cases separation. Often, the hope for a better education is the gift that keeps parents fighting for a better life.

Joining anthropology and the field of education, I stitch together a working definition of *education as currency of love* to explain how parents articulate their commitment to their children's education as a backdrop for migration. Families in this research asserted that to migrate is to care. The concept homes in on articulations of reciprocity between families and their newfound home, but also accounts for the role of institutions (U.S. government, public schools, police, hospitals, employers) in complicating or facilitating migrant families' everyday lives. This dynamic concept of education as currency of love surfaces in the gratitude and loss expressed by families upon arriving to the U.S., but also in the often unspoken expectations they have of their children. When parents make the constrained decision to migrate, they often justify it as intended to provide a better life for their children. However, when pressed about what it means to provide a better life for their children, parents anchor those hopes in education—a good education—as a possibility for advancement in their children's lives. Thus, the idea of education as currency of love, as a way that love can be exchanged between parents and children, emerges. When parents enroll their children in U.S.-based schools, when they watch their child go into a building that they assume is safe and provides children with the best possible start to their lives, when children are able to graduate, learn to read and write, challenge themselves in schools—that is where much of parental love is located. To provide a quality education is to love.

The context advanced in this book is based on three major disruptions in the lives of 16 families over three years: leaving their home countries, being detained and/or separated at the border, and facing a global pandemic. Taken together, these three dimensions exacerbated existing educational inequalities for migrants in the U.S. and were connected to breakdowns in care structures at home and the challenges that came with remote schooling. This complex constellation of stressors has also been referred to in psychological literature as compounded trauma (Garcini et al., 2024) and compounded loss (Cardoza, 2021). I borrow from this literature to map out a framework based on how families discussed their experiences: as a "series of emergencies" or "new nightmares," but maintaining their affirmation, "Now we are here." Caregivers and children, when telling their stories, started with their reasons for leaving their countries of origin in the first place. They then spoke about the pain and grief that detention and separation brought about for them, only to be hit by a pandemic that directly affected their hopes and dreams for a better life. Families discussed the *multiplicity* of ways in which their lives were affected by uncertainty, but their focus, dedication, and resolve never wavered.

Migration Studies

This study is situated within the sociohistorical context of U.S. immigration policies, the effects of which ripple across the border and throughout Latin America. In an era of heightened immigration enforcement, migrants have little stability or certainty in their migratory routes or settlement possibilities (Abrego, 2014a; De Genova & Peutz, 2010; Meyer & Boggs, 2016; Zatz & Rodriguez, 2015). What happens when people migrate? Sociologists of im/migration located within the field of education have long argued that there are patterns associated with how Latinx immigrants live their lives in the U.S.

Traditionally, sociologists of im/migration and education have focused their studies on modes of incorporation and assimilation once migrants arrive in the U.S. They have found that Latinx immigrants tend to migrate with lower levels of formal education, higher rates of undocumented status, and are more frequently from working-class backgrounds relative to other national origin groups (Feliciano, 2020; Lee & Zhou, 2015), causing Latinx youth to face greater incorporation obstacles (Telles et al., 2008). They have also argued that immigrant youth's educational performance and attainment outcomes are influenced by parental socioeconomic status (Bean et al., 2015; Lee & Zhou, 2015) and class mobility (Roksa & Potter, 2011), family structure and community dynamic (Cavanagh & Fomby, 2012; Rumbaut, 2005; Terriquez, 2012; Zhou & Bankston, 1994), and the preparedness of schools to receive them (Dabach, 2014; Hurie & Callahan, 2019; Rodriguez, 2019). These processes are uniquely marked by "illegality" for undocumented immigrant youth (Abrego & Gonzales, 2010; Gonzales, 2016).

Scholars have long sought to understand the adaptation processes of immigrant children whose lives are marked by vulnerable immigration status and the trauma of separation (Gibson, 1988; Portes & Rumbaut, 2014; Suárez-Orozco & Suárez-Orozco, 1995), as well as by im/migration policies that have become increasingly consequential in shaping how immigrant children adapt, come of age, and experience life in the U.S. (Gonzales, 2016; Suárez-Orozco et al., 2011). This book answers the anthropological question of what happens when families migrate, but it expands on this literature by engaging with an understudied population—detained and/or separated families shortly after reunification in the U.S.—and challenges fixed conceptions of assimilation and linearity that inform much of the rationale advanced in the sociology of im/migration.

Anthropological studies of migration have focused less on migration flows and more on how individuals respond to these global processes. The study of culture, which includes the study of the interaction between beliefs, behavior, and social relationships, has resulted in an emphasis on adaptation, culture change, identity, and ethnicity (Brettel & Hollifield, 2023). Studies suggest that migration challenges norms and ideals of family life that involve gender hierarchies (Coe et al., 2011), especially gendered roles and the division of household labor (Gálvez, 2011; Hirsch, 2009). However, women's roles in the household and outside of the home vary tremendously according to social and geographical locations (Dreby & Schmalzbauer, 2013).

Scholars of migration have produced an important body of work pertaining to newly arrived immigrants in the U.S. Areas of inquiry include parental narratives of sacrifice and hoping for a better life for their children (Boehm, 2016; Dreby, 2010; Gallo, 2017; Yoshikawa, 2011); immigrant mothers' advocacy for their children's education (Dyrness, 2010); transnational childhoods (Orellana, 2009); gender and health disparities (Gálvez, 2011, 2019), intergenerational care (Yarris, 2017); and the fate of unaccompanied minors (Heidbrink, 2020). More specifically, scholars of anthropology and education have provided deep ethnographic knowledge on the relationship between language, education, and im/migration (e.g., Bartlett & Garcia, 2011). Researchers have also documented the structures of care that are created when families migrate or are separated across borders (Dreby, 2010; Ehrenreich & Hochschild, 2003; Hirsch, 2003; Hondagneu-Sotelo, 1994, 2003; Hondagneu-Sotelo & Avila, 1997; Horton, 2008; Parreñas, 2005). This book builds on previous anthropological work on immigration that discusses parental care and sacrifice as ways to provide a better life for children. Within the anthropology of migration, I think with Yarris's (2017) concept of care as an affirmative moral stance, which is an expression from parents of unconditional support for their children.

To Migrate Is to Care

Initially, the study of care was the domain of medical anthropologists, who investigated the intimate act of caring for the body of another (see Smith-Morris [2018] for a review of four examples among many; also, Kittay [2011] for a discussion of the ethics of care and dependency). More recently, however, scholars have begun to pay attention to the cultural, linguistic, and political implications of caregiving, particularly as they pertain to transnational relations (Arnold, 2021; Baldassar & Merla, 2013; Ticktin, 2011). Ethnographic research on care in the context of migration illuminates the myriad ways people forge and maintain connections in light of the restrictions they face in their daily lives. Such research draws attention to both the personal and the public dimensions of carework, confirming the importance of care as a socially sustaining activity while showing how care-in-practice responds to broader forms of cultural and political mediation.

Care—in all its forms—is integral to social functioning, but it has also been a source of intellectual contestation (Buch, 2015). Care is typically understood as "a set of (ritualized) practices that are part of how people maintain and enhance relationships" (García-Sánchez, 2018, p. 168). Scholars have expanded on this idea to include the notion of obligation, describing care as an ethical commitment in which people feel compelled to "take care" of one another even when such actions run counter to or are otherwise distinct from individual interests (Engster, 2020). Feminist theorists situate this imperative within specific social and political contexts, drawing attention to how care's deep association with femininity affects its allocation and social value (Cockburn, 2005; Fisher et al., 1990; Gilligan, 1982). This perspective provides critical insight into care's relationship to lived experiences of inequity (i.e., who is obligated to provide care and how this affects care's perceived value). At the same time, feminist perspectives have been criticized for universalizing concepts developed via a myopic consideration of social norms observed in the West and Global North (Nadasen, 2017, 2021; Raghuram, 2016; Thelen, 2021; Yeates, 2012). As a corrective, other scholars have positioned the ethics of care in a broader political frame, defining care as an assertion of hope proffered in response to global economic, interpersonal, and ecological crises (Tronto, 1993). This understanding of care takes the same embodied practices configured elsewhere as emblems of "femininity" and uses them to develop language to explain how interpersonal actions articulate with efforts to craft a better future for one's community (Held, 2006).

Ethnographic Lens

This ethnographic study, begun in the fall of 2018 and completed at the end of 2021, illuminates the consequences that shifting immigration practices have had for families' lived experiences, children's educational experiences, as well as teaching in schools. As a method, ethnography offers a window into the complexities of real-world situations and highlights experiences, perspectives, and truths that are often silenced or sidelined. Ortner (2006) described ethnography in the following way: "Of course [it] means many things. Minimally, however, it has always meant the attempt to understand another life world using the self—as much of it as possible—as the instrument of knowing" (p. 43). Ortner explained that ethnographic thinness comes from a failure to understand internal politics of dominated groups and their cultural authenticity as well as from issues "surrounding the crisis of representation—the possibility of truthful portrayals of others (or Others) and the capacity of the subaltern to be heard" (p. 62). Edward Said (1978) argued that representations of *other* cultures are inherently political and tied to relations of power, meaning that anthropological knowledge production is not objective or value neutral. Anthropological knowledge, rather, served to "other" non-Western peoples and legitimize Western political and cultural domination. It helped justify colonial projects of control and influence.

A postcolonial, self-reflexive approach was thus needed to challenge taken-for-granted assumptions, acknowledge subjective standpoints, and elevate Indigenous agency and authority over cultural representations. Tuhiwai Smith et al. (2018) subsequently argued that Indigenous communities have long been subjected to having research done "on" or "about" them by external researchers, but rarely "with" or "for" them, perpetuating power imbalances. Following this tradition, the work by Alonso Bejarano et al. (2019) in *Decolonizing Ethnography: Undocumented Immigrants and New Directions in Social Science* proposed methodology like community-engaged research, participatory action research, and Indigenous research paradigms that promote self-determination and social justice.

I follow a long tradition of migration scholars who have conducted ethnographic work with populations with vulnerable immigration status through the development of trust and time (Abu-Lughod, 2000; Boehm, 2012, 2015; Brennan, 2018; Brettel, 2003; Dreby, 2010, 2015; Dyrness & Sepúlveda, 2020; Foner, 2005; Gallo, 2017; Gonzales, 2016; Heidbrink, 2014; Heyman, 1995; Levitt, 2001; Mahler, 1995; Menjívar, 2000; Parreñas, 2021; Smith, 2006). In keeping with this approach, I narrowed the focal topics of this research over the course of data collection as major events influenced people's lived realities (Blommaert & Jie, 2010). The key feature of ethnographies of migration and of migratory processes is that the researcher "moves" with the participants, adjusting according to how participants tell stories about their mobility.

The Work

I spent between 22 months and three years with a group of 16 families from four different countries in Latin America. The participants in this research were 30 children and youth ranging from 4 months to 18 years old living in the U.S., 24 parents, and 5 children and young adults living in their home countries. To that I added 18 teachers and community members with whom I interacted, resulting in at least 77 formal participants during those years. These families moved as a unit to escape complex contexts and encountered policies at the border that targeted their very existence—that threatened the integrity of the migrant family as such. Three main criteria were used to select families for participation in this study: (1) families experienced detention and/or separation at the border in 2018 or 2019, under the zero-tolerance policy and/or the Migrant Protection Protocols (MPP); (2) families asked for asylum upon entry at the U.S.-Mexico border; and (3) families lived in the state of Massachusetts and had at least one child under 18 enrolled in K–12 schools.

By its nature, ethnography lends itself to long-term work that is somewhat bounded. While sometimes these are physical boundaries, other times they can be relationship based. While I refer to countries of origin in this research, I move away from terms like "sending" and "receiving/hosting" communities commonly used in migration research. I do that as I privilege relationships over locations as a unit of study. Children in this research went to similar schools, after-school programs, churches, restaurants, hospitals, and so lived similar physical experiences. Establishing trust allowed me to observe their homes, schools, playgrounds, church events, among other celebrations. It was important that I could be in spaces with families in order to understand how they moved from one place to another and what spending time together looked like. In this research, I centered the relationships between family members, immigration policies, and the schools around them. Thus, the similarities among these families illustrate how the journey north and migrants' encounters with border policy coupled with a pandemic upon reunification complicate the survival and lives of these migrant families. The depth with which I was able to conduct this ethnography yielded high exposure (Small & Calarco, 2022). This means that I gathered much more data than I have been able to incorporate into the five data chapters in this book.

I conducted this research in the state of Massachusetts for several reasons. I live in the state, and at the time of research it was home to more than one million migrants who represented 16 percent of the state's population (American Immigration Council, 2020). Families in Massachusetts had united to sue Attorney General Jeff Sessions in the aftermath of the family separation policy in May 2018. The lawsuit detailed the stories of families from Guatemala seeking asylum in the U.S. Through a local nongovernmental organization and several school districts where I had previously conducted research with Latin American migrant children, I was able to meet families who had recently been reunified or released. I focused on 16 families: 7 from Guatemala, 5 from Brazil, 2 from El Salvador, and 2 from Honduras. Their children were enrolled in and attended different schools in similar towns (see table 0.4). The children interacted with a total of 18 teachers, 9 aides, and 8 specialists, in addition to principals, community center administrators, after-school program coordinators, and others who provided care for them.

As described below, I employed a collection of multimodal digital ethnographic tools in order to continue my fieldwork at the start of the COVID-19 pandemic in March 2020. I followed the tradition of digital ethnographers (Burrel, 2009; Dicks et al. 2006; Emery, 2018; Rodriguez Kerr et al., 2020) who designed their research studies as multimodal ethnographies. While we continued to face restrictions of mobility related to the pandemic, this methodology provided new ways for qualitative researchers and ethnographers who study migration to use both in-person and digital methods.

Data were collected in the following ways in 2018, 2019, and part of 2021: (1) twice-a-month unstructured interviews with the 16 families' parents and children. Participants' grouping varied in their homes, and sometimes I would spend more time with the children or the parents, or with the whole family having a meal, for example; (2) three semistructured interviews with each teacher over the research period; (3) twice-a-month classroom participant observation per elementary child and once a month per middle or high school child; and (4) every-other-week participant observations outside of school (home, church, doctor) per family. From 2018 to 2021, I spent four mornings or afternoons every week in the classrooms, schools, and homes of these families. Observations outside of school lasted between 45 minutes and 2 hours. I observed parents cooking, cleaning, working, and helping children with home-

TABLE 0.4 Participants.

Participation started	Family	Parent	Parent	Country of Origin	Children and Youth	BorderExperience
2020	Cruz	Yanet		Honduras	Jose (16), Jair (4), Josh (3)	Detained and released together (11 days)
2020	Ruiz	Fatima	Fernando	Guatemala	Rosa (18), Daniel (15), Vivi (6)	Detained and separated by gender (5 days)
2020	Martínez	Andrea	Javier	Honduras	Felipa (12), Daphne (11), Francisco (8)	Detained, separated, remain in Mexico (6 months)
2019	Rodriguez	Julio		Guatemala	Luz (5)	Detained and separated (72 days)
2019	Hernandez	Melanie	Edgar	Guatemala	Manuela (19), Lucas (14), Leo (5)	Detained and released together (6 days)
2019	Garcia	Edgar	Melanie	Guatemala	Javier (24), Augusto (21), Lina (20), Fany (8)	Detained and separated (41 days)
2019	Santos	Melissa		Brazil	Adriana (16), Juliana (14), Diego (13)	Detained and released together (6 days)
2019	Vieira	Cintia	Ricardo	Brazil	MariaClara (6), Pilar (3)	Detained and released together (6 days)
2019	Perera	Natalia		ElSalvador	Cesar (5)	Detained, separated, remainMexico (6 months)
2019	Morales	Daisy		ElSalvador	Cruz (7)	Detained and released together (4 days)
2019	Diaz	Dylan		Guatemala	William (8)	Detained and separated (18 days)
2019	López	Diana	Ian	Guatemala	Santo (5), Belen (2), Jimmy (4months)	Detained by gender and released together (17 days)
2018	Hipólito	Henrique	Emily	Brazil	Flor (6)	Detained and separated by gender (5 days)
2018	Silva	Gabriel	Jana	Brazil	Davi (9), Vinny (6)	Detained and separated by gender (21 days)
2018	DeLeón	Mimi		Guatemala	Augusto (7)	Detained and released together (14 days)
2018	Souza	Karina		Brazil	Giselly (14), Daiany (7), Carly (4)	Detained and released together (7 days)

Source: Author.

work. I accompanied families to church, to the park, to grocery stores, and to neighborhood festivities as part of these observations. I participated in meetings with lawyers, as well as parent-teacher conferences, and spent time with families at tutoring facilities and in sessions organized by the parental school outreach organization.

Who I am as a researcher matters. While positionality statements have gained traction in more disciplines and fields, the conversation about researchers' identities has always been an important one. Mario Small (2009), however, warns against the overreliance on identity match as a research strategy. Identity match refers to the degree to which a researcher shares social identities (e.g., race, class, gender) with research participants. Small (2009) argues that a higher identity match can help researchers gain access to communities and build rapport/trust with participants more easily. However, identity match alone does not guarantee high-quality data. Power dynamics related to identities like race or gender exist in any research relationship and must be navigated ethically and carefully. Identity match does not eliminate these issues. Leigh Patel discusses the concept of relationality in her book, *Decolonizing Educational Research* (2016), in which she advocates for a relational approach to research that centers connections and relationships between the researcher and participants. She critiques more traditional "extractive" research approaches that treat communities as objects of study rather than in relationship with the researcher and each other. Relationality—in contrast to the usual unilateral positionality statements—requires mutual learning, and relationships take time and care to cultivate. My relationship with participants was a familiar one because I had been researching immigration across the Americas for nearly a decade.

I was born and raised in São Paulo, Brazil, and Portuguese is my first language. I also speak Spanish, and so I never relied on translation or interpretation during my data collection. Being a teacher was part of my identity when engaging with participants. *Professora* or *maestra* were labels commonly used by parents, children, and youth when referring to me. In the U.S. I am often categorized as a person of color mostly because I was born and raised in Brazil. I am sometimes called Latina, Latinx, or Latin American. However, in Brazil, according to the census and sociocultural definitions, I am white. I speak English with my own accent, and while I have lived in the U.S. for almost 17 years,

I still feel very much like a foreigner or someone living in what Victor Turner (1969) has called a "liminal space." This liminality is a state of ambiguity: participants have left behind their previous status but have not yet been incorporated into their new status. Turner describes liminality as being "betwixt and between": neither here nor there, in a space that resists definition or classification according to cultural categories.

Thus, in many ways my identity as a U.S.-based university teacher, but also as a Brazilian migrant myself who was raising bilingual children and deeply missed her faraway family, merged in this in-between space. Parts of my identity became more or less salient depending on where I was. In schools I was sometimes mistaken for a K–12 teacher, but in teacher-parent conferences or in meetings with lawyers I was consulted and expected to have answers and solutions as an advocate. At participants' homes I was sometimes put into the role of a researcher, a babysitter, a tutor, a social worker, a mother's helper, a friend who stopped by to chat, and someone with resources that could support families' varied needs. Because consent is an ongoing process, my notetaking and recording served as constant reminders that I was a researcher and that I was registering our interactions. One parent, Yanet, described this process in the following way: "I sometimes forget you are taking notes and writing, but then you always remind us . . . you know you can stop telling us now . . . we see you a lot [laughter]!" I did frequently remind participants that they always had the right to have entire conversations with me that would never be written about. As Yanet's comment indicates, this process was sometimes too repetitive. Although no one ever asked me to leave anything out, reassuring participants that they had the right to set that limit was a key component of authentic ongoing consent.

Engaging in the myth of a detached objectivity while conducting research can be harmful to our work. Not acknowledging who the researcher is or omitting how they are perceived by participants would be a denial of our own humanity. Instead, I believe in being transparent and honest about who I am, and when asked, being sincere regarding how I feel about different issues. I have interviewed plenty of people whose perspectives differed completely from how I see the world. However, a rigorous ethnographer would not shy away from being in spaces that are contrary to their beliefs as long as doing so does not jeopardize their personal safety. Migrant families in this research differ in their religious and political beliefs. When I collected data with Brazilian participants there was more shared knowledge between myself and participants about the country, its states, sociocultural norms, and food than perhaps with other participants. There was also more difference in opinions about local and national politics, as well as about policies.

Ethnographers often romanticize the process of data collection and use words like "informants" or being "embedded" in spaces, thus depicting themselves as explorers going on adventures. This reflects anthropology's long legacy of exploitation. While I acknowledge these tensions in my own work, it sometimes seems as though the responsibility for engaging with our relationality, our ethical duties as researchers, and above all our commitment to the participants who allow us to even be able to write a book falls mostly to social scientists doing qualitative work. I hope this book contributes to continuing the dialogue on these topics and across all disciplines and methods that work with migrant communities.

A Road Map

Now We Are Here moves chronologically through the lives of 16 families. Chapter 1 describes how parents from across Latin America made the constrained choice to leave their countries of origin and undertake the journey north to the U.S. Families that experienced separation and/or detention at the border saw the possibility of enrolling their children in U.S. schools as a possible justification for hardships experienced at the border. The paradox, however, was the cost of this promise. Parents explained that detention and separation at the border forever haunted their dreams as they worried for their children's well-being after reunification or release. Was it worth it? What have I done? These were some of the questions parents engaged with after reunification.

Chapter 2 takes on children's narratives of how they understood their mobility, their parents' decision to migrate, and the journey north. Building on the previous chapter's focus on parents' struggles with guilt as well as the hopes that sent them north, this chapter centers children's accounts of what motivated their families' migration to the U.S. While children are frequently discussed in both policy and media spheres, they are rarely spoken to in their own individual contexts. In contrast, this chapter centers children as the experts of their own lives.

Chapter 3 focuses on children in classrooms. Children are the supposed beneficiaries of their parents' decisions to migrate, but they have varying levels of institutional support to succeed academically. While children talked about their migrant journeys in the classroom and offered glimpses of their experiences of detention and separation, teachers were hesitant to engage fully with these experiences. The result was what I call a "pedagogy of silence," which made many children feel invisible and uneasy about sharing their stories with teachers at school. Teachers, on the other hand, described a type of constrained care in which they felt they could not fully care for their students. Parents, meanwhile, worried that disclosing too much information about their migrant journeys could make their children visible and therefore vulnerable.

Chapter 4 illustrates how the caregiving structures available to migrant parents broke down in 2020 and how those breakdowns shaped children's schooling experiences. By early 2020, many of the focal families had found their footing in the labor market: they were experiencing steadiness in their jobs and consistently sending remittances to their home countries. When schools closed on March 12, 2020, parents—many of whom were essential workers—had to figure out how to care for their children during the hours they would be working outside the home in a context of already-strained household resources and infrastructure. The promise that educational opportunities would open the door to a better life was threatened and tested again.

Chapter 5 focuses on families' articulations of what they lost and found during the three years they had been in the U.S. As newcomers who hoped to thrive and provide a better life for their children, they seemed to face constant hurdles. The unstable economy and breakdowns in care deeply influenced how they perceived their ability to care for the family members with them in the U.S., as well as those who had stayed behind. Will things get better? Have we made the right decision? This chapter is dedicated to narratives of recovery in the face of a global pandemic, but not without mourning the losses experienced along the way.

Finally, in the conclusion I offer a look forward: short- and long-term reflections and recommendations that consider the multiple emergencies experienced by families that arrive in the U.S. from all over the world. To migrate is to care, and continuing to survive and to live is a complex task for these families. While the conclusion is the end of the book, these families and more families continue to push forward and attempt to build a life of dignity and purpose.

Why is it that the right to a good life is reserved for some and denied to others? The reflections in the conclusion are about education and immigration policy, but ultimately, they are about how children and parents resist oppressive structures that constantly strip away their right to exist and persevere. This is not a romanticized view of migration, but rather a response to what Adriana said in the beginning of this introduction: is it a crime to care?

Who cares? Parents care. Children care. Educators care. The decisions and motivators of families' departure from their homelands included parents' commitment to the possibilities a life in the U.S. could offer their children. On the other hand, children were the assumed beneficiaries of their parents' decision to migrate but experienced hardships in U.S. schools. While parents had high expectations of how transformative their children's formal education would be, immigrant children existed in an in-between space of resisting in classrooms and schools, and existing at home. Teachers', principals', community workers', and school staff's attention to immigrant children's needs and their asset view approach to children are acts of care. While children's stories of migration were not always welcomed in classrooms, many educators worked to build meaningful relationships with families. Teachers care.

Harsh border policies coupled with a pandemic put families' expectations on permanent hold. Migrant parents were essential workers during the pandemic. Uninsured, afraid, and with little social safety net, they pushed through for their children. They also experienced loss and replayed their decisions in their heads over and over. Migration brought a heightened sense of dispossession and loss for parents and children; they met hardship with unwavering hope for the future. The triad of compounded losses—leaving home, border detention, and a pandemic—tied parents' and children's prospects for a better life to education. Family migration is an act of care, and love is expressed through providing stable formal educational opportunities to children. The hopefulness expressed through *Now We Are Here* should not be mistaken for naïveté, a lack of agency, or docility. Parents and children are agentic beings pushing through the suspended nature of their existence—waiting for court decisions about their future.

During one of our final interviews, Julio, a father from Guatemala who migrated with his daughter Luz, asked, "I wonder if they will care?" When asked what he meant by that question, he explained: "Do you think if the government, lawyers, teachers all of the people would care if they knew about all the things we have been through . . . I'm not saying we are victims, I am saying we are fighters . . . I wonder if they would care about Luz more, you know?" This lingering question remains crucial to understanding the multiple disruptions that so deeply affected the lives of families and children. *Who cares?* The pandemic's tragic disruption highlighted how recent policies have shaped the educational experiences of migrants in the U.S., demonstrating that states and public schools can lead the change for families who now are here.

ONE

Parental Migration and the Promise of an Education

PARENTS FROM COUNTRIES ACROSS Latin America have made the constrained choice to leave their country-of-origin homes and undertake the journey north to the U.S. In 2018 and 2019, as migrant families sought better lives and survival, many of them encountered U.S. government policies that would forever shape their lives. In this chapter, I focus on parental narratives to show the factors that motivated parents to leave their homes and trek north. What do parents' and children's narratives about migration and education tell us? What do these narratives say about the lives migrant families want to live and what they are willing to do for a brighter future?

When they decided to migrate, parents envisioned improving their children's lives and discussed educational opportunities in the U.S. as one asset that could immensely contribute to that vision. While parents explained the need to escape poverty, violence, and untrustworthy governments, they also stressed the promise of a U.S. education. Education, while not the direct motivator for migration, was the promise parents pinned their hopes to. The paradox, however, was the cost of this projected promise. Parents explained that detention and/or separation at the border forever haunted their dreams as they worried for their children's well-being after reunification and release. Was it worth it? What have I done? These were some of the questions parents engaged with after reunification.

Migration motivated by the desire to provide a better life for one's children through education is not a new facet of U.S.-bound migratory movements. Through in-depth ethnographic and qualitative studies, several immigration scholars have shown how education as a concept becomes central to parents' narratives of departure (Abrego, 2014a, 2019; Dreby, 2010, 2015; Gálvez, 2011; Gonzales, 2016; Oliveira, 2018; Rodriguez, 2023; Smith, 2006). The families in this research, however, encountered government policies in 2018 and 2019 that impacted how they made sense of their motivations to leave their countries of origin. A closer look at how families articulated their losses and their hopes shows the complexity of the immigrant bargain (Louie, 2012).

Julio and Luz

It took weeks for Julio, a father from Guatemala who migrated with his 5-year-old daughter, Luz, in 2018, to speak to me about the 72 days he spent separated from his daughter. Julio, like many with similar experiences, explained his departure from his home country as the single most effective strategy available to him to stay alive:

> There were pressures from the groups you know the people that steal and kill for a living... I needed to live. I could have come by myself, but then what would be my daughter's future? Her mother didn't come because she was sick. She could have suffered a lot in the crossing... but for Luz, she needed a better future. I also know we come as a family they understand it better in the U.S. they will not hurt children... I thought.

When I asked what "a better future" for Luz meant to Julio, he explained: "[to] have better conditions to live, study, have a shot at being someone with an education." To him, having an education meant obtaining formal schooling from at least kindergarten to grade 12, with the chance of pursuing higher education. However, his and Luz's experiences at the border left Julio wondering if he had made the wrong decision by bringing his daughter along with him, especially because he had thought that officials would not harm children asking for asylum in the U.S.

While Julio was detained in Texas, Luz was at a shelter in New York. They communicated very little: "Once or twice during the whole time, but the first time I talked to her was not until weeks after." As we sat outside the two-story apartment building where he lived on one floor with his brother, nephew, and an older lady from Guatemala who stayed there three nights a week and who they referred to as the "babysitter," he told me: "I think she [Luz] thought I had abandoned her . . . how would she know?" Julio discussed feeling guilt and shame over what he described as his responsibility for putting Luz in that position:

> I have so many thoughts . . . think about this as a parent you do what you think is best. Then the worst thing happens, the worst . . . they take her. I feel . . . how do you say . . . *culpa*. I feel like it hurts my stomach and my heart. And when I tell people I feel . . . like they will say "you're bad parent." We leave for a better life for something worse to happen. I think we need help from a psychologist or a social worker, you know?

Julio and Luz started their journey from a small town in Guatemala located a few hours from the capital. Julio came from a family that worked in remote rural areas in the country. They raised farm animals and sold chickens, pigs, and food that they had grown. In his attempt to make more money in urban towns in Guatemala, Julio spent time working in construction and mechanics for different bosses. Julio felt pressure to be a stable breadwinner for the family. Carmen, Luz's mother, had diabetes, and while they were no longer together as a couple, he thought of himself as the financial provider. He borrowed money to start his own business but defaulted on payment when not enough clients showed up. The group that loaned him the money was involved with dealing drugs and began to pressure him, threatening Julio and his family if he did not pay them back and work for them.

In a panic, Julio started to contact family members and friends who lived in the U.S. to see if anyone could help him escape to where they were or even help with money. Members of the drug-dealing group began to show up at Julio's house and follow him and his daughter on their way to school. Julio recalled that when he tried to confront the group one Sunday afternoon when they came knocking, he was punched and kicked in front of friends and family. "It was a warning that they would do whatever they wanted," he explained. Julio explained that the group he had borrowed money from and did favors for—like fixing cars for free—was a large entity in Guatemala that he claimed even involved government officials. What happened in front of his family was a decisive moment for him: Julio decided then and there that his only way out of his situation was to leave Guatemala.

It took months for Julio to accumulate half of the $7,000 he needed to pay smugglers to take him and his daughter across the border to the U.S. Julio borrowed money from a cousin in the U.S. and from his family in Guatemala. The deal with the smugglers was that he would have to pay the second half upon arriving in the U.S. Julio and Luz left on May 1, 2018, on a bus bound for Mexico. In Mexico they were joined by other groups from different countries like El Salvador, Honduras, Brazil, and Venezuela. Julio was worried that Luz would witness violence as they made their trip across Mexico: "In her case she had to be with me, which sometimes it was hard because I was with many men. I was concerned . . . but there were women who helped her and other kids. But I had Luz with me the whole time, sometimes I would not sleep to be sure I was watching her. Nothing is made for a daughter and father traveling . . . the bathrooms, the sleeping conditions . . ."

Many families that endured the journey north experienced gender-based divisions in shelters and motels as well as in Immigration and Customs Enforcement (ICE) detention. Keeping a father and daughter together through all these spaces was no easy feat for Julio. For the 12 days that it took them to travel from Guatemala to their last stop at a shelter in Ciudad Juárez, their routine was to stay in church- or NGO-run shelters and find two to three meals a day and a clean place to sleep. Julio explained that Luz—then only 5 years old—cried often for her mom and missed home. But he told her stories about what life in the U.S. would be like, including a school, teachers, and friends: "I used to tell her about the good life we would have and that she would not believe the schools . . . how big and pretty, and the friends. And her cousins . . . I was just trying to have her not be sad all the time. But I kept thinking about the mistakes I made . . . like did I make a mistake even getting money from the people in Guatemala? Did I make a mistake bringing her?"

Later in May 2018, Luz and Julio, along with a group of 12 people, crossed into the U.S. and walked straight to Border Patrol officers. Julio described a commotion in which yelling broke out. He remembered different vehicles: pickup trucks, vans, even fire trucks. The group was told to sit down and to wait to be evaluated or checked. Luz and other children were asked to sit apart from their parents and caregivers, which caused the children to scream and cry. Julio described children getting up and running to their parents, but then being reprimanded and asked to sit down. Thankfully, Luz was sitting close enough to Julio, and he just kept telling her, "Esta bien, tranquila" (everything is fine, stay calm).

After what Julio thought to be an hour, about eight people, including children, were loaded into a van and transported to a processing facility in Texas. The ride took more than 30 minutes, according to Julio. Upon arrival at the processing center, passports and other documents were taken, and Julio and Luz along with other parents and children were told to wait in a room. They were fed frozen burritos and given Mylar blankets, similar to the foil wrappers marathoners use to protect themselves from the cold. Julio and Luz were allowed to use the bathroom and were kept with other families with young children. Julio described the scene: "There were so many lines ... and one officer interviewed us and then there were many papers to look at and to sign, I just said that we were leaving Guatemala because it wasn't safe. One officer said in Spanish that I would have to say that to a judge." Luz feared the facility. It reminded her of a prison mixed with a hospital, she explained: "There were sick people ... little babies crying and many men."

The same day that they were taken together to the processing facility, Luz and Julio were separated. Julio was sent to a detention center in Texas and Luz to a shelter in New York. Officers did not give Julio much information, only that the detention/separation was going to be temporary until paperwork was processed. Julio did not understand if he had any rights at that point and did not know if he would stay in the U.S. or be deported: "I prayed that they didn't send me to Mexico and Luz stayed. How would I ever find her again?" On the day they were separated, he remembered: "They [officers] told me I could bathe and dress her one last time ... [pause, clears throat] ... so I took all the time that I could bathing her in this small bathroom, putting her in clothes they gave us ... pants, t-shirt. Her hair was long, so I braided her hair like I remembered." But when the time came, a woman and a man took Luz by the hand and escorted her away from him. Julio explained that he was yelling as Luz was taken to a different space in what he described as the *hielera* (ice box). "I kept yelling 'no te preocupes hija, todo va pasar bien, te quiero'" (don't worry, my daughter, everything will be OK, I love you). All his dreams and the promise of a better life flashed before his eyes. Julio recalled thinking, "What have I done? My heart is out of my chest." This regretful thought—even as he reassured his daughter—was echoed by other migrant parents who experienced detention and/or separation at the border.

The cruelty of immigration policies—like the zero-tolerance immigration policy in place at the time of this research—is not novel. Families like Julio and Luz have been attacked, undermined, detained, and separated for a long time in the U.S. In *Separated: Inside an American Tragedy*, journalist Jacob Soboroff (2020) details the series of decisions and discussions that ultimately led to the formal adoption of the zero-tolerance immigration policy in 2018. This type of policy had previously been considered during the Obama administration. Soboroff chronicles the damages and suffering caused by the policy, but most importantly, he shows key historical continuities: the U.S. has a long history of enacting immigration policies aimed at undermining and criminalizing immigrant families as a form of deterrence, independent of which political party or politician was in power.

The families in this research were affected by varying degrees of policy implementation at the border. Thus, while I focus on the events that took place between 2018 and 2019, families had been subjected to detention, deportation, and separation before the Trump administration's specific policies took effect. The importance of telling these stories transcends any particular policy, government, or single politician to encompass how the U.S. has historically understood its role at the Mexico-U.S. border and across the Americas. It is paramount for us to understand the multiple ways in which policy impacted families from different nationalities as well as their post-migration trajectories.

Cintia, Ricardo, Maria Clara, and Pilar

Cintia and Ricardo, who migrated from Brazil, crossed the border a few months before the 2018 policy was in place but experienced detention nonetheless. In the beginning of 2018, Cintia and Ricardo left the state of Minas Gerais in Brazil with their then-6-year-old daughter, Maria Clara, looking for a better life in the U.S. Cintia was six months pregnant when they arrived in Mexico City by plane, carrying the money they had been saving for years, and they boarded a bus that would take them to Ciudad Juárez.

In Minas Gerais, Ricardo had worked as a mechanic and Cintia as a cashier at a small grocery store. They lived in a small town but had to travel into urban areas to work. Cintia explained: "I had been robbed so many times in my town, and it felt like the prices kept going up and our salaries were not, I had a sister living here [the U.S.] so she said she could help us find work. She also said my children would just grow up with more opportunities . . . you know, the American dream [laughter]." Cintia was nervous about traveling while pregnant, but she and Ricardo were determined to find a better future in the U.S. Ricardo had sold his most prized possession, his car, to pay for the plane tickets to Mexico City. Their flight had a layover in Panama City, which Maria Clara remembered made her a little nervous: "I didn't know when the end was going to come. Is it now? Are we in America yet?" The family was guided into the U.S. by individuals Ricardo referred to as "the people who help us cross, sometimes they are called coyotes in Spanish I think." For Cintia, Ricardo, and Maria Clara, the total cost including plane tickets was $9,000 (almost 30,000 *reais* in Brazilian currency at the time). They paid half of the money before arriving at the border, and the rest was to be paid within a few months of their arrival in the U.S.

This family's border experience was different from Julio and Luz's experience but reflected other draconian immigration policies aimed at families. Ricardo described the strategy he was told about before leaving Brazil: "They already said that if you arrive with little kids, they will let us through, it's what they call *cai-cai*. That means that in order to get into the United States you have to bring your kids, they won't hurt your kids, and the kids are the most important thing." This practice, *cai-cai*, continues to be a common strategy for Brazilian immigrants trying to avoid immediate deportation. The idea is that family units are less likely to be deported than single adults who arrive at the border.

While the number of Brazilians crossing the border has dramatically increased in the last five years (Montalvo & Batalova, 2024), Brazilian nationals have usually arrived in the U.S. on tourist visas and then overstayed, becoming undocumented once their visas expired. However, when U.S. immigration policy became more restrictive, Brazilian nationals started to arrive in Mexico in higher numbers, looking for asylum or another immigration status that would allow them to enter the U.S. According to U.S. authorities, over 2.5 million migrants were encountered at the U.S.-Mexico border in 2023. In 2021,

Customs and Border Patrol (CBP) registered 17,000 encounters with Brazilian nationals at the border (Waters & Batalova, 2022). This was a dramatic increase from the mere hundreds of Brazilian migrants encountered in the years prior.

In March 2018, Cintia and Ricardo were detained together as a family unit in Texas. They stayed in the facility for 12 days before they were released to a shelter in El Paso, where they spent 7 days and were finally released with the help of a sponsor, Cintia's sister. While Ricardo said that the process "could have been worse," Cintia quickly corrected her husband and stated: "Maybe for you; I thought I was going to die, I thought I was going to lose the baby and I know Maria Clara was traumatized, the girl was traumatized, you know that." Ricardo paused and played with his coffee cup on the table of their one-bedroom apartment: "I know, but look, we are here now, now it's here, and everyone is fine, they tried, but they didn't break us." Holding her younger daughter, 1-year-old Pilar, Cintia got up from the table and went to the bathroom. Ricardo then told me, "I know it was scary, we were all scared, but it was months ago, and our family stayed together." As we continued our conversation, Maria Clara picked up a book in English and asked if I wanted to hear how she was already learning to read in a language other than Portuguese. I was excited to hear her and to give Cintia and Ricardo a break from one of the many conversations we had about their journey into the U.S. When Cintia came out of the bathroom, she put Pilar down and said, "You always think: had I known, would I put my babies through this again? For what?"

While Cintia and Ricardo had different feelings about what had taken place at the border—Ricardo thinking that it could have been worse while Cintia openly questioned if it had been worth it to bring their daughter and unborn baby through the border—they shared the guiding value of gratitude. Cintia explained: "So many thoughts I have Gabi . . . so many about all of it. I was pregnant with Pilar, can you imagine a pregnant woman going through all of that? I couldn't believe that I did that, that I agreed! I have to say, look we are here now in this apartment, we have health, school, we have to be grateful . . ." Ricardo interrupted: "That's all I am saying, we can't deny that we are here with opportunities even as I have to go to court still, we have to stay positive, *ser grato* [be grateful]." Ricardo, like other men in this research, left the detention facility with an ankle monitor and a date to appear before a judge. The date was pushed back multiple times: "I don't know if I will show up to court . . . I have friends that went to a river and cut the ankle monitor and threw it in the lake . . . I just have to focus on working, surviving, giving my girls a good life and teaching them to pay it forward."

The families interviewed brought up their gratefulness even as they described the fears and horrors of their arrival experiences in the U.S. They held on to the promise of a better life, which to them meant that their children would have a shot at good schooling, stable jobs, and a life without the fear of poverty and violence. In fact, as I discuss in chapters 4 and 5, even as the pandemic raged and many families lost their income and loved ones, narratives of needing to make things work because of the hardships their families had endured remained prevalent.

The Meanings of Sacrifice

Different versions of border deterrence aimed at criminalizing, traumatizing, and discouraging people from crossing into the U.S. affected families before and after the infamous zero-tolerance policy of April 2018. However, even the cruelest policies have not deterred people from seeking a life of hope and dignity. Heidbrink (2020, 2017) and Abrego (2014b) have long discussed the connections between narratives of sacrifice and migration. Sacrifice, as articulated by Joanna Dreby (2010, 2015), has roots in narratives of religion and culture in Latin America. Dreby discussed the connections between narratives of sacrifice in Mexico and cultural norms that represent the stoic man as a soldier and the woman as the Virgin of Guadalupe, La Malinche, or La Llorona—a self-sacrificing martyr for her children (Paz, 1961).

In my previous work, *Motherhood Across Borders* (2018), I discussed the meanings migrant Mexican women attached to their role as caregivers, even as they remained separated from their children. In her book on Nicaraguan families, Yarris (2017) showed the moral duty grandmothers felt when their grown children migrated and they became their grandchildren's caregivers. According to Yarris, this arrangement was both a feminine role imposed by structures of society and a role enacted by the women in charge. Migration is rarely ever an individual decision with ramifications confined to the person who leaves. Often, entire families or transnational care constellations (Oliveira, 2018) are involved in the decision and implementation of departure, as well as in the everyday operation of care once people arrive and settle into their new homes. However, meanings of sacrifice become more nuanced and complicated when parents are faced with memories of detention, separation, and a continuous sense of guilt over the events of their migration journeys. Like Cintia, they ask themselves, had I known, would I do it again?

Melanie, Manuela, Lucas, and Leo

Melanie, a mother from Guatemala, experienced the remnants of family separation policies upon her migration north. When she arrived at the border in early 2019, she told border agents she was seeking asylum due to domestic abuse in her home country. She was separated from her 14-year-old son Lucas for several days after they were detained together for a few hours in the ICE box (*hielera*). The explanation she was given by officers concerned Lucas's age and gender: because he was a boy in his teenage years it was "not safe to be mixing with young girls," she remembers being told. While her separation from her child was not as lengthy as those experienced by other participants in this research, Melanie had no idea at the time if those days would become weeks or months: "If I talk about it, even though he is right there next to me . . . still hurts . . . still hurts."

Melanie had lived in Guatemala City with her first husband, Leon, and three children: Manuela (19), Lucas (14), and Leo (5). She described Leon as an alcoholic and their 20 years of marriage as a violent sequence of abuse and neglect. She also described him as a good father and explained that he had never hurt the kids: "But with me . . . he hit me a lot. I was always bruised. Covering the bruises . . . I left because I didn't want to die. I didn't want to die. If I had stayed, in my view, I would have been dead." Melanie had a cousin in Massachusetts who told her there was work for her if she wanted to travel north. Her cousin, Marisa, told her she would get Melanie some money to start her journey. Melanie's biggest decision was whether or not to leave her children behind. Her 5-year-old son had a severe heart disease and had been hospitalized multiple times. "If I can make money there [U.S.], I can send him money. It's painful, but it's the only way for a better life," she explained.

Not only for me, but also for herself, Melanie practiced telling herself and her family members that leaving a child in her home country and traveling to the U.S. was the right decision. While telling me the story across her kitchen table, Melanie asked if I wanted to talk to her son Leo in Guatemala and see him. "I'm going to call him, so you can see him, OK? You will see how he is doing much better . . . that maybe it was good I left to send him money." She tried to call him over FaceTime three times before her mother-in-law picked up the phone. An energetic boy popped up on the phone while his grandmother held the device. "Say hi to your mom," Leo's aunt who was around nudged him, "Oh, and her friend too." Leo said hi and showed his toys and a plate of food to his mom. "Mira, mamá, mira eso que tengo ahora" (Look, mommy, look what I have now).

Tears ran down Melanie's face as she reached for a paper napkin. It had been nine months since she had seen her son in person, and the pain of separation had not subsided. This type of FaceTime call repeated almost every week I was at Melanie's house. She was proud to always call Leo and ask how he was doing. Another time when I visited her, as she washed the dishes while rice cooked on the stove, Melanie described her pain: "As if someone opened your chest and took your heart out, you have your babies, imagine." I think often of the immense privilege I had to sit across the table from a mother who FaceTimed her 5-year-old thousands of miles away while I went back to mine every night. Melanie reminded me of it and tried her best to explain the pain: "Do you feel it now?" she inquired putting her hand on her heart. I did. I do.

Melanie was able to work in the U.S. and send money home, which gave her a tremendous sense of accomplishment. "Once you have children, you are responsible for them, forever. There is no forgetting, no abandoning, no stopping. I will work to give them a better life until the day that I die. For my boy here. For my boy there." Melanie had worked as part of a cleaning crew in Guatemala City, and when she decided to leave, her eldest daughter, Manuela, took her job. Manuela decided not to accompany her mother to the U.S. because she wanted to stay with her own baby and husband. Melanie also knew she couldn't take Leo with her. She feared he would not survive the crossing. So, her attention turned to Lucas, her teenage son: "He could come with me, I thought. He can go to school in the United States, and he will be able to even start sending money to his grandmother one day. He can do it."

While Melanie's plan included her middle child, they didn't know what would happen at the border. Multiple friends and family members had attempted to cross, and Melanie and her family had heard about people being detained, but Melanie decided she couldn't continue living under the circumstances in her home country. I asked Melanie if she had thought her then-husband would be OK with her decision, and if his opinion mattered to her at the time she made it.

> GABRIELLE: How did you think he would react?
>
> MELANIE: I knew he would be mad, so I had to keep it a secret. And my son and him didn't get along at all, so my son was OK keeping it a secret. So, one day I went to work and had my son meet me after work and we left from there. I remember kissing Leo in the morning. God protect me I thought, God protect my son, my little baby, I begged. And there it is... and that's how it was.
>
> GABRIELLE: When your husband didn't see you coming back...
>
> MELANIE: He called... and I didn't answer. I don't talk to him anymore.
>
> GABRIELLE: And Leo and Manuela?
>
> MELANIE: Now, because I send money, I think Leon is fine with me being here, he also has someone else. He always had... but now I know I won't die in his hands, and he won't touch my children. He will not. He was always a good dad, but with many demons. I think my son [Lucas] doesn't like him because he saw him doing things to me... I try to say, he will still be your father.
>
> GABRIELLE: And how is Leo doing?
>
> MELANIE: [Pause] you know he was born with a heart disease and almost died. He has had three surgeries in his five years of being alive. In my mind, God has been keeping him alive, so it's God will. It's in God's hands for him to still be alive [Melanie pulls up a picture on her phone], look at him in the hospital for his second surgery... so brave, this little boy [tears start coming down]... I know he knows I love him so much; God will always protect him.

Melanie was in a new relationship with Edgar, a man from Guatemala who migrated to the U.S. with his 7-year-old daughter, Fany. Edgar and Melanie met in the U.S. when they were working at the same perfume packaging facility. The facility had grueling hours, and Edgar and Melanie bonded over their concerns for their children's health—those in the U.S. and in Guatemala. Melanie, Edgar, Fany, and Lucas lived together in a one-bedroom apartment in a four-story building. Their kitchen was the largest room in the house, and that was where they all congregated when possible.

Edgar was reserved and didn't like telling stories like Melanie did. Melanie always asked me to try to talk to Edgar because she thought it would be good for them if Edgar told someone else about his journey. When Edgar decided to talk to me about his experiences, I started going to see the family more often to make time for both of them. In one of our first conversations he explained, "You take one out [referring to himself leaving Guatemala] to help everyone else that stays, it's the sacrifice we can do for ourselves and for our children and parents, especially the ones who are ill." When I asked Edgar whom he was referring to, he answered that so many of his siblings, friends, and cousins had been getting ill over the years and always needed money to pay for healthcare bills. His migration was tied to many better futures, many better opportunities, and he felt responsible for all of them.

Edgar and Fany

Edgar and Fany had migrated before Melanie and experienced the cruelty of the 2018 family separation policy in its full dimensions. They arrived at the U.S.-Mexico border after enduring tremendous challenges on their journey. Like Julio, Edgar and Fany traveled from Guatemala in the back of a windowless truck with almost 50 other people. Families traveled crammed together with young babies, pregnant women, toddlers, teenagers, and a few elderly folks. He described feeling thirsty, his daughter feeling thirsty, feeling drowsy and dizzy, and "thinking this is how I go! And for what my God, for what?"

Edgar was 48 years old and had three other children in Guatemala, all of whom were older than 8-year-old Fany. Javier was 24, Augusto was 21, and Lina was 20. He had not been with his partner for several years before he migrated. Edgar didn't think he could convince his other children to trek north with him, but he was adamant that to survive and pay the bills he needed to bring Fany with him. "A person works and works my whole life... then I got robbed, stolen from, and I was left without money. I got a loan and the people who gave me the loan started threatening me. It is on me, my fault, I got involved... They were going to take my house, and who knows... people were getting killed over money." Like other fathers in this research, Edgar described the pressure to be a stable breadwinner coupled with the complicated choices he faced regarding how to secure money. Loan sharks, organized crime, urban violence, and potential unemployment were direct threats to men's ability to provide for their families. The threat of not being able to be a breadwinner and stoic caregiver hit at the core of the definitions of masculinity held close by these men.

Along with these issues, Edgar brought up the concept of honor. In Guatemala he had worked as a mechanic and co-owned a shop with a friend. The business went bankrupt when, according to Edgar, his friend stole money from the business to repay his personal loans. Edgar then also took out loans from the "wrong people" who may have been involved with weapon and drug trafficking. "You hear about people getting in trouble and you never think... ah it will be me. No. You judge them: how could they be so stupid? Until it's you." Edgar had a hard time convincing Fany's mother to allow Fany to leave Guatemala and head to the U.S.: "No mother wants to see their child leave, but she understood that for Fany this would change her whole life . . . forever. It was painful, but Fany will be able to go see her, God willing."

Fany's mother, Noemi, sent Edgar many messages via WhatsApp. The audio messages were long, 10 minutes sometimes. Fany called her often, and Edgar sent money to Noemi every month. Melanie understood Noemi's constant calls and messages; she had similar contact with Leo. The bond developed by this family was unique in how they traveled similar, mirrored paths: heartbreak, loss, hope, and care within and across borders. In one of Noemi's messages, she said to Edgar: "Listen, now you are there, you have to make it work for our daughter Fany. You don't have a choice, give her the world." In the U.S., Edgar found himself in a similar predicament to the one he had experienced in Guatemala, in which he felt pressure to be a stable provider. But having a family with Melanie was also a stabilizing force for him. Melanie was loving with Fany and treated her like her own: "Here [pointing to her heart] everyone fits."

Upon entering the U.S., Edgar and Fany were separated. Similar to Julio and Luz's experience, they surrendered themselves to CBP and were taken to a processing center together. Within hours Edgar was informed that his daughter would be taken elsewhere in Texas to be with other children like her. Edgar explained that he was shown paperwork, and he almost signed it, but he thought the paperwork said he would not be able to find Fany again. The American Civil Liberties Union has documented this practice in which parents with deportation orders have been offered forms to sign that waived their right to be reunified with their children (Sullivan, 2018). Edgar did not sign.

Edgar and Fany's separation lasted 21 days, and according to Edgar, they were only able to reunite because "President Trump stopped the processes." During the days they were apart Edgar had no access to Fany but was able to get free legal representation through a pro bono organization. Edgar said he couldn't eat or sleep while away from Fany. He pictured her on her own, afraid. Fany was in a facility with other children in Texas; she was never told anything about her father's whereabouts, even though she asked. Edgar spent his days trying to find more information about his daughter, and in between meals he told me he begged officers for any information they could share about where Fany was. At one point the lawyer supporting his case was able to locate Fany and assure Edgar she was healthy and well. "We were not prisoners, but we were prisoners, does that make sense? The problem is that you have no contact, no help, who do you trust? And part of me thought she was sent back to her mother in Guatemala. I just kept thinking, what have I done?"

Melanie, who supported Fany in their home in Massachusetts, explained: "The poor little girl has nightmares every other night. I sit with her and pet her head and I tell her, 'It's OK, it's OK, you're safe now,' and then she goes back to sleep. I tell her, 'I love you like a daughter.'" This care arrangement was important for this family unit to regain confidence regarding their reasons for leaving Guatemala. Parents Melanie, Edgar, Julio, Cintia, and Ricardo all lived with the difficult thoughts that came from their sacrifices. Although I never prompted, all participants offered "what if" questions during our conversations. Should I have done this? Was it worth it? Those thoughts were quickly followed by a description of the situation in their homes. "No one actually wants to leave their homes," offered Melanie. "Well, some people have an idea that everything here is better, so they do want to leave," responded Edgar. Melanie replied, "Yes, but if both places are equally good, no one would want to leave their homes." The three of us sat in silence at her kitchen table, the fan oscillating left and right as they looked down into their cups of coffee. "I need help!" Fany yelled from the bathroom. "I'll go!" Melanie responded quickly.

Now We Are Here

Present thinking that also involved future planning—planning for a better future—was a feature of parental narratives once families arrived in the U.S: "Now we are here." The "now" signaled the present, the immediate, a break with the past. The "we" brought in the entire family unit, meaning no one would stay behind or be excluded from the plan. And finally, "here" meant in the U.S., but more than that, it signaled opportunity, hope, promise. Parents' doubts, reflections, and regrets informed their focus on present thinking. Dozens of newspaper stories and migration research have documented that the normative response to the question "why did you migrate?" is usually "to provide a better life, a life of opportunities." However, here parents' narratives revealed the intricacies of what may initially seem like a linear thought or a straightforward choice to pursue a better future. "What have I done?" they asked. "Now we are here," they responded. Migration literature usually pays little attention to migrant families casting doubt on their decisions and struggling with the events that brought them to the U.S. Not least, members of each family went through the motions of migrating differently. It is insufficient to merely pay attention to how parents told the story of their migration. We must also understand the constellation of thoughts and perceptions they experienced about the decisions they had made and situate those decisions in a heavily constrained environment.

Ideas of what constitutes "here" and "there" have been discussed at length in the migration studies literature. Hondagneu-Sotelo and Avila (1997) titled their seminal piece on transnational motherhood "I'm Here but I'm There." Therein, they examined how Latina immigrant domestic workers transformed the meanings of motherhood to accommodate spatial and temporal separations. The temporal aspect of migration was particularly salient. The migration experience of parents in this research was informed by the relationship between their present and their future, when they would be providing a better life for their children: "Now we are here." Their past justified their departure, but detention and/or separation sparked questions and fears about the decisions they had made. In my previous work (Oliveira, 2018), I wrote about how migrant Mexican mothers remained connected with their countries of origin in part because they were raising their children at a physical distance. In this case, while the families in this study had transnational ties with family members in their host countries, focusing on being "here" helped them make sense of their journey north. Parents also centered education as a path to a better future. Going to school in the U.S., regardless of all the critiques one may have of American public education, represented the possibility of social mobility and the possibility of breaking intergenerational poverty.

Pandemic and Sacrifice

Melissa, a mother from Brazil, and I had scheduled a time to meet in person in March 2020, but both decided we would be safer meeting through a video call. I had been visiting Melissa and her children for all of 2019 and early 2020, but that day in March we decided not to meet in person not knowing that months would pass before we saw each other again. Melissa's face popped up on my phone screen when I swiped to answer her call. I could see her three teenage children, Adriana (16), Juliana, (14) and Diego (13), walking around or watching TV in the background. We shared the agony of those first weeks in March when we had no idea what was about to happen in the world. Our kids stopped going to school. I was working from home and Melissa, now working as a home and office cleaner, did not return to work for the next two months.

During that call, Melissa still had some bandages on her face from burns she had suffered while working at her previous job in a restaurant kitchen. In 2019, she had been making caramel at work when the contents of the pot exploded; she sustained first-degree burns on her face. While the restaurant's insurer provided her with a stipend and money to pay for reconstructive surgeries, Melissa was not able to go back to working in the kitchen. She was nervous and in pain and struggled to work in a rigid 9 am to 6 pm environment standing over boiling pots every day. She switched occupations and began cleaning homes and offices with a crew.

Melissa and I had talked about her accident before, and I had met her before it even happened, so her recovery, surgeries, and financial issues were part of our everyday conversations. However, now with a pandemic looming I asked how she was feeling about the accident, her work prospects, recovery, and hope. She explained:

I burned myself. Period. That fact is not going to win over me. It's only I that need to know how to learn to live with his. It is me that see myself every day in the mirror. After all of the effort, money, and frankly seeing my children be happier here, we have to be grateful we are alive. Now we are here, so we must take care of each other no matter what. We come here to work and work, and the kids to study and study. When I lost that [work] I did think: now what? And then I told myself, "Well, Melissa, now you are here. You make it worth it!"

Melissa was from a small town in the state of Minas Gerais in Brazil. She explained that she had gotten married at age 16 when already expecting her first daughter, Geise. Her husband owned a small store that sold cleaning products and a range of food items. Melissa had her other three children in Brazil and consistently felt like "ia faltar para eles" (there wouldn't be enough for them). She described her life in Brazil: "There I worked so hard, and I got nothing. I had no money to take my kids out, to take them to the dentist, to live a normal life. I always felt like there would not be enough." The idea to migrate to the U.S. was thus closely related with Melissa's ideas about where opportunities were: "In the United States even the worst is better than in Brazil. For example, the schools my children went to in Brazil . . . they were public and terrible. Here they are public and great . . . there is no better feeling than seeing your children do well in a good school." For Melissa, the best way to cope with the trauma of the trip to the U.S. was to talk about how happy her children were in U.S. schools. Melissa had migrated with her then-husband in early 2019, but he left her shortly after their arrival in the U.S. She became a single mother overnight and in a completely new environment. Her ex-husband didn't pay child support at first, but after many months he started contributing to Melissa's total income of $1,500 a month.

Even so many years after what had happened, Melissa still described her entry into the U.S. as a traumatic event. She explained the detailed strategy provided by the coyotes and showed me the notes she had taken. I have translated them from Portuguese to English here:

Run as fast as you can into the United States. That is to prevent the Mexican police from arresting you first.

Se entreguem, surrender yourself to U.S. border patrol officers.

Don't lose your passport and make sure you know a phone number by heart.

Make sure they see you have children with you.

Melissa had written the rules on a tiny piece of paper. The night before her crossing, she recalled being paralyzed by the prospect of having to cross on foot and risking her children's lives: "It's one of those things, do you stay and let your children not have a chance, become drug addicts, and get shot by a stray bullet, or do you travel north and risk being arrested, shot, and deported? It's more of the same . . . more tragedy." Her route north started in Brazil, through Peru, Mexico, and the U.S. When I asked about traveling within Mexico, Melissa explained: "That part I can't remember." Her son, Diego, echoed her words: "Never remember?" Melissa finally conceded: "I think it was too traumatic and they disappear from my head. You know that?" The trip through Mexico involved staying in many religious-based shelters, not sleeping during nights, being mugged, being accosted by the police, feeling nervous about kidnapping and rape while trying to safeguard all of the documentation and money they had secured.

After surrendering herself and her family at the Ciudad Juárez-El Paso, Texas, border, Melissa was detained with her two daughters and separated from her husband and son for 17 days. First, they were separated at the ICE facility, then she described being put on a bus and traveling for hours to a detention center where she and her daughters were held for more than two weeks. Melissa described "the agony" of not knowing whether her husband and son were safe or whether they had been sent back to Mexico. She also expressed feeling responsible for the panic her daughters experienced: "I saw in their faces, they were so scared. But you know, kids trust their parents so much. They trusted me. I told them, 'We are going to make it, we are here now.'"

After those weeks, Melissa and her daughters were finally reunited with her husband and son in a shelter in El Paso where they stayed for five days until the family was able to travel to the Northeast U.S. Like other parents in this study, Melissa described the cost of trying to provide a better life for her children. The changing nature of border policies between 2018 and 2019 was more dangerous than Melissa had thought it would be. However, Melissa anchored her narrative in the present, repeating the words "now we are here." Parents in this research always followed their reflections on separation and detention by reiterating that their now or present was better than their past. Julio described this feeling in the following way: "If one stops too often to think about leaving a home, putting young children through this trauma, then our minds will be always clouded by doubt, questions, and what ifs. So, one must protect the mind from the bad thoughts of what have I done?"

To migrate is to care. Mothers, fathers, caregivers in this research elaborated on both their reasons for leaving—the structural conditions of their home countries—and their hopes for the future—to provide an opportunity for their children to receive an education that would change their future. The easiest analysis is to stop there and portray migrant families' quest for better lives as a singular narrative of striving. Here, however, I have shown additional dimensions of that narrative: first, how the promise of an education is used to counterbalance the experiences of violence, fear, and loss on the way to the U.S.; second, how the self-doubt, personal guilt, and fears of having made the wrong decision haunt parents; and finally, how even within family units, degrees of questioning and commitment to a life in the U.S. vary. However, it is in the articulation—"now we are here"—that we come closest to understanding what it means to migrate.

(Un)Fulfilled Promises

While detained and after release, parents spent time rethinking their decision to leave their home countries, challenging their own assumptions of what it meant to be a "good" parent. In all cases of detention—together or separate—the U.S. government employed the strategy of enacting the unknown: not knowing how long it would take to be released, not knowing the whereabouts of their children, not knowing if representation would be available, and not knowing if deportation orders would be put in place—all functioned as ways to confuse, undermine, and hurt families. Caregivers were left to fend for themselves and individually figure out how to find their family members or be released.

Julio recalled walking around at the detention center he was kept in for 72 days and finding a pamphlet attached to the wall that read: "Do you need a lawyer? Call this number." He picked up the flyer and memorized the number.

When he had a chance to use the phone, he called the lawyer. Until then, Julio had not had a lawyer assigned to work on his case. The number on the flyer connected him with a nonprofit that helped parents and children reunite after being separated at the border and, ultimately, with a lawyer named Justin. Julio remembered resisting pressure from U.S. agents to sign a paper that he thought meant he would be deported without Luz, similar to Edgar. Julio used his phone time every day to call Justin and tell the lawyer his story. Justin immediately validated his preoccupation with signing papers and told him not to sign anything until they could meet in person. Julio explained: "They [ICE agents] insisted that I sign papers I think it was so that I could be deported . . . I think . . . I am not leaving my daughter, one can't break a promise, I made a promise to her." When I inquired what promise he had made, Julio answered with his hand in the air indicating the numbers, "The first one was that she was going to be OK, then a better life, more opportunities, a good education."

With his lawyer's help, Julio was able to speak to Luz a couple of times—after six weeks of no communication. Julio asked agents on a daily basis, "Where is my daughter?" The response he usually got was, "We don't know, the paperwork needs to be processed." Julio described witnessing dozens of detainees signing paperwork and then not seeing them again. He feared his time was coming and being sent back to Guatemala without his 5-year-old daughter was his worst nightmare. After two weeks working with his lawyer, Julio was notified that his reunification with Luz was imminent. Julio said that his reunification with Luz was possible because of "God, the president of the United States, and my lawyer, Justin."

Luz and Julio were reunified in Atlanta, Georgia, after more than two months apart. Julio remembered hugging Luz and crying but feeling like her hug back was not very strong. He described her as having sad eyes and a confused face. At that time, authorities told Julio they would release him with an ankle monitor only if he could show proof of a sponsor. Julio had a cousin in Massachusetts who confirmed his role as sponsor with U.S. immigration officers. Julio and Luz boarded a plane together to the Northeast and settled in a town where they knew people, but Julio wondered if he would ever have a real shot at fulfilling his promises to his daughter: "You are so happy when you are together . . . in my mind I was worried if she was going to be with traumas for the rest of her life . . . and I am the one with guilt."

Andrea, a 38-year-old mother from Honduras, described similar feelings as she reflected on her trek north with her three children: "It has been a huge change for my children, and I don't trust that doctors and psychologists and teachers can help them. I don't trust them. But they need support to recover from so many disruptions; after all, we are here to do good, no one wants to hurt anyone here." Andrea came from a small town in Honduras near the border with El Salvador and Guatemala. She migrated with her three children in November 2019 and because of a policy called Migrant Protection Protocol (MPP)—commonly known as "the remain in Mexico policy"—stayed in Ciudad Juárez for one year before being authorized to enter the U.S.

Andrea's husband, Alberto (42) had been deported when caught by the Border Patrol trying to cross the Rio Grande before Andrea tried her luck with her children. Andrea opted to surrender herself and her children at the border because she feared one of them could drown or die on the way to the U.S. Andrea described living a quiet life in rural Honduras until a group of *pandilleros* moved into her town in an attempt to hide from competing criminal groups. "When they first moved, they were not bad, they didn't cause any trouble with us," she said. "But then they started to come to our house and demand to take everything we grew ... chickens, vegetables, fruits ... and then there was a bad incident with my husband and we decided to not let the kids play outside on their own anymore."

In the incident she referred to, Alberto had confronted members of the gang and told them they could not take things from his family. As in other migrants' stories, the gang members beat him right in front of his house. Andrea remembered screaming at the men who were punching Alberto to stop. Her children also witnessed this senseless act of violence. After what Andrea described as several minutes, the *pandilleros* left Alberto on the ground with a bleeding nose and two broken ribs. Alberto explained that he felt angry, but also felt a sense of shame for having let his family down: "We are supposed to protect them, our kids, and provide for them. They saw me on the ground."

Andrea described a multitude of armed conflicts in her town, stray bullets and police officers being called but paid to say nothing. She started to worry. She asked a sister already living in the Northeast U.S. for money to support her trip north with the children. When Andrea decided to leave in 2019, she planned it so the whole family would go: "No one will stay behind." When adults and youth decide to leave their homes, often they speak to others who have taken the leap to travel north. Facebook and WhatsApp groups are common ways to retrieve information, figure out routes, get alerted if anything has changed or if there are better or worse shelters along the way. Andrea looked for as much information as she could and paid for a service to bring her and her family to the border.

Her journey had three phases: Honduras to Guatemala, Guatemala to Mexico, and the trek to the U.S. border. Andrea described the journey between Honduras and Guatemala as less harsh than the trip through Mexico to the border. Because she already lived so close to Guatemala, traveling through the neighboring country did not seem as daunting as traveling through Mexico. Most migrants traveled by night in Mexico, which made them easy targets for organized crime members and police officers who wanted to exploit them and steal their money. That was also true for Andrea's family. She had spare money ready for any extortion attempt and paid off three police officers during her journey through Mexico before she arrived in Ciudad Juárez. There, they stayed at a shelter for immigrant families run by nonprofits and the Catholic Church.

Andrea thought she had made a mistake arriving at Ciudad Juárez instead of Piedras Negras or another port of entry bordering the U.S. When she and her three children arrived at the border, Migration Protection Protocols (MPP) was in place. The MPP program was initiated in 2018 and quickly implemented in Ciudad Juárez. Under this program, certain individuals who arrived at the Southwest border were returned to Mexico pursuant to Section 235(b)(2)(C) of the Immigration and Nationality Act to await immigration proceedings under Section 240 of that same act. In practice, the MPP program created a huge bottleneck of migrants in Mexico waiting to appear before a judge on the U.S. side. The program also left migrants in a vulnerable position as they awaited news from the U.S. Migrants in Ciudad Juárez were often victims of kidnapping and theft, and parents worried about letting their children play outside or enroll in a public school.

Issues with the program mounted. People subjected to MPP usually lacked legal representation. According to the American Immigration Council (2022) only 7.5 percent of individuals subject to MPP ever managed to hire a lawyer, though the true representation rate may be even lower because that estimate includes individuals who were initially placed into MPP and later taken out of the program and allowed to enter the U.S. The lack of counsel combined with the danger and insecurities individuals faced in border towns made it nearly impossible for anyone subject to MPP to be granted asylum. By December 2020, of the 42,012 completed MPP cases, only 638 people had been granted relief in immigration court (American Immigration Council, 2022).

Every day that Andrea and her three children stayed in the shelter in Juárez she felt farther and farther away from fulfilling her dream of providing them with a better life. Andrea explained: "Those were very difficult days. I was afraid for my children, I didn't have a phone, so I had to buy a Mexican number to try to talk to my husband. I didn't know if he was going to try to cross again. My kids lost almost one year of school, because I couldn't send them in Juárez." She emphasized: "It's hard not to be able to fulfill the dream to enter the United States, and worse having your children witness it." In her last months before entering the U.S. Andrea was able to enroll her children in the local school in Ciudad Juárez. According to her, they never complained and were happy to be able to leave the crowded shelter to go to school. Andrea echoed Melissa's words about feeling the weight of her children's trust: "Our children, they look at us and think we have the answers, they can trust us. And the truth is their dad did the wrong thing, crossing into the U.S.; that's a crime, it's wrong, it's our fault. That's why for me it was important to show that I was trying to do the right thing for them, it is my duty in life, to care for them."

Parents struggled with the realities they faced at the border. The nightmares commonly referred to by children continued to the present day. When parents migrated alone and endured the hardships of border crossing—the violence of police officers in countries of transit and the fear of rape, death, and deportation—they kept those experiences to themselves or shared them with peers (Oliveira, 2018). However, when families migrated together, parents struggled with the fact that their children witnessed and experienced the pain of detention and/or separation at the border as well as the other dangers of the journey. These experiences undermined parents' sense that they had fulfilled their duty to care for their children; instead, they worried that they may have put their children in danger. These mixed feelings of guilt and hope permeated their existence, even as they were reunified far away from their home countries and the border.

Conclusion

The experiences that children and parents suffered before migration and during their detention and/or separation at the border have generated long-term trauma. Parents and children continued to cope with the hurt caused by this process and grappled with their new realities in the U.S. In this chapter I have shown how immigrant narratives of sacrifice—the hardships, selfless acts, and exhaustive efforts immigrant parents endured in the hope that their children would have access to better schools and brighter futures—shaped their experiences of crossing the border. I contend that overlapping experiences of poverty and violence prior to migration, coupled with traumatic experiences at the border, resulted in parents reflecting on the costs of their sacrifice. While much of the literature on migration frames sacrifice as the reason for migration, here parents challenged their own assumptions regarding the payoff of this sacrifice. Was it worth it?

Parents' identity as caregivers and providers came first, so their decisions to leave, to migrate, to remove their children from a place where they no longer thought their families could thrive, was the ultimate motivator for all parents in this study. As Julio and Melanie feared for their lives, they also pondered what their children's lives would be like if they were no longer there. As Melissa and Edgar reasoned, they knew that their children trusted them to know what was best, even as they doubted their own judgment. Andrea and Cintia felt their children's pain when they were kept from their partners, not knowing if they would ever see them again.

Parents relayed this message in different ways. To survive and provide a better life for their children, parents migrated north. Parents defined that better life as one in which their children would have enough food to eat and a house to live in, would not experience violence or poverty, and would receive a good education. Education was the most specific benefit parents articulated when they imagined their lives in the U.S.: schools equipped with teachers, books, chairs, a cafeteria, and specialists who would help students and their families. To paraphrase Warsan Shire, their judgment that the water was safer than the land—and no one would put their children in a boat unless it was so—shaped parents' decision to trek to the border between the U.S. and Mexico.

However, parents did not fully anticipate the reality of crossing the border with their children. Through separation and detention, parents felt compelled to rethink what had spurred them to leave home. Time and time again, Edgar and Julio reflected on what Julio described as "putting her through so much" or what Edgar deemed as his "responsibility" for his daughter's well-being. Andrea remembered thinking to herself as she waited at the border: "Patience, patience, at least we are alive, we are making progress, we are closer to freedom and the right to a good life."

TWO

Im/migrant Children's Embodied Narratives of Immigration

WHAT HAPPENS WHEN CHILDREN and youth are the storytellers of their migration histories? While in the social sciences the notion of agency has been used with increased frequency in research with children, replacing traditional assumptions about young children's roles as mere recipients of adults' arrangements, there is still room for complex work that honors children's and youth's experiences. Thus, the concept of agency is helpful as both an educational aspiration as well as a signifier of a strong rights-based political commitment to countering views of children as lacking capacity to understand, explain, and teach us complex topics (Guo & Dalli, 2016; Silver, 2020).

Immigrant children's voices rarely guide media coverage of the so-called immigration crisis; however, their images are overused to evoke empathetic responses from a wider public. During 2018 and 2019, several news outlets reported on how children were being cared for at detention facilities along the border and in the U.S. On July 10, 2019, a hearing took place before the Subcommittee on Civil Rights and Civil Liberties in the House of Representatives titled, "Kids in Cages: Inhumane Treatment at the Border" (2025). Oral statements were collected from experts on child well-being as well as a parent, Yazmin Juarez, whose toddler—Mariee—died weeks after she was released from the Immigration and Customs Enforcement (ICE) facility in Dilley, Texas. As in this case, for legal and logistical reasons, adults are often the ones who hold space for testimonies and storytelling about children and their well-being.

By contrast, in this chapter I take on children's narratives of their own mobility, their parents' decision to migrate, and the journey north. Here I explore children's accounts of what led their families to leave their homes and travel to the U.S. in the first place. I also focus on children's stories of what happened at the U.S.-Mexico border as they were detained with or without their parents, often separated, and sometimes handed over to the Office of Refugee Resettlement (ORR). Migrant children's accounts differed from their parents' narratives. In a much more localized way, children made sense of their parents' sacrifice by expressing what they saw and heard, but also by explaining how these moments made them feel. While children are often the subject of policy and media discussions, they are rarely consulted. Children are the experts of their own lives, and through narratives of the ruptures and continuities wrought by migration, we learn how the journey north took place from their perspective. Whenever scholars write about the perspectives of children and youth, a common critic's comment is that children are told things and then they repeat them. It could be. But that observation does not discount the knowledge children and youth contribute about their migratory processes.

In her recent book *Drawing Deportation*, Silvia Rodriguez Vega (2023) argues that there is an "implied disposability of children's lives when the political strategy for immigration policy relies on family separation" (p. 14). The drawings Rodriguez Vega collected show the importance of listening to children and centering their perspectives even as adults are the ones who make decisions. A growing number of projects by UNICEF, KIND, and other organizations focus on making space for immigrant children to tell their stories. However, research that doesn't just "add" children to the mix of sources, but rather homes in on their knowledge from a learner's perspective, is occasional.

In the next section I briefly engage with frameworks and literature that help conceptualize children's role in migration flows. Without being comprehensive, the goal is to show that centering children's and youth's perspectives, narratives, and thoughts in research endeavors increases nuance and strengthens our findings. However, it is not enough to include or engage children in research. We must change how we conceptualize our own understandings of who gets to tell what story and our assumptions of the structures these stories must follow (Oliveira & Gallo, 2021).

Childhood Studies

Early iterations of childhood studies align neatly with dominant trends in anthropology and sociology writ large. Namely, childhood studies provides a window into how scholars conceptualize people's complex relationships to processes of "socialization," with children providing a kind of ideal test case of enculturation. This literature thinks of "childhood" as the period of time in which young people are learning how to be part of the societies to which they belong. There are varying approaches to this question, which also mirror broader trends in social science. For example, theorists have alternatively embraced models such as determinism, functionalism, and constructivism, each of which offers an independent vision of the tensions that emerge when the study of dominant norms (i.e., "cultural practices") rub up against the inherent diversity of engagement that humans exhibit (for a detailed overview of these movements and their relationship to the study of childhood, see Corsaro, 2015).

Analyzing the development of this theoretical tradition over time reveals two big aims. One branch of research attempts to account for how society changes or molds children. Another branch does the inverse: this research seeks to understand how children impact or change their surroundings. These are each distinguished from constructivist views, which see attempts to distinguish childhood from other life stages as a reflection of societal norms and values, not of biological, intellectual, or developmental reality. Both branches of literature demonstrate that studying childhood can provide researchers with a way to understand broader patterns of social organization (Prout & James, 2015).

Children are not passive members of the cultures and communities in which they are embedded. Rather, they can (and do) instigate change through the same relationships that reveal patterns of social behavior. Early theories of socialization and enculturation largely treated children as the passive subjects of a process that would continue to take place independent of their existence, but which manifested in its most concentrated or identifiable form in relation to them (Handel, 2011). Over time, this approach to childhood studies has largely fallen out of fashion, as social scientists have embraced the notion that children, while vulnerable, are agentive participants in the phenomena researchers study (Bluebond-Langner & Korbin, 2007).

Researchers have investigated children's agency to different degrees: research has focused on young people's ability to make choices within the cultures and institutions that contain them, on their understanding of the complex sociopolitical phenomena that shape their worlds, on instances of "rupture" that challenge a society's norms, and on the potential existence of distinct versions of reality that are different from but exist in tandem with the adult world within which research is ordinarily situated. Focusing on children's agency has been critical to establishing an international rights framework that recognizes the importance of involving children in the decisions that affect them (Baraldi & Cockburn, 2018; Bluebond-Langner & Korbin, 2007; Moody & Darbellay, 2019). At the same time, some scholars have dismissed "agency literature" as basic and call for theorization that goes beyond simply recognizing children's ability to act—an ability that all people have (Hammersley, 2017; Mason & Hood, 2011). These writers argue that this approach often stops at recognition, failing to further the field in a way that substantively "advanc[es] theory" or "improv[es] the lives of children" (Lancy, 2012, p. 13).

Young people have never truly been absent from anthropological and sociological research. Their presence has always been noticed and, indeed, central to any analysis of social and cultural life. However, their silence has been noteworthy: while children have been present, their perspectives have often been left out of accounts of their lives (Prout & James, 2015). Deeper research conducted on and with children demonstrates that they hold unique viewpoints and ways of being that push the adults around them to confront alternative versions of "truth." Scholarship that contends with these aspects of children's existence draws inspiration from other "standpoint theories"—most notably, feminist theory—to articulate the importance of accounting for the unique viewpoints children hold as a result of their position in a world largely run and described by adults (Bluebond-Langner & Korbin, 2007). "Child standpoint theory" (Mayall, 2002) argues that, like women and other "subaltern" groups, children possess a unique perspective on the worlds they inhabit: a "standpoint" that inevitably differs from that of a proximate, dominant group (in this case, adults).

Alongside related intellectual traditions, such as Black feminism, Indigenous frameworks, Global South epistemologies, and Borderlands writing, this version of childhood studies forces scholars to think through the lived experiences of "alternate personhood" and its implications both for children and for society writ large (Nagasawa & Swadener, 2017, p. 217). Importantly, this approach to childhood studies does not simply see children as a counterperspective through which dominant social trends are illuminated, but rather recognizes "children as people to be studied in their own right, and not just as receptacles of adult teaching" (Hardman, 1973, p. 504). In some cases, this might mean approaching childhood as its own cultural system—one that overlaps with and responds to broader (adult) societies, but which is still an exclusive dimension with its own values, practices, and order of beliefs. In others, it might mean seeking a way of understanding how children's position in society influences their interpretation of complex intersocietal and intergenerational events.

Child standpoint theory has faced several critiques, chief among them is that it tends to collapse the experiences of all children around the world into one monolithic perspective, which is often dominated by Western cultural realities (Wells, 2021). This limitation is augmented by the temptation to draw rigid boundaries around who "counts" as a child for the sake of clean comparison. This impulse can extend and reify culturally specific notions of when one stops being a child and enters a new life stage. Like feminist theory, child standpoint theory has also suffered from a lack of intersectionality, failing to recognize the diverse factors that influence children's experiences in different social and political contexts.

Linking childhood studies to feminist scholarship also risks recreating some of the problematic traditions to which the latter initially sought to respond. More often than not, women's experiences are analyzed in relation to children's experiences—whether they choose to have and care for them or are asked to defend the decision to abstain from motherhood and caregiving. Entangling women's perspectives with children's risks reinforcing the supposed "naturalism" of the relationship between these groups. Political efforts to support the needs of women as caregivers can rub up against efforts to recognize women in their own right and advocate for them apart from their role in children's lives. This is further complicated by how women are often portrayed as childlike (at least, until they bear their own children). At the same time, "concerns have been raised that this conceptual antagonism reduces the complexity of adult-child relations—which can include joy, love, and reciprocal care—solely to that of work and burden," when in fact the relationship among women and children is multifaceted and multidirectional (Twamley et al. 2017, p. 251).

In the sections that follow I focus on the narratives of children and youth. While I run the risk of putting children's and youth's narratives in direct contrast with their parents' narratives, the juxtaposition of children's and youth's choices regarding what to share and focus on with the parents' narratives explored in the previous chapter is striking. On the one hand, parents discussed a localized, individualized guilt regarding the decision-making that brought them to the U.S. Children and youth, on the other hand, had expansive explanations that centered policy as well as the Mexican and U.S. governments as actors that had impacted their experiences.

They Took Me Away

Luz, 6, was separated from her father, Julio, for 72 days. When I first met Luz in 2018, she was about to join a kindergarten classroom in a bilingual school after having been in the U.S. for some months. She was excited about going to school after being reunified with Julio. A week before she started school, Luz showed me the outfit she had chosen: a dress with a bow in the back. Her school had a dual language program, which meant she would be speaking in Spanish with some of her teachers and peers for at least half of the school day. Luz was interested in books, and every time I came to see her, she would ask if I had a new book to bring her. I always did.

Luz enjoyed school while she could attend in person. She described her classroom as "colorful," her teacher as "kind," and the playground at her school as "big" and "fun." She often told me about how different her current school was from her previous one in Guatemala. "The bus here is yellow and big, and everyone is always singing," she told me with a big smile on her face. Luz also discussed how much she wished her mother could see her school in the U.S. "She loves to hear me read," Luz said of her mom. The promise of the American experience of schooling and education permeated the opinions of Luz's family members in Guatemala. Luz explained: "I know that in my country people say, everyone comes here so they can go to this big pretty school I go to! I wish my cousins could come too."

Luz and I often talked about her time away from her father after they surrendered themselves to Border Patrol at the U.S.-Mexico border. When I first asked her why she thought her father decided to migrate to the U.S. and bring her with him, she paused for a minute and then said, "To give me a chance for a better life." Her answer resonated deeply with those from her father and other parents I talked to, but Luz's thoughts also differed from those of the adults around her:

> In truth sometimes I think about my country and my mom and I think about how everyone is doing there . . . I'm happy there too, and I am happy here, I think about my bike . . . I want to ride my bike and play . . . the only place I didn't do that was when I was with the señor y señora in their house for all the days . . . but you know what we had pancakes and cereal for breakfast every day.

The *señor* and *señora* Luz mentioned were a couple that looked after her and other children under the age of 10 when she was in U.S. government custody. Luz recalled that the woman, who she said was from Puerto Rico, was always "angry" and "yelled a lot" at the kids. In her narrative, Luz alternated between framing and locating "here" and "there." However, she pointed to the moment when she was detained as an exception in her happiness and freedom to play: it was "the only place I didn't do that," she explained. Every now and then Luz asked me or her dad if we knew the fate of the children who were with her for those 72 days. "Did they find their parents?" she once asked me as we made pizzas and cupcakes with Play-Doh.

During the more than two years I interviewed and observed Luz, she never stopped asking questions related to her experience in 2018. Over time, she offered me various pieces of her experience of migration, separation, and detention. She sometimes offered these narratives unprompted, especially if something we were doing or eating reminded her of those experiences. One late morning in June 2019, while Luz and I were eating a meal of rice and chicken at her kitchen table with some books in Spanish waiting to be read, she told me:

> LUZ: For lunch sometimes there was rice with chicken because she, the one who took care of us, was Puerto Rican she would make food that was Puerto Rican . . .

GABRIELLE: Do you remember her name?

LUZ: No... I don't.

GABRIELLE: But did she play with you and help you?

LUZ: Well with me and with the others sometimes she would get very mad because of what we did...

GABRIELLE: Mhmm.

LUZ: I couldn't sleep with anything on my bed, no toys, none of this [showing me a teddy bear that was on a couch close by the kitchen table].

GABRIELLE: That is hard, not being able to sleep with your toys.

LUZ: It was just... I don't know... I was thinking, why couldn't we? What was bad about it?

GABRIELLE: I agree with you. It's good to sleep with our favorite things.

LUZ: Now my bed has one million toys [laughter]...

[WE BOTH LAUGH AT LUZ'S COMMENTS ABOUT HAVING A MILLION TOYS ON HER BED.]

GABRIELLE: What about your clothes, did you have clothes to wear every day?

LUZ: When I arrived there, they gave us a few clothes, but we didn't have many and it was getting cold. But when we arrived there we arrived with a bag of clothes... in the plane!

GABRIELLE: Wow! So you flew in a plane, was it your first time?

LUZ: Yes! And I was not afraid of the plane. I didn't know where I was going but I heard Nueva York! And it was so far... I had to use the bathroom in the plane.

GABRIELLE: It must have been a very long flight.

LUZ: I didn't sleep in the flight and they gave us some crackers, but I didn't sleep.

GABRIELLE: Did you sleep when you got to the house?

LUZ: Yes and others they were *chiquitos* [small kids] too they were with me.

GABRIELLE: I see, were you all in the same room?

LUZ: Not all of us, I mean, not all of us slept together in a bed, but we slept in bunkbeds and there were little kids that were 2, 3, 4 years old. They were little. Sometimes at night they cried "mamá mami mamá" but not me. I knew they took me away, but I was waiting to see my papi. It wasn't his fault they took me away.

After saying this, Luz got up from the table to get paper and markers for us to draw and write. Usually, I didn't ask her questions about the past unless she started a conversation about what had happened to her. When she offered a sentence or two, I followed up with questions that ended up helping me understand her experience better. Luz finished our dialogue by getting up and changing the activity. She also put her own experience in contrast with the younger children who were with her—"not me"—affirming she knew she would see her father again. That moment in time was temporary; she was just waiting.

Luz expressed concern for the children she had been with in New York City as well as for children who lived near her current home in the U.S. Her apartment was a two-bedroom unit on the first floor of a four-story building. When I came to her house, there would often be multiple children playing in the outdoor area of the building's top floor. Often, two young toddlers would be there, walking around and playing in only t-shirts, without diapers. They were also from Guatemala and lived with Luz's cousin and uncle in the building. Luz was aware of her surroundings: "I don't know why they are not wearing clothes, it's cold, we need to help take care of kids. There were some kids in my house [the shelter in New York] that were always dirty, and they didn't change their diapers, or help them. I can help them now." I understood Luz was mentioning the shelter she lived in when she said "my house" because I immediately asked, "Which house, where?" to which she replied, as if she was stating the obvious, "In New York!"

My sustained, multiyear interaction with Luz allowed me to follow up when she referenced a location or moment in her life related to her journey to the U.S. Since she narrated those experiences at moments that felt important to her, they varied in time and space—in the U.S., in Guatemala, or in detention.

The intertwined memories of "here" and "there" entered and exited Luz's narratives often. Once, at a playground in 2020, Luz was swinging next to a friend. I was sitting at a bench nearby with her father, Julio. She was laughing and playing when we saw her schoolteacher with her own children on the playground as well. Luz came running to me and to her dad to tell us that Ms. Gonzalez was there. Luz was a little nervous about going up to her teacher and saying hello. When I asked her why she felt uneasy, she explained, "I don't think she knows about everything that I tell you. Do you think she knows..."

When I followed up with "She doesn't know that . . . ," Luz jumped in whispering, "Que me llevaran" (that they took me away). By the time we were finishing our conversation, Ms. Gonzalez had walked over to say hello. I already knew her, as she had participated in interviews for this study. Luz spoke to her briefly about the nice day off and how she was going to get back on the slide. Ms. Gonzalez tried to talk to Julio about how well Luz was doing in school, and he just repeated, "Gracias, maestra, que bueno maestra" (thank you, teacher, that's great, teacher).

After the interaction Luz and I debriefed about what she thought Ms. Gonzalez didn't know: "Some things I say in the class, but somethings I don't know if I can say. There I'm reading the books and playing. But I don't know if she knows where my mom is. Maybe she does . . . do they know that I came from Guatemala, the police, the house, the plane . . ." Julio held Luz's hand and told her not to worry, that even if the teacher knew, everything would be alright. Luz asked if they could go get a popsicle and Julio said yes. For Luz and other children in this study, the experiences of separation and detention stayed with them well beyond reunification and release. The daily reminders of a past that they did not often share or that even felt secretive due to the delicate nature of their immigration status were present in their daily lives. Children articulate the impacts of immigration policies on their lives differently than adults, however. The only way to improve the support children receive is to listen to them on their own time.

In my conversations and interactions with Luz she focused on institutional spaces that contributed to her experiences crossing the border: the shelter, the school, ICE detention. She also separated out her dad, Julio, as someone who had not "put" her in danger, contrary to how he thought about it. As a 6-year-old, Luz showed critical knowledge about the external, structural forces that contributed to her migration trajectory. She explained: "It's that no government wants us. Guatemala doesn't want you, Mexico doesn't want you, U.S. doesn't want you. So, one has to escape, hide, it's dangerous." While we had this conversation we sat on the floor of her family room, coloring and practicing her handwriting together. I asked, "Why do you think that . . . that no government wants you?" Without missing a beat, Luz answered: "How do I say this . . . we don't have much and if one doesn't have much they don't want you." I pressed again, curious about Luz's rationale here: "What is it that you don't have?" She responded: "Ay maestra [laughter] cosas y dinero . . . y cosas como una casa, y eso" (Ah teacher things and money ... and things like a house, and that). Luz explained that poverty was a major determinant of whether a government would want you in their country. For Luz it was not Julio who put her in danger, but the governments that didn't want them.

Migration and Childhood

Children's well-being—present and future—is often positioned as a primary motivation for migration. This phenomenon has been well documented by anthropologists working in a variety of geographic contexts (Boehm, 2008; Cuevas, 2019; Dreby & Stutz, 2012). Even when immigrant families experience challenges in the aftermath of migration, visions of providing an "ideal childhood" to one's descendants retain their power (Horton, 2008). Children and youth are well aware of these dynamics and often identify feeling a sense of "indebtedness" (Gu, 2021; Kang & Raffaelli, 2016) toward caregivers who sacrificed so much to provide the next generation with safety, security, and future opportunity (Chao & Kaeochinda, 2010; Enriquez, 2011). This pattern is evident even among children who stay behind when parents leave to migrate. These children adopt a similar framework to justify parental absence as an investment in their future opportunities (Hu, 2017; Oliveira, 2018).

Transborder movement can also bring families into contact with alternative understandings of childhood, as they move between contexts with different practices and assumptions regarding young people's place in society. This dovetails with research that seeks to identify transhistorical or cross-cultural comparisons of the changing value of children as a depersonalized, moral concept (Lancy, 2014) or social construction (Prout & James, 2015). Migration may require that groups develop new ways of organizing themselves in response to unprecedented challenges, manifesting new ways of "dealing with" children in the personal, political, legal, and academic sense.

In her recent book, *Migranthood: Youth in a New Era of Deportation*, Lauren Heidbrink (2020) teases out these different dimensions of young people's involvement in migration and their implications for scholarship on youth and childhood. Heidbrink finds that youth have their own understandings of and narratives about migration—narratives that often differ from those produced by their family members, their teachers, and the governments tasked with their well-being. For young migrants, mobility is a "cultural elaboration of care" on par with that undertaken by adults who move across borders (p. 33). At the same time, Heidbrink identifies children and youth's unique position in global and national imaginaries, extrapolating both how young people and their families are socialized into migration and how their movements are pathologized at an institutional level. Within Heidbrink's definition of migranthood, children vacillate between centering their own needs and wants and resisting larger assumptions of their role, while situating themselves in relation to broader immigration policy. It is in this context that listening deeply to what children and youth tell us reveals a nuanced, nonlinear version of migration and mobility.

Because It's My Parents

Felipa (12) was sitting on the porch outside her house. She had just gotten out of the shower and her hair was wet. Since we met regularly, at least every other week, she was waiting for me. It was May 2020, so while we had met consistently from January until the pandemic shutdown in March, we waited until May to meet outside in person again. Between March and May, we FaceTimed frequently, and she would send me recorded messages through her mother's WhatsApp. Daphne, Felipa's 11-year-old sister, also came out onto the porch. She was also fresh out of the shower and holding a container of cut-up cantaloupe and a few cans of ginger ale and seltzer water. Their little brother, Francisco, greeted me through the window holding an iPad, but said he wanted to finish playing Roblox before he came outside. Their dad, Javier, was home and their mom, Andrea, was at the restaurant where she worked as a cook.

Felipa mentioned that she was tired of doing online school and asked me if people in Brazil were also doing online school. I responded that, yes, but that not everyone had access to a computer or internet. She then told me:

> FELIPA: I wonder how the kids in my town in Honduras are going to school. Are they going? I don't know...
>
> DAPHNE: I wonder about my friends, our friends, we made in Mexico, are they going to school? We had a little school in our shelter... the volunteers helped.

GABRIELLE: I don't know, I think most countries are still doing online schooling... I think, but I don't know.
FELIPA: It's funny because here we are, now we are here to be doing things on the computer.
DAPHNE: Yes, but at least we have the computer!
FELIPA: I know we have a computer, but we didn't think we would not be going to school in the United States.
DAPHNE: Remember Caro that worked at the house we stayed in Mexico? She went to college, maybe we could find her... she was a college student here in the U.S. Is she doing online too?

I answered Daphne saying that at the college where I was working at the time, our students were all online.

We stayed on that porch talking and hanging out for about an hour and went inside after to eat together. I had brought bagels because Daphne had mentioned she had them once and wanted to try them again. The girls also wanted to show me all their homework for school. Often, I would try to help them with homework, mostly explaining the directions and breaking down the steps. I had informed their teachers that sometimes they asked for my help. As I looked at their homework, I could see that both Felipa and Daphne had been doing some writing in Spanish on their own. They each had a notebook decorated with stickers, hearts, and their names in bubble letters. Felipa and Daphne asked me to read their entries. They had written in those notebooks almost in the form of diary entries: reflections on the past, present, and hopes for the future. "Today I did all my homework but couldn't go out to play much. My parents don't know many people here yet, and we are learning English. I wish I had my friends here with me. I don't know if I will ever see friends again that are not in the United States," Felipa had written in one entry. "Why are some people not nice at school? Sometimes I feel so different because of what happened to me. And someone said maybe they don't have the same president next year," wrote Daphne about the possibility of President Donald Trump losing the 2020 election.

Felipa wanted to show me her math homework, but Daphne asked if she could go first. The two sisters argued often. Felipa's personality was more reserved, and she described feeling scared about walking down the street by herself or going into a convenience store on her own. She didn't like when her parents were gone for too long and waited by the windows and door with a phone in her hand. Daphne was the opposite. She was outgoing and described different moments in her life—including the journey north—as "adventures." The family had relatives in the U.S., and before migrating, Daphne told me she had always wondered what her cousin's life was like in the U.S. When the time came for her parents to leave Honduras, she felt ready.

Whenever I asked the sisters if they knew why their parents had decided to come to the U.S., they often responded: "To give us a good life here, to have school and for one to be safe," Daphne began. "Yes, our mother and father always wanted us to have a different life than they did . . . and for one to get more education, try to have good jobs," finished Felipa. While the sisters provided similar answers, their descriptions of the migratory journey were different. Thus, although families may go through the departure, getting stuck, apprehended, detained, and released together, each member of these family units experienced these "compounded losses," a term used by scholar Margarita Alegria, in different ways (Cardoza, 2021). When we untangle the individual perspectives of youth and children from those of their parents and siblings, research in immigration yields complex findings that defeat the stable, assumed notion of linear success, mobility, and academic achievement.

In many families, adults told me grueling stories of their journey and what happened to them before they migrated in their living rooms in front of their children (Oliveira, 2018). The idea of what children ought to know and how they should participate in grown-up life differed from family to family. However, in the cases I discuss in this chapter, children not only participated in these conversations, but they were also central to both the family's decision to migrate and to how the journey took shape. For instance, Javier explained that because he traveled by himself—a single male adult—the decision to walk in the desert for days made sense. However, he did not want his wife and children to experience the same, so they took a different route to the U.S.

When I first met Felipa, Daphne, and Francisco, they had just settled in their new home in a town in the Northeast of the U.S. They had been stuck in Ciudad Juárez for almost a year before being allowed entry into the U.S. In one of our weekly conversations, Andrea pulled out her phone and showed me videos of her with her three children on a motorboat crossing a river in Mexico.

In the footage, Felipa's face was frozen, her expression concerned as she held on to her seat. The camera panned to Daphne, who had a big smile on her face and clapped her hands saying, "We are getting closer!" Francisco was nestled in his mother's lap, hugging her very hard, with his eyes wide open. As I finished watching the footage, I asked Felipa about her take on the trek north. I said, "It seems here you were nervous about the boat, is that right?" Felipa responded:

> I didn't like any part of the trip. It was sad to leave. It was sad to travel, it was sad to stay in Mexico, it was sad to say goodbye to friends we made in Mexico, and now we are here. The part that I hated the most was this boat trip. The boy driving the boat was my age, he was going fast, and the whole time I'm thinking, where are we going? Are we going to be alive? Because of my parents we go, you know? Not because of me. I told my mom I didn't want to ride on the boat . . . but she said for me to stop worrying.

Daphne quickly jumped in and explained that she did not fully agree with Felipa's assessment. She didn't think everything was as sad as Felipa was describing. Daphne had made good friends while at the shelter in Ciudad Juárez. When Daphne talked about the volunteers that helped her there and how she kept busy, her eyes welled up with tears. For Daphne, it was the gunshots outside of her house in Honduras that haunted her. "So many times in front of my house we would be playing and then cars would drive by shooting at each other, we had no peace. My mom and my dad knew that. I almost died there!" Javier described the event Daphne referred to during another interview: a time when a car almost hit Daphne. If she had not jumped out of the way, she would have been hit. To this day they believe the car drove toward her at full speed on purpose, because threats had signaled that the family was in danger. For Daphne, the construction of the decisions to leave her home was more obvious and straightforward than for Felipa. While Felipa questioned most of her parents' decisions and did not express much hope for the future, Daphne felt that she was finally safe once she left Honduras.

Francisco (6) told me: "I don't even remember my house in Honduras . . . I remember a lot more in Mexico. I played so much with everyone's phones, but I don't remember my room anymore in Honduras, I remember playing outside, and eating the cake at abuela's house . . . a colorful big cake, remember?" For Francisco, the journey north felt scary. In Mexico, he slept in the same bed as his mother the whole time they were there. They shared a single mattress, while the girls shared a room. Francisco only ate with his mother, only slept or bathed if his mother was around or in sight. He explained: "Because it's my mamá... I just want to be where she is so that no one can take me from her." Francisco had nightmares and felt scared while they were traveling from Honduras to Mexico. Francisco vividly remembered one incident when his mother had to pay a bribe. The bus they were traveling on was stopped, and men dressed as police officers demanded money. In his words the "bad guys" pulled a gun on his mother and yelled at her. He remembered her crying and giving the "bad guys" a lot of money.

When Francisco told the story of his journey between Honduras and Mexico, he pulled from different memories, sometimes mixing up times and places. For example, he mentioned that he loved his teacher in Honduras called Carolina, but Daphne quickly jumped in and said, "She was a volunteer at the shelter!" Or when Francisco said that he liked to ride his *patineta* in the street in Mexico, Felipa corrected him, "That was in Honduras." Now, what was clear to Francisco was his love for the toys protectively tucked up in his room. The family lived in a two-bedroom apartment on the first floor of a three-story townhouse. Francisco continued to sleep with Andrea, but he now had a dedicated storage space for his things. He explained about how many toys he had in his storage space: "Because my parents gave me things... sometimes because I was feeling sad because we left... my mamá had to leave so we can be here with health." Immediately after finishing this sentence Francisco stood up from the floor where we were playing with cars, ran to his mom in the kitchen and gave her a bear hug. She rubbed his back with her arms, sparing her hands. "They are covered in garlic," she yelled out.

However, Francisco also offered poignant critiques of structures that failed to protect him and his family. During a game of hide and seek in his house, Felipa and Daphne were hidden and Francisco was looking for them. I was seated on the couch talking to Andrea about their upcoming meeting with their lawyer. Francisco walked around the house looking for his sisters who agreed to one game of hide and seek and one game only. When he finally found Felipa, she jumped out from under the table and scared him. Francisco reacted: "Nothing scares me anymore! You don't scare me, the police doesn't scare me!" Andrea yelled at Francisco: "What police talk is that?" Francisco replied: "Ay mamá sí sabe . . . la policia que asustó nosotros . . . pero ya no pueden con nosotros, no nos ayudan" (Ay mamá yes you know . . . the police that scared us . . . but now they can't scare us, [they] don't help us). I turned to Francisco and asked when they (the police) didn't help them. He told me, ticking events off on his fingers: "In my home, in Mexico, and here." Andrea disagreed with him almost immediately: "It's not like that, *hijo*, there are good people helping us here." Francisco ran after Daphne who was also hiding in another part of the house.

Felipa, Daphne, and Francisco all articulated their parents' awareness of the dangers in Honduras. It was clear to them that their parents had some power over the decision to migrate to the U.S., but they also recognized that the idea to leave was connected to protecting them from harm. Felipa questioned these decisions when she asked, "Are we going to be alive?" Daphne explained that she almost died in Honduras and affirmed that "my mom and dad knew" about the dangers of staying. At another moment at the house, Francisco reflected on his family's decision to leave Honduras: "I think I will get a new tablet here maybe for my birthday. If I do well in school, if I am good and I learn . . . nothing bad will happen to any of us . . . because I am the superhero, want to see?" He picked up action figure toys from where we were playing and enacted a battle—"bang-bang, boom"—as if one toy figure was killing another.

The three siblings enjoyed school and found safety in their routines in the U.S. Of the families in this study, this one had spent the longest amount of time at the border in Ciudad Juárez waiting for the resolution of their asylum case. For this reason, their storytelling compared three realities: Honduras, Ciudad Juárez, and the U.S. Under Andrea's supervision they had engaged in school-like activities in Juárez. The shelter where they lived for months had university-affiliated college-age volunteers who were eager to play, teach, and spend time with children. Daphne missed the volunteers and credited them with "helping me not forget what I had learned in school." Felipa preferred the school in the U.S.: "I didn't like leaving, I didn't like staying in Juárez, but I think at least I am safe here . . . still not easy to just start a school in a new place." When I asked Francisco to draw what his experience leaving Honduras and arriving in the U.S. was like, he drew El Paso on one side and Juárez on the other side of a wall. He drew crosses on the ground on both sides because, he said, "Some people they die there." He also explained that there were so many children together in Juárez and he loved playing soccer with them. He drew the mountains in El Paso because the landscape and some buildings were what he could see from the shelter and included an airplane because that was how they left the border and made it all the way to the East Coast (figure 2.1).

One afternoon in the spring of 2021, Felipa, Daphne, and I were painting our nails together on their porch and we started talking about people that we had all met in the past in different geographic locations. We wondered how they were doing. Daphne asked me if I knew what my sister in São Paulo did every day. I told her I had an idea because we talk over WhatsApp so much. Felipa paused and looked up:

FIGURE 2.1   Drawing by Francisco, Age 6

Source: Author.

> I don't think we will know what people end up doing, like the people we met, or we knew in Honduras, or in Juárez ... I don't have their numbers ... our parents may know them. But because of my parents, I don't always mean bad thoughts, but because of my parents we are here ... I told them to get everyone's numbers, but I didn't know if our numbers would be the same ... and I was right, they are not.

Daphne continued the thought: "Yes, but it's OK, it's not only their fault [the parents]." The two sisters locked eyes with each other, shrugged their shoulders, and returned to painting their nails in bright neon colors. While some may call these "moments" of reflection or "glimpses" or "windows" into children's conceptualizations of their selves and family, I argue that these daily articulations are how they live. Instead of analyzing them as moments in a narrative, I understand these as constant verbalizations of what was, what is, and what is hoped for the future.

Somos MPPs: Policy Embodiment in Children's Expressions

Children and youth conceptualize and describe the so-called "push and pull factors" in migratory movements differently than do adults. They also articulate the impacts of immigration policy on their lives by identifying external forces, such as the U.S. government or the Mexican government, as important actors in their displacement, detention, and fate. Children and youth, while sometimes critical of their parents' decisions to leave, were fairly protective of them. Leaving home and taking on a long, uncertain journey together created multiple dynamics between parents and children.

Adriana (16), Juliana (14), and Diego (13) were immigrant youth from Brazil. Their mother Melissa was a single mother from the state of Minas Gerais and had migrated with her children to the U.S. through the U.S.-Mexico border. When I interviewed them, the three adolescents were in middle and high school in the U.S. and lived with their mother in a two-bedroom apartment. Since Melissa's burn accident (see chapter 1), Adriana had started working sporadically babysitting for neighbors and walking dogs to help with income. When we discussed the hardships of having to study, work, help their mother with health concerns, and other pressures of everyday life, Adriana explained that their experience at the border forever shaped how she understands "hardships." She recalled one moment in detention that stuck with her:

> So... whenever I think things are bad, I always think, maybe it's never as bad as it could be. At the jail at the border you know they were not that bad with us, like, they could have been so much worse, I saw so many people crying, babies crying, moms with the babies, pregnant women, little kids sleeping on the floor... you know there were some people who were MPPs and were stuck, and they wanted to be *cai-cai*, but they couldn't... we got through [*nós passamos*], imagine now they could send us back with the other law.

Adriana referred to particular policies established during the Trump administration when she considered the relative nature of hardship. The first policy she mentioned was MPP or Migrant Protection Protocols, a program that had been established by the U.S. government with the support of the Mexican government that went into effect in January 2019. Migrant Protection Protocols (MPP 1.0)—often referred to as the "remain in Mexico policy—was responsible for sending almost 70,000 migrants back to Mexico before it was suspended and then terminated after President Biden took office, only to be reinstated on December 6, 2021 (American Immigration Council, 2022).

Adriana used MPP to describe some of the people she met in detention. For thousands of people, being in the MPP program meant that their asylum cases would never be heard by a U.S. judge and that they had to stay in Mexican border towns like Juárez, Nogales, and others while they waited for their court dates. This setup generated concerning breakdowns in communication. For example, if families were given an appointment but had not registered a phone number or an address where they could be contacted, they would lose their spot. And if they lost their spot in line, the U.S. government might permanently close the family's asylum application case. Figure 2.2 is a screenshot from a message received by the Perera family from El Salvador, who waited in Mexico for their hearing under the MPP program. Their case was dismissed without any prior communication, and lawyers advised them not to appeal. This result was devastating for so many migrants. Adriana pointed to this catastrophe at the border when she considered what constituted a hardship.

Daphne also explained what MPP meant to her in a narrative of how her embodied experience of policy contributed to her understandings of self. She wrote in her journal entry in Spanish and here is a translation to English:

FIGURE 2.2   Screenshot of Message Regarding the Status of Immigration Cases.

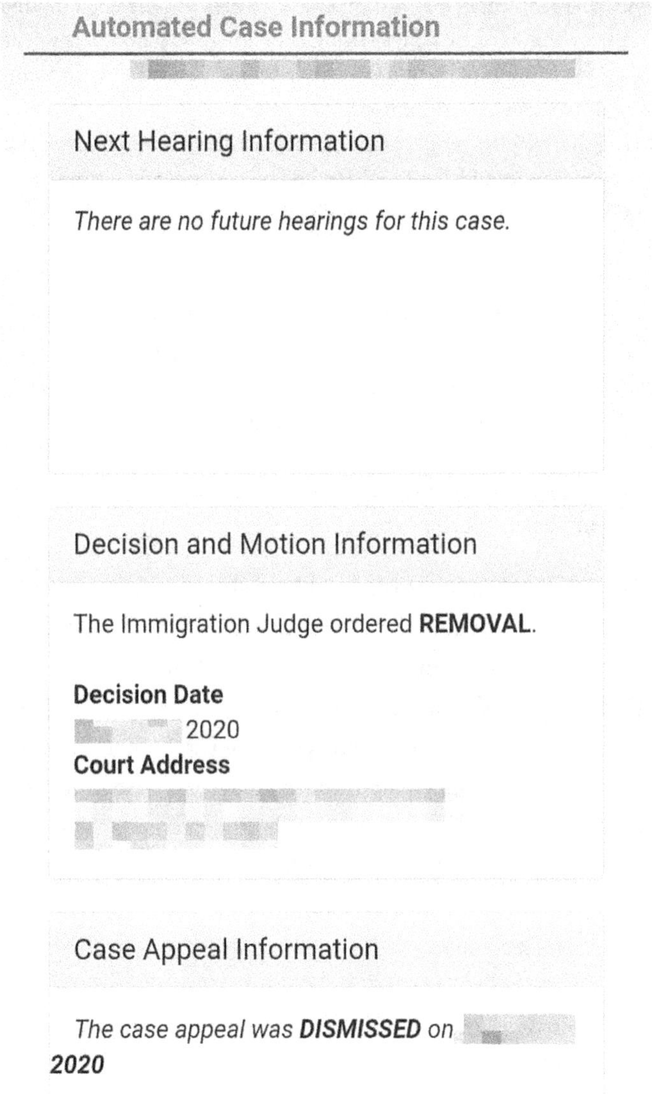

Automated Case Information

Next Hearing Information

There are no future hearings for this case.

Decision and Motion Information

The Immigration Judge ordered **REMOVAL**.

Decision Date
2020
Court Address

Case Appeal Information

*The case appeal was **DISMISSED** on*
2020

Source: Author.

The cold was intense.

And there it was the moment to cross, we went through a water canal and finally we were caught by the Border Patrol.

The experience in Migration is horrible, it was very cold, they moved us from one cell to another and we didn't have an idea of time you couldn't sleep [and] we were there for two days. Things did not go as planned they returned us to Mexico through MPP, we were very scared and filled with sadness ... they took us to Casa del Migrante.

There I shared with people of many nationalities, the experience there was pretty ... I made a lot of friends, with who I played and spent time.

Respecting the rules that were in place.

We were there for six months, we went to two [immigration] courts and they sent us back to Mexico.

Cristina, a friend of my mother invited us to live in a house with better spaces and we were going to be able to go to school, there were four families and more volunteers from the USA ...

In this house I lived beautiful moments, people that helped us were excellent.

With the change in government, he gave us the opportunity to enter and today I am in a beautiful city in the USA.

In this journal entry, Daphne explained how she and her family were kept in Mexico for months through MPP. She also pointed to the change in government as a possible explanation for why they were ultimately allowed entry into the U.S. Daphne provided a chronological description of their interactions with different law enforcement structures in the U.S. When she explained the journal entry to me, she said: "Es porque somos MPP, o no, fuimos MPP" (It's because we are MPP, oh no, we were MPP). This particular embodied signaling of the policy was echoed by other children who were detained, separated, or deported at the border. This articulation of the combination of agency and structure characterized many children's expressions regarding their border experiences.

Every child participant in this research offered one or more articulations of how migration policy shaped, at least discursively, the trajectories of their lives. Cruz, who was 7 years old, had migrated with his mother and father from El Salvador and referred to his experience in a similar way: "Depending on what happens at the border the people in the government can decide what they do with you." He explained how his fate and his parents' fate depended on policies and their implementations when families arrived at the border. William, an 8-year-old migrant child from Guatemala, explained that he noticed a difference between the colors of the uniforms of the "police officers" when his family first arrived at the border: "Some of them had brown clothes, some had black clothes, some people had normal jeans and a t-shirt, but they were also police."

William described these distinctions during one of our many interactions on the terrace of his home, where he enjoyed playing with cars. While he was playing with his cars, I asked if he had seen those types of pickup trucks in real life. William, who was separated from his father at the border for 18 days, said that he had ridden in many different vehicles in the last year: "This one belongs to the police on this side [showing how the vehicles were organized] and that one is with the one that wears brown clothes." Border Patrol agents usually wear dark green uniforms on the job, while Immigration and Customs Enforcement (ICE) agents usually wear black ones. These moments of encounter at the border remain with children long after the event of separation and detention.

Häkli and Kallio (2021) have argued that there is a politics of encounters centered on the body when it comes to analyzing refugees' agency and the governing structure where they are. According to the authors, "the term [politics of encounters] captures well both the eventful coming into contact by bodily subjects and the broader contextual forces that mediate and shape these encounters" (p. 683). Building on Plessner's theorizing on social embodiment (1975), the authors call attention to the duality in these encounters where there is embodied political agency in relation to governing bodies. Children in this research articulated their understanding of the array of ever-changing policies at the border, but their recollections also show how it became deeply interconnected with their sense of identity and (dis)placement. Ramsay and Askland (2020) define displacement as "not only a matter of physical or material security but a phenomenon that is deeply connected to the sense of security of the self within past and future temporal trajectories" (p. 2). The authors continue by explaining that "whether evolving from migration or stasis, or resulting from personal catastrophe or societal change, we argue that displacement fundamentally involves having one's sense of purposeful being and purposive connection to place, time, and social worlds—that is one's teleology—ruptured" (p. 3). These displacements, then, are not just about place and space, but are also deeply related to purpose; the purpose of being able to move for the idea of a better life.

Adriana also drew the parallel with yet another border-crossing practice known by Brazilians as *cai-cai*. As explained in chapter 1, *cai-cai* stands for the migration strategy in which a family is caught and released together by U.S. law enforcement, through a policy that was enacted by the Obama administration. If immigrants are trying to cross using the *cai-cai* strategy, they arrive at the border with underage children—who must be first degree relatives—and request asylum. These families can be released into the U.S. with the promise that they will attend scheduled court hearings. Some adults are released with ankle monitors that can only be removed if they appear in court.

To Adriana's point, some families wanted to enter the U.S. with children and assumed that they would be "caught" but would not be imprisoned, jailed, separated, or deported. Their hope was that they would be released into the U.S. together. This practice dramatically changed in 2018 when the Trump administration practiced zero-tolerance family separation at the border. However, Adriana articulated the embodied nature of "being" *cai-cai*—or participating in the catch and release government strategy. The policy's use as an identity marker was a salient feature of how children discussed immigration. In comparison to their parents, children freely spoke about the role governments and policies had in their lives.

Conclusion

"I love your Brazil shirt," Cruz said, referencing the t-shirt I was wearing one day that had the colors of Brazil. "Oh thanks! What do you like about it?" I asked him. He replied that he loved all the soccer players on Brazil's national team. One by one, Cruz started to recite their names out loud as we sat at his kitchen table: "Neymar, Felipe, Thiago Silva, Gabriel, Firmino . . ." I said to Cruz that it would be great to see a game live one day, especially if it was a match during the World Cup Championship. Cruz got up from his seat: "That would be a dream! We don't really have a good soccer team that can make it far in the World Cup," referring to his home country of El Salvador. I made a joke that they were better than the U.S. men's soccer team. Cruz let out a belly laugh, amused at my amateur comparisons in the men's soccer world.

Then he told me that he had seen children playing soccer across Mexico and eventually at the border with the U.S. His parents had left El Salvador because of the violence, lack of opportunities, and the fact that Cruz's grandmother already lived in the U.S. Before they left El Salvador, Daisy, Cruz's mother, had not seen her own mother in over a decade and Cruz had never met her in person. I asked Cruz if he played soccer at all as he traveled north with his parents. Cruz answered that he really wanted to, but they were always nervous about the Mexican police and being outside for too long. He explained that he had witnessed someone having a negative interaction with law enforcement in Mexico: "I saw a man giving money to the police in Mexico and then my parents were worried they would take our money too. I wanted to play, but I think my mom said we have to keep our eyes alert in case we see the guards. Sometimes they are not there to help a person. So, it can change very fast . . . what happens to you." Cruz presented a nuanced perspective on law enforcement in Mexico. The idea that police officers may not be helpful sometimes and the fleeting nature of interactions between migrants and law enforcement were and continue to be features of migrant experiences. Cruz spoke about what he wanted to do—"play"—but instead followed both the advice his mother gave him—"keep your eyes alert"—and the evidence he had observed for himself.

Children articulated uncertainty related to encounters with guards, the police, law enforcement, or with policy itself. While as children their identity did not reduce to their status as migrants, this dimension of their existence had daily implications. The very act of migrating brought children a sense of constant interaction with the law and with ever-changing public policy guidance at the border, both of which were not only potentially dangerous, but were also characterized by sheer ambiguity. The categories of migrant, refugee, or asylum seeker were met with migration regimes (in Mexico and in the U.S.) that worked relentlessly to contain, control, and organize where and how migrants appeared at the border. Ramsay and Askland (2020) describe the displacement suffered by refugees as a "disruption of one's sense of existential continuity and stability" (p. 2). In the same way, children who were deemed asylum seekers by the U.S. government witnessed and experienced not only their parents' criminalization as they attempted to cross into the U.S., but also a sense of displacement, since whether or not they would be allowed into U.S. territory was deeply connected with which policies they encountered.

The vulnerability faced by migrant children when they encountered the laws that contributed to how they were treated in Mexico or in the U.S. must not be confused with a lack of agency. In this chapter I have elaborated how children's narratives of migration, detention, and/or separation were embedded in larger structures like parental decision-making and border laws. However, children's articulation of how policies and their parents shaped their understandings of the rupture of leaving one's home and arriving in the U.S. demonstrates the subtle forms of agency that are otherwise concealed by their assumed embeddedness in everyday experiences. The interplay between agency and structure serves as a backdrop for children's narratives of entanglement between parental decision, border policy, and their own ideas of belonging. Barker (2012) defines agency as "the capacity of individuals to act independently and to make their own free choice," while "structure is the recurrent patterned arrangements which influence or limit the choices and opportunities available" (p. 126). Beyond analyzing how much agency migrant children have in an increasingly punitive migratory system, this work is concerned with how children articulate sophisticated understandings of the impact of those larger systems on their lives. Adults shouldn't be surprised by the elaborate, powerful analytical takes of children and youth; instead, they should listen closely and learn from them. For adults, these understandings demonstrate how children's narratives resist the linear descriptions of migration for a better life and the important implications of broader policy and parental decision-making in their lives.

THREE

Pedagogies of Silence

ONE WINTER DAY IN 2019, morning meeting—the first scheduled activity of almost every day of elementary instruction—began in a first-grade classroom. Children formed a circle on the rug and were encouraged to sit "criss-cross apple sauce" or, in bilingual classrooms, teachers would call it either *joelho com joelho* (knee touching knee) in Portuguese or *sentaditos de piernas cruzadas* (seated with your legs crossed) in Spanish. Morning meeting was a moment at the beginning of the day when teachers connected with the whole class. Some teachers used this time for students to share things that happened at home, others used it to review the day's plan, while still others checked in with students regarding basic logistics of the school day. Morning meetings were somewhat flexible compared to other more structured moments in the classroom routine later in the day. These 6- and 7-year-old students looked excited, tired, and ready to talk to one another, and to offer their own perceptions and knowledges. That practice, however, did not always go as smoothly as a teacher would want.

In this chapter, I show how migrant children's experiences were often left unengaged in structured and unstructured classroom instruction, as educators tried to comply with school curricula and expectations. I call these dynamics "pedagogies of silence." While young children sharing and talking about issues that are not deemed "classroom appropriate" is not a phenomenon reserved to migrant children, I paid specific attention to the stories and narratives students brought into the classroom that pertained to immigration. As teachers rerouted, skipped, or ignored what children shared in the classroom, I show how children resisted these dynamics and made space for their experiences to be discussed inside classrooms and schools. Finally, I consider how immigrant children were positioned between school and home, between promises and expectations, and how they were often left to reflect on their experiences on their own.

As explained in the introduction, I observed both bilingual (Portuguese/English and Spanish/English) and monolingual (English) classrooms. My classroom location depended on which child I observed on a given day and which program that individual child was enrolled in. Most bilingual classrooms I observed were in the elementary grade levels, while in the middle and high school grades I primarily observed English-language only classrooms. The language predominantly spoken in the classroom contributed to—but did not necessarily determine—the language spoken in teacher-student and student-student interactions. Recently arrived immigrant children and youth who had the opportunity to enroll in bilingual programs were able to speak in Portuguese and/or Spanish in their classrooms for part of the day, thus allowing their reflections, thoughts, reactions, and conversations to flow more freely in their first language. When classroom instruction was primarily in English, newly arrived migrant children and youth were not as participative and thus spoke less in general as they were learning English.

I observed each child and youth included in this study for a minimum of 80 hours and a maximum of 120 hours over 18 nonsequential months of schooling in person inside their classrooms or at their schools, and for an additional 15 months online or in the hybrid modality (chapter 4). The onset of the COVID-19 pandemic in March 2020 shifted my observations online and then to a hybrid modality until I was able to return to in-person observations in the late fall of 2020 for the remaining 13 months of data collection. Observations typically lasted between one and four hours each week per student. These observations took place inside classrooms or hallways, during recess, lunchtime, specials, after-school activities, and evening events. Since all children and youth attended similar schools or ones that were close by, I was able to observe two or more children each time I visited a school.

While conducting participant observations in these schools, I came to know the teachers, administrators, and other educators in the buildings. I was inspired by so many of them—by their hard work and care for the children they taught. It is important to understand these findings within the constraints experienced by the educators in this study. These educators were under pressure to deliver a prescribed curriculum that packed the school day from start to finish. Every minute counted toward their lesson goals. Educators' wiggle room was short and quick, and the time they could make to listen and learn from students was constrained. I have written elsewhere (Oliveira, 2021) about the concept of "constrained care" as a framework that teachers have experienced in classrooms. The concept refers to how teachers care deeply about their students and their stories, however, once out of the classroom, teachers' care becomes limited and constrained as they cannot facilitate or support discussions at home.

Many educators were uneasy about engaging in issues related to immigration, but willing to center discussions of racism, gender, different family units, and (dis)ability in their lessons. For many of these topics, teachers explained that they had been trained or attended a professional development session, or even reported having curriculum available to use in their teaching. Immigration felt like a harder topic to take head on. Being a public school teacher is no easy feat. I commend and applaud the tireless work of so many teachers to find the wiggle room, the spontaneous sharing moments, the less rigid times, and allowing space for children to bring their knowledges and perspectives into the classroom. Not just learning happens in these unstructured real moments; it is also where children build trust with teachers.

The Role of Educators and Young Migrant Children

Young migrants often experience trauma in their country of origin or in the course of their transnational journey (Bemak & Chung, 2017; Goodman et al., 2017; Talleyrand et al. 2022; Thibeault et al., 2017). In addition, they may encounter unexpected difficulties after arriving in the U.S., such as poverty, food and housing insecurity, and discrimination, alongside the loneliness and isolation associated with adjusting to life in an unfamiliar place (Suárez-Orozco et al., 2008). Teachers are often aware of some, but not all, of these experiences

(Gándara & Ee, 2021; Turner, 2015). Moreover, they are not always prepared to respond to the nuanced experiences newly arrived children and youth bring into the classroom (Damaschke-Deitrick et al., 2022; Frankel et al., 2021; Gitlin et al., 2003; Goodwin, 2017; Hamman-Ortiz, 2020; Hamman & Zúñiga, 2011; Hopkins et al., 2015; Rodriguez et al., 2020).

Many adults—including school leaders, administrative staff, and classroom educators—have the power to affect when, how, and under what conditions newcomer students are able to communicate about their experiences. In alternating moments of engagement and silencing, adults in school settings draw implicit boundaries around which stories students are "allowed" to share in different contexts. How teachers and school personnel respond to children's attempts to talk about their immigration experiences in turn constrains the knowledge they can gain about the circumstances shaping students' engagement in classroom learning. Educators' responses can affect newcomers' sense of belonging and their ability to process the different emotions that arise as they adjust to their new schools and communities.

Numerous studies have sought to understand how teachers can best meet the needs of immigrant students to facilitate their engagement in classroom activities. While well intentioned, research and professional development resources that focus on the "problem" of immigrant education often reinforce deficit frameworks, rather than investigating the circumstances that shape immigrant students' involvement in different school activities (Rodriguez, 2015; Roy & Roxas, 2011; Sharma, 2018; Watson & Knight-Manuel, 2020). For example, educators may express concern that newcomer students are not actively asking questions in class and take their silence as an indication that they need additional intervention (Patchen, 2005).

In reality, there are myriad reasons why newcomer children might be more hesitant to engage in one-on-one conversation with an instructor, including different cultural norms around classroom behavior or feelings of intimidation or discomfort (Kiramba et al., 2021; Ryu, 2013). By beginning from the premise that student engagement must be actively solicited, these approaches may miss moments in which children are already trying to communicate details of their lives and academic experiences in ways that make sense to them. It is in this context that pedagogies of silence emerge as a common practice in classrooms.

Migration Stories Inside Classrooms

Back on the rug during morning meeting that winter day in 2019, the classroom teacher, Ms. Andrade (Brazilian, veteran first-grade teacher), went around the circle asking if the children had brought lunch from home or if they were going to buy lunch at school. She did so in Portuguese—the target language of instruction—and in English. She began:

> Agora eu vou perguntar sobre o almoço de hoje [Now I will ask you about today's lunch]. Hoje, se vocês quiserem comprar o lanche quente temos Fajitas [Today if you want to buy hot food we have fajitas]. Fajitas são como uns vegetais quentes e também carne enroladas num pão bem fino que chama tortilla [Fajitas are like hot vegetables and meat wrapped in a really thin bread called tortilla]. I really like it. OK, let's start, Pedro, lanche de casa ou da escola [lunch from home or from school]?
>
> PEDRO: *de casa.*

Ms. Andrade pointed to next child, asking her to respond to the same question and taking notes on a small pad.

> CHILD 2: *de casa.*
> CHILD 3: *escola.*
> CHILD 4: *de casa.*
> CHILD 5: *de casa.*
> FLOR, 6-YEAR-OLD FROM BRAZIL: My lunch is from home and my mom made um *misto quente* which is a sandwich we eat in Brazil and they didn't give us that when we were in a jail, I think they gave us this thing you just said Ms. Andrade . . . this fajita thing. I think that it was that thing . . . it was very cold . . . and . . .
> VINNY, 6-YEAR-OLD FROM BRAZIL: Flor, I know the food you said, the food they give to eat . . . and . . . that is cold one and . . . the rice inside is ice . . . and . . .

Ms. Andrade jumped in and addressed Flor: "Ok, thank you, Flor, we can talk about this later, OK?" Flor nodded her head yes and the children continued answering Ms. Andrade's question: *de casa* and *escola.*

Flor had been in the U.S. with her family for five months (since November of 2018) at the time I observed this exchange. She arrived with both of her parents via Ciudad Juarez, Mexico, across the border from El Paso, Texas. Flor was detained with her mother, but they were separated from her father for a week. While her family was not detained in the height of summer 2018 when the family separation policy was at its zenith, a few months later some practices were still in place, like the separation of families by gender. During the normalcy of a morning meeting when teachers usually tried to organize the day's basic logistics, Flor broke with the accepted order of things. Between other students' "from home" and "from school" responses, Flor quickly made a connection between the food she brought with her, which she associated with Brazil, and the food offered at school, which she associated with her experience at the border, and drew a comparison between the two. While teachers were used to elementary-age children blurting out seemingly out of context answers or comments during the school day, Flor's apparent non sequitur provided context about her life. Her comment was not an isolated event: in hundreds of hours of observing dozens of migrant children and youth in their classrooms, moments like this one happened constantly, often interrupting the order of business in schools.

My colleague Sarah Gallo and I have called for "listening re-alignments" (Oliveira & Gallo, 2021) when moments like this happen. While researchers and educators may skip over children's responses or thoughts spoken out loud, we argue that researchers must change how they understand the arc of a seemingly linear story, allowing for twists and turns and connections that may seem out of place. This moment with Flor during morning meeting realigned my listening to attune to instances in which children carved out space or made use of wiggle room to share their migratory experiences. I was attuned to a child's elaboration of events happening in the present (responding to lunch preferences), how they linked the moment with events related to their immigration journey (connecting with the food they ate at the detention center), and the response of teachers and school staff who interacted with the child. This pattern in which immigrant children offered unprompted glimpses into their past experiences took place in a multitude of ways.

Vinny, the 6-year-old from Brazil who chimed in on Flor's story, had arrived in the U.S. a month after Flor. They lived close to one another in the U.S. and their parents knew each other. Vinny had an individualized education plan (IEP), and his parents worried he had disabilities that were not being supported at school. During that morning meeting, he was quick to corroborate Flor's story even as Ms. Andrade interrupted and brought the focus back to choosing lunch. Vinny and Flor debriefed after the period was over as they walked to their physical education (P.E.) class. "You also ate that . . . aquela coisa gelada horrível [that horrible cold thing]," Flor said. Giggles ensued. Vinny responded, "Eu comi, todo mundo comeu, mas seus pai já falaram para você guardar segredo?" (I ate [it], everyone ate [it], but have your parents told you to keep a secret?). Teachers and educators asked the lined-up students to be quiet as they made their way to P.E. Flor and Vinny stopped their conversation, but now they were connected: "Aconteceu com nós dois né? [It happened to both of us right?]," said Vinny.

During math period in Ms. Andrade's class on a different occasion in 2019, Vinny was trying to figure out how to solve 7 + 6 on a math worksheet. The class had been using manipulatives on the floor to understand addition and subtraction. The classroom was loud and students worked in pairs or trios. While Vinny spent some time on the ground working with cups and blocks to signify the quantities, he then made his way back to his table where his worksheet was. After looking at the paper in front of him for a few seconds, he looked up and put his pencil down. He then raised both hands in the air and made the number seven with his fingers: holding five fingers up in one hand and two fingers up on the other hand. He told himself, "Guarda o sete na cabeça" (Keep the seven in the head), closed his eyes and proceeded to add six, starting from eight: "Oito, nove, dez, onze, doze, treze . . . é treze, tia?" (eight, nine, ten, eleven, twelve, thirteen . . . it's thirteen, aunty?). He called me *tia*—a common way Brazilian children refer to adults in their close circle or at school. Even though I was one table over, Vinny waved me over and asked me to sit with him to check his answers.

As I sat down next to him, he said: "You take a lot of notes, you are also a teacher, right? A teacher of adults." I nodded my head yes as I looked at his math problems. Vinny then asked me if I lived in Brazil, and I responded to him that not anymore. "Now I live here," I told him. Vinny then explained to me: "Did you know that in Brazil there is violence, and a lot of people die, like 10, 20, so many people die there, they have kidnappers, and people disappear, it's dangerous." Ms. Andrade, an experienced teacher who advocated for her *brasileirinhos* (little Brazilians) to have to access to a bilingual program at her school, looked at me and whispered, "He talks about these things a lot." I turned to Vinny and asked, "How do you know there is so much violence there?" Vinny quickly fired back at me: "I lived there, right? And we left because it was so dangerous and people were stealing and then we get there . . . to the other place where they speak Spanish, and they put us in a place like we are bad, they put us in jail there." The dialogue continued:

> GABRIELLE: Where was the jail?
> VINNY: You know, after you travel a lot and you arrive in an airport and then you go in the bus, and then you sleep, then you go go go go and you go to the jail.
> GABRIELLE: Did it make you nervous to be there?
> VINNY: We were all together, the food was bad and I had pain in my ear, a lot of pain in my ear, because of the cold air there. My mom thinks it's because I slept on a cold floor with my ear touching the cold floor . . . she said that . . . I don't know.
> GABRIELLE: Aham.
> VINNY: After we went to another place that I played soccer with more friends, they had a room with toys, then another plane, another plane . . .
> MS. ANDRADE: Vinny you are safe OK, we talked about it. You are OK, everything is fine now, OK?

I looked at Ms. Andrade, and she shot me a look that I understood to mean "don't encourage." I wanted to continue my conversation with Vinny, but at the same time, it was not my classroom.

Ms. Andrade cared deeply about her students. More often than not, she would arrive early to school and leave late to be sure she was available for parents and children. However, if children spoke about their experiences in ways that she saw as returning them to a place of suffering and loss, Ms. Andrade was quick to put a stop to those conversations. After each observation, Ms. Andrade wanted to debrief with me. She was genuinely interested in any insights or real-time feedback I could provide her, although I was the one learning from her. At the end of that day, I asked her what she thought about Vinny sharing his migration journey during math. Ms. Andrade explained,

I consider myself ready to discuss these issues. I can take them on. I just don't think every other child in the classroom is ready. So I will open Pandora's box if I start listening and talking about every single child's trauma. The other children will talk about it at home, and I am not home with them to help support these conversations. So it feels irresponsible to me. It would be a mistake to look at this situation as me not caring about my students. I care. But this classroom has to be a safe place for all.

Vinny chased me down the hallway when it was time for lunch. He wanted to finish the conversation we had started during math period: "I know that many people don't want us here. My dad tells me all of the time that I can't get in trouble, because they will send us away in the plane again. So I can't tell these things to everyone. You will write this in your notebook? Don't forget to write it!" I didn't forget.

Similar dynamics occurred in other classrooms. In a third-grade class, Davi, Vinny's 9-year-old brother, brought up his migration experience. Ms. Brito (Brazilian, veteran third-grade teacher) kept a drawing and a writing piece Davi had done to show me. When I arrived at her classroom, she called me to her desk: "I think you will be interested in seeing this. I saved it for you." His work read: "My wish is to return to Brazil because I don't like America, my family is in Brazil and I am in America." The activity prompt had been to "make a wish for what you want for Thanksgiving," accompanied by a picture of a wishbone. The lesson had explained the tradition involving the wishbone from the turkey carcass: two people each hold a side of the wishbone and pull the bone apart while making a wish. Whoever breaks off the larger part of the wishbone will have their wish granted.

In the drawing Ms. Brito showed me, Davi had drawn a map of the U.S. and a map of Brazil and connected the two with a dotted line. Ms. Brito had put a Post-It note on Davi's drawing that read: "Dear Davi, changing countries is not easy, but soon you will get used to it and will be happy here as well! ☺" I asked Ms. Brito if I could be around when she returned the drawing with the note to him. She said yes. When Davi received his drawing and writing back he read the Post-It note and put his hand on his face. I was sitting next to him at the round table. He tapped me on the arm and showed me the drawing. I asked if he was still feeling like he wanted to go back to Brazil and he answered:

"The problem is that my grandmother is there, my dog, my friends. We left so fast and then we were so sad when we got to America, because it was not what we thought." I asked what he meant by that. Davi explained that arriving in Mexico and then at the border, riding in buses, feeling scared, didn't feel like the safe place his parents told him about before leaving the state of Minas Gerais in Brazil. "It was like we were criminals," he said. Ms. Brito approached and said, "But will you look at the beautiful cursive writing this boy has!" It was indeed beautiful. Davi turned back to his work and began to line up his pencils and pens in preparation for the next assignment.

Mentions of children's migration journeys came up during almost every classroom observation. These moments in the classroom offered windows into children's lived experiences related to migration, longing, fear, and potential trauma, and showed the saliency of what they had gone through (and continue to go through). The fact that migrant children share parts of their journey with their teachers and peers is not a novel finding (Gallo, 2021; Oliveira, 2018; Rodriguez et al., 2022). However, these observations reveal that children often encountered adults who stifled their narratives, changed the subject, or decided that this type of politicized knowledge could be dangerous or complicated to discuss in the classroom (Gallo & Link, 2015; Gallo & Dabkowski, 2018). Children, nonetheless, resisted. In every observation there was at least one mention of an incident, moment, artifact, or story that brought children's thoughts back to their countries of origin or to the border. Children and youth did not stop bringing up their migratory experiences despite the fact that educators did not always know how to center their narratives, engage with them, or capitalize on them, and even gently discouraged discussion of them. Flor, Vinny, and Davi were not discouraged by the lack of follow-up from the adults in the room. Their experiences and memories continued to be central to their everyday lives, and teachers' responses did not change that.

Dual language classrooms avoid some of these issues by giving students the opportunity to translanguage (García-Mateus & Palmer, 2017; Palmer et al., 2014; Takeuchi, 2015). In such settings, children can use different languages as they engage with course content, but students are still often limited regarding what topics they are permitted to discuss. While they are encouraged to use multiple languages in the classroom, the use of those languages is typically constrained to "academic" content (Cervantes-Soon, 2014; Hamman, 2018;

Park, 2021; Somerville & Faltis, 2019). Similar phenomena are evident in English as a Second Language classrooms. While these spaces are more likely to foster opportunities for newcomers to process their experiences than are other learning spaces, teachers might still impose limits on the information shared and the circumstances under which students are encouraged to discuss sensitive issues with one another (Dabach, 2011; Park, 2021). In each of these cases, teachers have been observed to establish topical constraints that restrict students' ability to bring their full selves into the classroom. However, teachers in turn were constrained by the structure imposed in schools.

Past as Concern

William, an 8-year-old boy from Guatemala, had migrated to the U.S. with his father, Dylan, in 2018. William was Luz's cousin (stories in chapters 1 and 2) and arrived a few weeks after then–Attorney General Jeff Sessions and then–President Donald Trump had agreed to end the family separation policy that had been in effect in April and May 2018. In July 2018, William and Dylan were separated for 18 days at the El Paso–Ciudad Juárez border. William was sent to a shelter in New York City, and Dylan stayed in a facility in Texas, much like Luz and Julio's experience of family separation.

 William and Dylan described the separation experience as a "nightmare." While their separation was shorter than Luz and Julio's, in the midst of separation, caregivers, parents, and children had no idea if it would last one day or several months. William stayed in a shelter with older boys and remembered: "Some of them became my friends and helped me when I was sad at night. At night was difficult because I tried to sleep and I woke up in the middle of the night . . . like many times." Dylan found a lawyer who visited the detention center and represented many other people who were detained like him. His biggest concern was that he would be deported: "If they sent me back . . . I wouldn't see William again. I wouldn't forgive myself. I thought I didn't give him the future he deserved, and I made his life worse." They were finally reunified in a city in the northeastern U.S. in August 2018.

 Upon reunification, Dylan's first task was to enroll William in third grade at the same school as his cousin Luz, in a bilingual program where Spanish was the predominant language used throughout the day. William, like most children in this research, had been in school before migrating to the U.S., although his schooling had been interrupted during the summer of 2018: for weeks as they traveled from Guatemala to the U.S., as well as the three weeks of separation. Administration and educators in the district where he was enrolled were getting used to receiving large numbers of migrant children, and the city's enrollment screening had become more attuned to contextual issues in families' pasts.

William was quiet in class at first, and his teacher, Mrs. Diaz, described him as an introvert. I didn't get to observe William until the spring of 2019 when we first met, but Mrs. Diaz told me from the beginning that he was one of her students of "concern." She was concerned he wasn't focusing during class, that she was never able to get ahold of his father, and that the "boy is without his mother here." Mrs. Diaz explained: "I am sure something really bad happened to him, his past is a cause of concern for all of us, but I need to be sure he is doing well on his day-to-day." For teachers and other educators, concerns that the past would bleed into the present constantly reminded them of the hardships and vulnerabilities of the immigrant children in their classes.

In the spring of 2019, I was at the school one day during recess. William and another student had a disagreement while they were playing soccer. William wanted to play goalie, but the other student said it wasn't his turn yet. William yelled at the other boy, saying that he said that every day, so it would never be William's turn. Both boys went at one another physically and pushed each other for three seconds. I started walking toward them and yelled out for them to stop. The recess teacher ran and intervened, getting in the middle of the boys and saying, "OK, enough, go see your teachers." If you spend enough time in schools, this scenario is not rare when 8- to 10-year-old students get into heated disagreements. The recess teacher reported the incident to Mrs. Diaz, who told William, "I will have to talk to your dad about this, OK? We don't condone violence, no matter what." William was visibly upset and explained to his teacher what had happened in Spanish. After he left, she asked me if I had observed what William described, which I had. Dylan, William's father, received the phone call later that day, and after he was done speaking to Mrs. Diaz he sent me a text message: "De nuevo es un problema de sus experiencias pasadas. Dicen que como que tenga mucha ira que está tratando de sacar debido a lo que le sucedió" (Again it's the problem of his past experiences. They say it's like he has a lot of anger he is trying to get out because of what happened to him).

However, in the classroom William was quiet and shared bits about his past with his teachers and friends. These glimpses into his past were not necessarily engaged directly by his teachers but were sometimes pathologized. William drew the Guatemalan flag several times on his notebook; his teachers never inquired about it. One day he wrote in his weekly letter assignment about wondering how people were doing in faraway countries that don't have internet or quicker modes of communication. He also hoped people had homes that wouldn't flood. In another instance when children were engaged in "pair and share" for a literacy assignment, he shared with a friend that his dad had to wear an ankle monitor for months after he was released in the U.S. The class was about to be dismissed, and I was sitting next to his group of boys getting ready to put my stuff away. As usual, I had my notebook and recorder.

> ANDREW (CLASSMATE): You always write about what we say or do you only write about what the teacher says?
> GABRIELLE: Both! It depends how fast I can write everything down or if I can record.
> CARLOS (CLASSMATE): What do you study?
> GABRIELLE: Many many things! Now I am studying . . . trying to understand what happens when people move from different countries to the U.S. . . . how does it feel . . . what is your experience like . . . And especially what happens to kids in schools.
> WILLIAM: My dad had a thing on his ankle for some months after coming here . . .
> ANDREW: I had a neighbor that had one too . . . but you know what he did . . . he went to the lake and cut it with a knife and threw in the water! He wanted the thing to drown!
> WILLIAM: You can't do that.
> ANDREW: My neighbor did . . . tell your dad. So the police don't come.

Mrs. Diaz approached our table and complained about the boys being loud. She overheard the last three sentences of the conversation and said, "I don't like this kind of talk here. I don't need anyone else feeling scared, OK? It's in the past!" The boys looked at one another and Andrew whispered again to William, "Tell your dad."

Pedagogy of silence is the act of decentering the experience of marginalized communities in the classroom. Educators engaged in this pedagogy of silence to shut down or set aside information children volunteered in school settings. It is important to highlight that educators were not actively seeking to hurt or ignore children when they did this. More than anything, teachers wanted their students to feel supported in the present moment and understand that they were now safe. Teachers felt compelled to enact the promise of a better life for their students in an environment they deemed appropriate, like the classroom. Living in the past was both a problem and a distraction for educators whose goal was to include children in classroom learning.

In his book *Pedagogy of the Oppressed*, Paulo Freire outlined a new approach to education, one that was designed to empower people who have been marginalized and oppressed. Freire argued that traditional education, in which teachers hold all the power and students are passive receivers of information, reinforced oppressive power dynamics. Instead, he proposed a "dialogic" approach to education in which students and teachers engage in a collaborative and democratic exchange of ideas. From this perspective, children's conversations or creations (writings, drawings) in classrooms and schools offered a window into their painful pasts. Most teachers observed in this study tried to create culturally responsive classrooms along the lines of Paulo Freire's teachings. However, it was also important to them to keep children anchored in a positive present and oriented toward a fruitful future. The past was cause for concern; the future held promise.

The Lopez Family

Santo, a 5-year-old kindergartner from Guatemala, migrated to the U.S. with his father, Ian, in February 2019. His journey to the border was filled with fear. Santo and Ian left a small town in Guatemala in 2019 because, as Ian told it, "They make you work for them and if you don't they don't let your children go to school and you can't even cross the street if you don't pay . . . they come and knock on your door and demand you work for them or give them money." Ian was referring to the criminal gangs that control small towns in rural Guatemala. Diana, his wife, came to the U.S. a month after Ian and Santo with their 2-year-old daughter, Belén.

Ian and Santo endured a complicated and dangerous trek through Mexico and to the border. The high cost of $8,000 for father and son to cross and the potential dangers of the journey informed Ian's decision to go first with Santo and then send money for Diana and Belén. Santo and Ian crossed the U.S.-Mexico border into California by jumping over a fence that divided the territories. The Tijuana–San Diego location has a roughly 18-foot fence commonly known as the "floating fence" or the "Sand Dragon." Ian remembered that members of his migrant group used a tree to help them climb up to the top of the fence. Ian carried Santo on his left arm and shoulder and climbed up the tree first before transitioning to the fence. He would take a step up and pull Santo up with him, then he would secure Santo on a branch and climb up some more. As he told me the story of their crossing in front of Diana she couldn't help but cry and wipe her tears with the back of her hand while holding her youngest on her lap. "It never stops being sad to me," she explained. When Ian and Santo finally reached the other side of the fence, Santo fell a few feet from Ian's arms. As Ian described it, Santo slipped from his arms as Ian was coming down the fence on the U.S. side. Ian tried to reach quickly to at least grab some part of Santo's body to prevent the fall, but Santo fell on the ground. He scraped his arm and legs, but otherwise he was okay. Santo remembered not crying when he fell: "I didn't cry, I didn't cry," he explained. Ian thinks Santo was shocked: "The boy had his eyes wide open in shock looking at me. I just kept saying he was doing good. He weighs maybe 20 kilograms so I thought I had him, I thought I did."

Santo and Ian continued to walk with the group for a few more days until Border Patrol agents found them. Santo described the encounter: "They came from everywhere, lights, sounds, and screaming loud . . . they pulled my dad from me, and they kept screaming at everybody." Ian described the moment as terrifying. He didn't know if Santo would be taken from him, and he didn't know where they would go. They were taken together to a processing facility where they stayed together for two nights. These facilities often separated men and women, including adolescents, even if they were together as a family unit. After those two days, Santo and Ian were taken by bus to a detention center where they stayed for 12 days. They were released to Ian's brother who agreed to pay their airfare to where he lived in the northeastern U.S.

After arriving in Massachusetts, Santo attended a preschool between April and June of 2019. His parents enrolled him in summer school, and he started kindergarten in the fall of that year. Diana and Ian both described the scene when Santo rode the bus to his first day of preschool: "He cried the whole time when we put him in the bus." I asked Santo why he felt so sad, and he answered: "I thought they were leaving me... leaving me again." Ian quickly jumped into the conversation and explained to me: "It made him think about the crossing and the detention, even his teacher mentioned it." Santo was wary of being left with people who were not his parents. "It was like when the police took us, I didn't like the bus, and saying bye, I didn't like it," he explained.

The family and the school worked on an adaptation plan in which Santo would only attend half of the day. But while Santo's preschool was attuned to his family's needs, when he started kindergarten the structure and expectations of teachers and schooling dramatically changed. Full days, bus rides, more children in the classroom, and as Santo put it, "they didn't let us sleep anymore"—referring to the fact that most kindergartens in U.S. public schools don't have nap time. His new kindergarten class was also exciting, however. It was part of a bilingual program, so his teacher spoke in both Spanish and English. Diana and Ian were excited to share a language with their son's teacher.

It wasn't long before Santo started to speak about his past experiences in the classroom. One morning in his classroom, children were drawing their homes. They labeled each person in the drawing as "mamá," "papá," "abuela," or "tía," etc. Some children were already writing in the fall of kindergarten, so they wrote more words and names. Some kids would not write at all and just drew instead. Santo was able to do some writing. He drew a yellow house that had two floors and a large backyard. As his teacher moved around the room checking on children's work, Santo said, "Aquí es mi casa en Guatemala, una casa amarilla" (Here is my house in Guatemala, a yellow house). His teacher, Mrs. Gomez (Puerto Rican, veteran teacher) was interested and said, "Quién vive en tu casa, Santo? Puedes dibujar?" (Who lives in your house Santo, can you draw?) Santo responded: "This yellow house was in Guatemala, and the second floor I was not allowed to go to. My mother would not let me go, because she thought I was going to fall. I always wanted to go upstairs, but she said no. There were other men outside always looking looking looking, so she said, in the house, stay in the house." Mrs. Gomez replied to Santo: "Oh, thank you for sharing, Santo. Can you draw the house here in the United States?" Santo got another piece of paper and proceeded to draw his house in the U.S.

Before he finished, time was up, and the students had to bring their drawings and writing to their teacher. Santo lamented that he couldn't finish his second drawing and wondered if the first would count: "Do you think she will think the house in Guatemala is OK?" I responded that I thought she would.

Mrs. Gomez was a caring teacher who always showed interest in her students. Santo's class included a mix of children who spoke Spanish and were born in the U.S., some newcomer migrant children like Santo, and children who had no connection with a Spanish-speaking country but whose parents wanted them to learn Spanish. Mrs. Gomez felt conflicted regarding the support she could provide to her students. She explained to me:

> The problem is that I know a lot of these children are arriving here traumatized. I can't imagine the things they went through. It's terrible. But I also have a responsibility to teach all of the other kids, so sometimes I have to stop a conversation or change the subject to keep it moving for all of my 5- and 6-year-olds. I am responsible for all children's well-being, and some of them I have to help with language and the others I work more as a social worker. I have to help them see the now and the here. You know?

This was a common concern for teachers who felt themselves to be under enormous pressure to perform and comply with bilingual programs. Just as migrant parents were focused on the present tense of their existence—the "now"—so were teachers. For Mrs. Gomez, "here" meant Santo's life in the U.S., the one he should be focusing on. During the three years I observed Santo's schooling in the U.S., I noticed a steady decline in how much he referenced Guatemala. However, he continued to refer to the border and his migration journey. While Mrs. Gomez engaged with Santo, even in a limited fashion, her pedagogies focused on teaching *all* children. Mrs. Gomez found ways to counter pedagogies of silence in her instruction: she made room, even if briefly, for children to speak and build trust in her classroom. The drawings activity was one example of many in which Mrs. Gomez tried different ways to engage with children's past, present, and hopeful future.

Santo's mother, Diana, and his sister, Belén, arrived in the U.S. a month after Santo and Ian. Their crossing experiences were also complex and painful. After Santo and Ian were settled with Ian's brother, Ian decided to send money so the rest of his family could join them. Ian said, "I wanted to make sure the path was safe for them to come . . . and I thought that they will be better with a mother and daughter because they are bringing the little baby girl." Belén was 2 years old when her mother brought her to the U.S. Diana explained the decision to leave:

> These groups go door to door asking you to give them money. And if you don't give them they will cut your access to water, to school, and they told us that when Santo was 16 he was going to have to work for them. And when they leave to go "work" you don't know if they will come back dead or alive . . . we lived in a humble place, but I wish that it was without conflict . . . what do the children have to do with this? What do their education has to do with this?

Families consistently offered descriptions of close contact with forms of organized crime in their towns. Their involvement or how pressured they felt to be involved varied across contexts in the Americas. Diana told me, "I think we made mistakes too. Getting close to people that were not good . . . and it was not always like that, it's not true that we come only from violent criminal countries . . . because then we leave as criminals and arrive as criminals, not true." Diana's concern was crucial to understanding the home contexts of the migrant families in this study. Gross generalizations of rampant crime in migrants' home countries often contribute to the erroneous assumption that people had absolutely no *everyday* life prior to migrating. These families, however, had to make the constrained choice to migrate in order to attempt to live a life with more possibilities.

When I asked Diana if the government in Guatemala did anything to assist or support them while their towns were under siege by this criminal activity, she explained: "The government came for 40 days just to say they did something . . . then they left, and we are back to the same thing. I never understood why they were trying to take something that wasn't theirs in the first place, like my children's education. And I tell you, you know what they will never take from us and it's funny? Our education." Diana had been a stay-at-home mother in Guatemala and Ian had worked in construction; he found similar employment in the U.S. Diana had been to therapy since arriving in the U.S. She said that her doctor had diagnosed her with severe post-traumatic stress disorder. Thus, whenever she told the story of her crossing it came in bits and pieces. She explained that she had suppressed a lot of it: "Lo bloqueé" (I blocked it), she repeated. We had been meeting regularly for weeks before Diana told me more pieces of the story. By that time, she was eager to talk to me about her journey and share her thoughts on being in the U.S. On almost every occasion we started by talking about the border. I usually paused, almost interrupting her, and offered, "We don't need to and don't have to talk about any of this." She finally told me half giggling, "I want to. I want to! If I don't want to, I will tell you."

When Diana and Belén embarked on their journey north, they left with a group of eight people. Diana didn't know any of the members of her group, but there were three children including Belén. They rode on buses from the Mexico-Guatemala border all the way to the Ciudad Juárez-El Paso border. When she arrived at the border with her toddler, the leader of the group told them they would have to cross the Rio Grande to make it to the U.S. on the other side. Diana remembered looking at the water and feeling nervous about getting in as she told me. What would she do with her daughter? What about her clothes? Was there a current? She was apprehensive and told me that she didn't have much time to hesitate. She took her shoes and socks off as well as a sweatshirt and put them all in a black garbage bag handed to her by one of the leaders in the group. Diana did the same with Belén, taking her shoes, socks, and sweatshirt off and placing them inside the same bag.

Belén was nervous and started to whimper, throwing her arms around her mother's neck so hard that Diana had to gently loosen her grip. The water was cold. She explained that the water came up to her nose and she kept treading water to be able to safely carry Belén with her. She asked for help and a man in the group took turns carrying Belén so she could catch her breath. Belén didn't want to go with the man at first, so Diana felt that she had to be stern with her about following directions. It was early in the morning, and they were all cold.

> We were crossing the river and I told Ian this the river doesn't take you with waves, it drowns you, it pulls you down. So we were crossing and then the police on the other side [U.S.] appeared and said to me "Señora por favor no cruze" [ma'am, please don't cross], but I didn't have a way to go back anymore ... and that's when *la nena* fell in the water ... fell from my arms ... and I tell you, I don't know how but I went under water, I opened my eyes, and I grabbed her ... I grabbed her.

Diana referred to this moment of the crossing multiple times during our many interactions. Panic always edged into her tone when she referenced either her crossing or Santo's crossing. She continued:

> When I was leaving the water with Belén in my arms I was relieved that we survived the river, that we survived Mexico, the police officers even the one saying don't cross, *las pandillas*, I was certain help was on the way. But when I looked up what I saw were these electric pistols . . . the police officers were holding electric pistols, and next thing I know I felt it in my arm, stinging, and I fell on the ground.

I asked Diana if she was holding Belén when she was tased and she replied that yes, she was. Diana said that she thought maybe it hurt more because she was wet. She remembered her body being paralyzed, which is what a Taser does: it delivers a modulated electric current designed to disrupt voluntary control of muscles causing incapacitation. The image of a person coming out of the river holding a toddler only to be tased by Border Patrol is a reminder of the cruelty at the core of immigration policy and border security.

When she regained control of her body, the officers asked Diana to give any metals she had to the police officers. Belén was crying. Officers ordered Diana to board a small truck to be transported to a facility known as the *hielera* (ICE box). Belén continued to cry. Diana didn't remember how long it took for her and Belén to arrive at the processing facility. In her mind it was an eternity, "It was long . . . at the same time I thought: I lost my daughter, I am about to die, or now I am being jailed." After four nights in the processing facility, they were moved to a larger detention area where Immigration and Customs Enforcement (ICE) verified Ian's address to check if Diana and Belén could be released to a sponsor. Diana also talked about how much Belén cried during their time in detention. "*La nena* would cry and I would put my hand over her mouth, because I was nervous about her making too much noise. I didn't want to get in trouble." Diana explained: "Every time they released someone I would go and take the blankets the person left behind, not for me, but for Belén. I would roll her up like a taco with all of the blankets, you know those foil blankets? I rolled her in five!"

By the time they were reunified, the entire Lopez family had been through traumatic experiences that still formed part of their lunch or dinner conversations years later. One of the first things Diana did after arriving in Massachusetts was enroll Belén in preschool. That's when I met the family, two weeks after Diana and Belén's release. Belén attended the same preschool Santo had attended before kindergarten. Late one morning in June, I went with Diana to pick up Santo and Belén from preschool. It was only her second month attending, and Belén was crying at pickup. Her teacher was explaining to Diana that Belén wanted to keep playing on the playground, but time was up, and they needed to get ready for pickup. As we were talking to the teacher, she knelt down to Belén, put her hand on her shoulder and said: "Don't cry, there is no need to cry." At the comment, Diana froze for an instant and told Belén under her breath: "You can cry, it's OK." For Diana the freedom to cry meant something more than the teacher could possibly imagine. Diana tried to explain to the teacher: "It's because she went through things that can make her sad. And maybe she remembers?" The teacher, also speaking in Spanish, said to Diana: "I know, mom, but don't worry, let's not remind her. Here you are OK. You are OK. OK, mom? Have a good afternoon, OK?" Diana couldn't hold back tears. The teacher placed her hand on Diana's shoulder in comfort: "It will get better, I promise," the teacher finished.

Diana explained to me later in the day when I asked if she was feeling alright: "Remember I told you about having to cover Belén's mouth when she cried, how that sound could be bad for us, that makes me think of me covering her little mouth, I feel so bad I covered her mouth." The exercise of remembering what happened in the past—layering a school pickup with the border experience—was a constant reminder for families that their presence, their existence, and ultimately their experience in the U.S. had been marked by a multitude of structural factors: the inequality in their home countries, the constrained choice to leave and escape, the desire to provide a better life, and the cruel implementation of border security. Scholars in the area of mental health have described this phenomenon before. Alegría et al. (2017) have pointed to family contexts as factors that influence the relationship between immigration and mental health. Rios Casas et al. (2020) have described the different coping mechanisms used by Latinx women. They reported immigration-related stressors including unsafe migration, preoccupation about immigration enforcement, broken social ties, and limited access to health and social services as crucial reminders of their vulnerability in the U.S. These multiple disruptions contribute to how migrant families experience their newfound homes and schools.

It is important to contextualize suffering and sadness. Chronic silences or avoidance of discussing past experiences were not helpful practices to support families and children. While children were often referred to psychologists and social workers who would routinely visit families, there was a real disconnect between how students brought their charged past into the classroom and how much educators engaged with their stories. Every child has a past, and many children have complex upbringings: children who have not experienced a migration journey or been subjected to harsh immigration laws may also deal with poverty, violence, parental incarceration, and prejudice. However, by identifying the many instances when young children exercised agency or resisted the limits defined by adults in schools—as well as educators' avoidance and silences—we can change practices in schools and classrooms.

Prioritizing a teacher-centric model of "involvement" means understanding educators' preexisting beliefs about how children need to change in order to effectively participate in the life of the classroom—a mindset that leaves little room for students to demonstrate the different founts of knowledge they bring with them to school (Rodriguez, 2013; González et al., 2006). Efforts to "engage" newcomer students are often premised on students performing that engagement in a way that is familiar and legible to school officials (Kirksey et al., 2020). Classroom practices are deemed successful only when they result in behaviors that align with the school's or teacher's preestablished notions of how children should behave, what topics they should communicate about, and how they should connect with peers and instructors (Kiramba et al., 2021). Focusing only on these supposed "successes" reinforces the idea that students must adapt to the school's way of doing things in order for their contributions to be recognized as legitimate forms of involvement. This approach limits students' ability to assert themselves as active participants in the project of learning and hardens hierarchies of knowledge that prioritize the perspective of adults over the needs and ideas of the children they are charged with teaching.

This dynamic can be difficult to unravel, largely because it often stems from positive intentions. For example, teachers may provide a rigid format for class participation to help ease students' transition to a new learning environment, hoping to clarify the unspoken behavioral expectations of U.S. schools through a clearly delineated structure. However, in doing so they may reinforce the role schools often play in stifling diversity as part of a broader project of nationalist assimilation (Banks, 2008; Yoshino, 2007). Researchers have critiqued engagement approaches that seek to integrate immigrant students into homogeneous ways of "doing" school, pointing out how this framework draws on assimilationist ideologies that undermine students' complex transnational identities (Abu El-Haj, 2015; Sánchez, 2007). Scholars have discussed the broader implications of such unequal power relations to show how efforts to constrain students' in-class behavior bolster hegemonic ideas about national belonging (Lee et al., 2017). Such an approach can not only restrict students' involvement in school, but also affect their sense of "home" by implying that they must bifurcate their identities to succeed in school (Jaffe-Walter & Lee, 2018).

Youth and Activism

Many middle and high school youths were vocal about their migration journeys and transformed their experiences into activism. While young children found spaces in everyday classroom routines and responded to prompts from teachers in ways that connected their present to their past, youth were more intentional about their participation in school.

Siblings Rosa (18) and Daniel (15) were both enrolled in high school. Rosa was in her last year of school and had become an outspoken advocate of students categorized as English Language Learners, including herself, particularly expressing critiques of how her schedule didn't allow her to fully participate in the same academic opportunities as her peers. Rosa and Daniel also had a younger sister, Vivi, who was 8 years old. Their family had arrived in the U.S. in February 2019. Originally from a town two hours outside of Guatemala City, this family of five journeyed to the border to escape violence in their hometown. Like others who migrated from Guatemala, these children and their parents, Fatima (42) and Fernando (45) had lived in a small town that they described as controlled by multiple kinds of criminal activity. Before they left Guatemala, their house had been robbed. While the children were playing inside and Fatima was cooking, a group of four men rang the bell and, armed with what appeared to be firearms, pushed into the house as soon as she opened the door. The men screamed at Fatima and the kids and asked for her husband, Fernando. She explained that he was out working, and she didn't have anything to give them. They took the family's cell phones, television, and the equivalent of three hundred dollars they had kept in a drawer in the kitchen. I asked why they kept that kind of cash in a drawer and Fatima explained, "Because of a situation like this." She meant that in a highly volatile context it is better to have something to give than to frustrate any member of these groups.

After that incident other threats followed. The children were followed to school, they felt unsafe in their house, and whenever someone would ring the bell, Vivi—who was 7 at the time—was paralyzed with shock. Fatima explained, "Nosotros tenemos un caso dificil, esta bien peligroso donde somos nosotros, también asaltaron a ella" (We also have a difficult case, it's very dangerous where we are from, they also robbed her). Fatima pointed to Rosa, who explained:

> They robbed me in my town, took my phone, pushed me to the ground ... I still have a scar on my knee. Then when we finally left [Guatemala], we arrived at Ciudad Juárez and that was also dangerous for us. We stayed in Juárez for eight days, finally when we crossed over *nos entregamos* [we turned ourselves in] to the police. But they also scared us and separated us ... Daniel and my father stayed together and Vivi, my mother and I stayed together. But then they put me in another space because I wasn't a "small child" that needed support ... but I needed it. I could write a book about this moment.

Fatima wiped tears from her face as Rosa told the story in her own words. Flor looked up: "It's like ... I never heard her talk like this ... all of the suffering, you know?" Rosa quickly looked at her mother and consoled her, "It's not your fault, mamá, no es tu culpa, ya te dije" (It's not your fault, I already told you).

Daniel didn't talk about his past as much as Rosa and Vivi did, but he once described the journey north: "A veces no teníamos agua, y mucha gente sufriendo con niños chiquitos que lloraban mucho" (Sometimes we didn't have water, and there were a lot of people suffering with young kids that cried a lot). During another interaction, he mentioned that they arrived in Massachusetts in the winter so there were no leaves on the trees. The trees were and continued to be a symbol of the seasons for Daniel. He appreciated the snow but explained that in Massachusetts the winter felt long: "I like when I can see the leaves," he said. Daniel brought up contextual descriptions of his experience in Guatemala and at the border in different moments of our interactions. Sometimes he was the last one to contribute a thought when we were all talking, taking his time and waiting to offer his feelings.

At school Rosa and Daniel engaged with peers and teachers in different ways. Rosa was in the Latinx Club and was an active member of the student council. While she described her English as "not as strong" or as she put it "not good English," her language skills did not stop her from voluntarily participating in English-only environments. At one student-organized high school event that Rosa participated in, youth read essays or poetry, performed a song or a dance, or displayed a piece of art. Rosa was an organizer and proudly wrote all the communication in Spanish for parents and families attending the event. Her English language arts teacher explained: "It's fabulous to see the go-getter attitude, we are proud! But Rosa has to put more effort on becoming fluent in English. I am not saying that it should cost her Spanish, and trust me this is not coming from a critical stance, I just don't think she will be able to go as far as she can without the fluency, so maybe put more time into becoming fluent." Many teachers shared this thought: fluency in English was an important skill for children's future. This particular thought, plus education requirements and the structure of school schedules, contributed to students being pulled out from elective classes and spending more time in English instruction classes.

In her first year in the U.S., Rosa turned in several assignments written in Spanish that discussed her experience migrating to the U.S. Her ELA teacher returned the first assignment with a note saying how happy she was that Rosa was comfortable enough to share how sad it felt to leave friends and family behind in Guatemala. Rosa was motivated by this response and wanted to read books and essays in class by others who had experienced migration. Her English language teacher, Mrs. Dawson, responded to her by saying that some things are better left to the clubs or after-school activities. The teacher explained that not everyone wanted to relive or talk about what happened in the past. Mrs. Dawson said she needed to think about everyone's experiences and that not every student in her class had a complicated journey to the U.S. The argument that *all* students must be considered when teachers are teaching is an important one. However, the mistake is to think that individualized experiences cannot also be part of general instruction that considers every single student in a classroom.

Rosa described feeling shut down by her teacher's response. She explained:

> I am about to finish high school. I hope I can finish. All I was trying to say is that it's OK to talk about how we feel not just with the psychologist. They contain us to certain spaces. Our stories can't cross borders. Why are we just talking about the hardships with some teachers but not with others? I think I am always trying to show that I am more than a person who needs to learn English. But I am so happy here. I love it here, I just wanted to be real.

Rosa was vocal about this idea that students should be seen as more than a label. In fact, she wanted to start an apparel line called "more than a label" that would have t-shirts, sweatshirts, and notebooks. In the U.S., public schools orient themselves around the *needs* each student has, which makes labels important. In this structure, labels trigger services that are assured by law. For example, if a child is considered to have special education needs and the school labels the child as such, only that label allows families and students to access services they may need.

Fatima often spoke highly of her youngest daughter Vivi's English learning abilities. She once said at the lunch table,

> Todos están encantados con ella . . . por mi nena. Los maestros de Vivi siempre quieren hablar conmigo, como cinco maestras quieren hablar de como están encantados con ella. Ella es la que sabe más inglés, ya está empezando a escribir, habla y entiende. Los maestros se quedan más preocupados con los otros dos por el inglés.
>
> [Everyone is enchanted with her . . . with my baby girl. Vivi's teachers always want to speak with me, like five teachers want to talk about how impressed they are with her. She is the one that knows English the most, she is starting to write, she speaks and understands. The teachers are more worried about the other two because of English.]

According to Toppelberg and Collins (2010), using the work of Alejandro Portes, "due to the assimilative forces that propel children of immigrants to learn English quickly, language shift and/or loss starts occurring as soon as they begin school. Second generation immigrants are more likely to lose their first language than to remain bilingual" (p. 4). Thus, since Vivi was younger when she migrated, her English exposure was longer and more sustained in comparison to her siblings.

When I asked Daniel's and Rosa's teachers whether they had knowledge of what these students had experienced before enrolling in school, their answers were all over the place. Daniel's science teacher explained: "He is so quiet so I try to focus on the content to help him when he talks, I just have to take the opportunity and ask, 'Do you have questions? Can I help?'" Rosa's English language teacher said she was nervous about discussing legal issues that could potentially hurt the family: "How do I talk about legal status and other stuff in the classroom? What if someone uses that information to harm her?"

Many teachers and educators felt this sense of responsibility and care. However, educators also often fell into a common trap of curtailing immigrant youth's potential participation in classrooms and schooling. School personnel more commonly focused on academic concerns such as grades. Rosa's grades fell within the school's average range, while Daniel's were slightly below average. Many teachers seemed to feel that Rosa's and Daniel's expected academic trajectories in the U.S. were not being realized. These pedagogies of silence were anchored in deficit thinking either because of educators' preconceived ideas, or because educators tried to protect and care for students. Teachers and counselors focused on youth's ability to learn English or to raise their average grade in other disciplines. One of the counselors at the school described Daniel: "He is timid. He likes to ride his bike, and talk to his friends. I think it's better to keep his deeper conversations to professionals, like with me, you know kids in classrooms can pick up on things and run with them, I would like for him to have more self-confidence on his academics, so he can be motivated for the future."

This concern was present in all the teachers' narratives: they wanted to *close the gap*. Teachers wanted to be sure the playing field was similar for immigrant and nonimmigrant children. However, most did so without engaging in the profound work of understanding the meaning of education and sacrifice for students and parents alike. In my own work with teachers across the U.S. and the Americas the number one request I get in professional development training is "Can you come talk about the children/students we serve?," so much so that I have given many sessions entitled "know the students you serve." In those sessions I am only able to provide historical context about the new demographics of migrant families as well as their country-of-origin contexts. But the everyday work of transforming assignments into windows into students' experiences, fostering a classroom where instead of rerouting and silencing we have purposeful engagement, really depends on the training, preparation, and support we offer teachers. They cannot be responsible alone.

Promises and Lies

"O problema é que ninguém entende a gente aqui, sabe?" (The problem is that no one understands us, here, you know?) Juliana (Brazilian, 14) explained as she described her experience in school. She continued: "O silêncio deles eu não sei se é porque eles não entendem a gente ou porque não querem falar sobre alguma coisa. Americano é diferente, né?" (The silence, I don't know if it's because they don't understand us or if it's because they don't want to talk about something. Americans are different, right?) We were sitting on a park bench on a warm fall day in 2019. Juliana had finished school, and I had been there observing for the hour before dismissal. When the bell rang, I asked if I could walk with her and talk about how her day had gone, and she was excited to take me to Dunkin Donuts for one of those sugary fruity drinks that I also happened to love.

We sat outside after I paid for the beverages. Juliana made the comment above in response to a question I posed: "Do you think Brazilian students feel like they belong in the classroom and in the school?" Juliana used the word *silêncio* (silence) to describe her interactions with adults in the building. According to Juliana, her siblings Adriana and Diego experienced similar issues. Juliana described a fight that had broken out on the school bus a few weeks before our conversation. She said someone yelled out that they had a knife, which prompted the driver to issue a formal complain to the school. Juliana and a group of other students were summoned to the principal's office. Juliana described the event:

> After the school bus fight, they got about eight of us in a room at school and said, hey we know it's hard to be in a different country, but you also have

to put effort into making it work. Like they didn't want to hear how we felt about the situation, they didn't want to look closely at the video footage from inside the bus to see that it was not us! They kept changing the conversation and I don't even know if they understood us to begin with. So if you feel like people don't understand you . . . I don't know . . . how would you feel? Then I still have to explain everything to my parents . . . like why the grades are not always perfect. You know?

In Juliana's view, the support she and other Brazilian students received from adults at the school was different from the support for the "Americans." She used "us" as she told her story to group herself with other Brazilian students. The conflict, according to Juliana, was already framed as "us" versus "them," an approach that was unfair to begin with.

While youth like Juliana thought about school sometimes as an unfair space, migrant parents frequently described their relationship with their children's schools as one grounded in gratitude. Gratitude was both expected from immigrant parents and demonstrated by them. For instance, Melissa—Juliana's mother—often discussed how she counted her blessings for the education her children were able to receive in the U.S. Melanie, a mother from Guatemala, often talked about how lucky she felt that even though they went through so many hardships leaving their home and crossing the border, school held a promise, a key to mobility and to more opportunities. However, her son Lucas (14) struggled to make sense of what was expected of him: "It's not like I can learn English in one day. And I can't always talk about the things that are in my mind. I think they [adult educators] listen more to the little kids, but with us, they assume we are bad and we need to just stop and adapt ourselves . . . like I hear 'stop making noise!' but then my mom gets nervous, because she's like this is what we have . . . 'you are so lucky, be grateful' she tells me." These parallel perceptions of (un)fairness and gratitude sometimes clashed.

Children and youth were often stuck between their parents' beliefs in the promise of an American education and their own experiences in school. Parents, teachers, and educators all seemed to believe in the promise of silence: that silencing the past at school and focusing instead on the present, on the now, would yield academic success, integration, self-confidence, and a better schooling experience. I asked more than 25 teachers what they thought was the most important thing to do when working with newcomers and immigrant students, and the responses echoed in a chorus:

> "Focus on the present and things will fall into place." (Mrs. Manning, white, U.S.-born, middle-school ESL teacher)

> "I know it's complicated, but they have to focus on the opportunity, on the second chance they got." (Miss Hopkins, white, U.S.-born, district educator)

> "They are already competing with their American peers who have a lot more cultural capital, they can't dwell in the past, they need to catch up." (Mrs. Peixoto, Brazilian school psychologist)

> "I know we should be able to talk about the complicated nature of being an immigrant, I am one too. But I need the parents to understand how to participate in schools and support their children now, we can't keep reliving trauma every day." (Ms. Machado, Brazilian elementary school teacher)

> "I don't mean this in a bad way. I think every child's history is important. My fear is that the immigrant students will stay too caught up in all the bad things and that they will not see the good. And there is good." (Mrs. Santana, Dominican middle-school teacher)

At school the expectation was that kids and youth would live in the present tense, valuing the opportunity and the chance they were offered and doing the best they could. At home, parents saw education through the lens of gratitude—gratitude for being alive, in good health, and with the opportunity to change the trajectory of their lives. While this paradox is not new for immigrant families and students (Louie, 2012; Suárez-Orozco & Suárez-Orozco, 1995, 2004; Bartlett et al., 2018), children and youth exist in this liminal, shifting space. A presentist approach to teaching and learning in schools denies immigrant children and youth a space to critically reflect on and discuss macro contexts that affect their lives, like the reality of immigration policies. Pedagogies of silence at school are met with politics of gratitude at home.

Authentic Engagement

One way to remedy the mismatch between politics of gratitude and pedagogies of silence is to engage in culturally responsive teaching practices that place explicit value on students' and families' politicized founts of knowledge (Gallo & Link, 2016). Gallo and Link (2016) assert that knowledge is not neutral, but instead politically and culturally constructed. Part of the battle for teachers in this situation is to create environments that allow for authentic connections, even as educators engage with a heavy daily script. Easier said than done. Anyone who has been in classrooms long enough will have seen both the deeply caring adults who chose this profession out of love and purpose, and a bureaucratic system that continuously adds daily tasks to teachers' docket that take away their joy and the time they have to spend with students. Teachers cannot be lone actors in a learning ecosystem. They need time, better pay, and space to engage authentically with students.

Asset-based approaches to engaging immigrant students require that teachers and educators decenter their own perspectives and experiences in order to allow children and youth to bring their holistic selves into the learning environment (DeNicolo et al., 2017; Jaffe-Walter & Lee, 2018; McDevitt, 2021a). Scholars have offered several models for such work, ranging from a "Lived Civics" curriculum that draws intentionally on the lived experiences of mobile marginalized youth (Cohen et al., 2018; Mirra & Garcia, 2020), to critical transnational approaches that seek to honor young people's connections to different places and contexts (Bajaj & Bartlett, 2020; Knight, 2011), and transborder thinking (Dyrness & Sepúlveda, 2020).

Teachers' approach to collaborative, culturally responsive education is directly shaped by their ideological perspectives on immigrant communities (Expósito & Favela, 2003; Haim & Tannenbaum, 2022; McDevitt, 2021b). Therefore, preparing teachers to develop inclusive, collaborative techniques involves unpacking how their personal identities intersect with those of the families and students they seek to engage while opening conversations about responsive teaching models that honor the equitable participation of all learners entering an academic space (da Silva Iddings & Reyes, 2017; Shirazi, 2018; Turner & Mangual Figueroa, 2019). Professional development efforts that draw on empirical research to help foster teachers' understanding of cultural theory can increase their confidence in integrating transnational frameworks in their classrooms (Trumbull et al., 2020). Schools that have developed promising practices in this area include those affiliated with the International Schools network, a collection of institutions that focus specifically on building safe, equitable, and responsive relationships with youth and their families (Hersi & Watkinson, 2012; Miranda, 2017). Similar techniques have been successful in other school contexts as well (Bajaj & Suresh, 2018; Jaffee, 2016; Murillo et al., 2021).

The techniques described above succeed when they prioritize relationships and allow students and families to take an active role in shaping classroom practices. This is deep and difficult work that teachers may not be able to prioritize given the other demands on their time. Many educators cite a long-standing ethos of care when reflecting on their work with newcomer populations (García et al., 2013; Häggström et al., 2020; Hos, 2016; Oliveira & Kentor, 2023; Saavedra, 2021). However, actualizing this dedication can be difficult when teachers are asked to meet administrative benchmarks that contradict the goals of collaborative, culturally sustaining pedagogy (Paris & Alim, 2017). Despite educators' commitment to forging relationships with immigrant students, there remains a dominant focus on measurable (i.e., quantifiable) inputs and outcomes (Lundberg, 2020). This is not to dismiss formal assessments, but it is to question time that must be spent on tasks instead of with students.

For example, discussions of how to engage newcomer students in schools often focus on language needs (Dabach & Fones, 2016; Hilburn, 2014). Educators regularly position getting students comfortable with English as the first and most important task to which teachers should dedicate their time. However, for newcomers who are not yet comfortable with English, the focus on language can cause additional anxiety, ironically compromising their confidence when it comes to participating in class. In addition, while many newly arrived immigrants are adjusting to learning in a different language, scholars have critiqued the conflation of immigrant and English Language Learner populations, emphasizing that not all immigrants are ELLs and, conversely, that not all ELLs are immigrants (Dabach & Fones, 2016; Hilburn, 2014).

In U.S. educational systems a label or a diagnosis is sometimes the only way to trigger student services that support learning. However, these labels can also dominate students' identities, thus compromising the development of their purpose and motivation. From English Learner (EL) to English Language Learner (ELL), and from English as a Second Language (ESL) to English as an Additional Language (EAL), the categories and acronyms used to describe English language learning may be subtly different, but they all have one thing in common: they can have serious impacts on the people they aim to describe. One of the biggest setbacks of overcategorizing students is to generalize not only a single student's experience, but also that of an entire population. Youth participants in this research often mentioned how their knowledge, expertise, and smarts were not part of *how* teachers perceived them. According to youth, many teachers *only* saw them as language learners, and not math lovers, for example.

Bilingual classrooms can be important spaces for children and youth to develop trust and belonging. However, experiences inside and outside of bilingual classrooms can erect implicit barriers around when multilingualism is acceptable and when it must be hidden (Dabach, 2014; Evans & Liu, 2018; Reynolds & Orellana, 2009), further constraining the conditions under which children feel they are able to express themselves in the way they desire (Garver & Hopkins, 2020; Park, 2021; Robertson et al., 2014). Language goals can thus eclipse squishier but equally important topics, such as discussion of students' feelings about their migration to the U.S. and preliminary experiences in their new neighborhoods.

A note of caution is important here. It would be impossible for schools across the U.S. to have spaces for or educators who spoke every language spoken inside a school building. Thus, while bilingual classrooms (in the cases here of Spanish/English and Portuguese/English) are important spaces for children and youth to build trust, feel as though they belong in the classroom, learn, and play, they are not always possible at every school. As professionals in the field of education we must do better and not expect that subjecting educators to sporadic professional development sessions will bring about a sea change in pedagogies. Teachers' and school administrators' preparation must include training in *pedagogies of possibilities* even if educators only speak English. That means that schools of education across the country must integrate into their curriculum the knowledge that one in four children in K–12 are children of immigrants, that immigration policy matters for understanding who is in the classroom and why, and that language learning, while important, cannot be the only focus of immigrant education (Bajaj et al., 2022).

Conclusion

Pedagogies of silence are practices anchored in the perceived well-being and care of a population, but in their implementation, they exclude, silence, and dismiss the very population they promise to benefit. In the context of the findings presented, educators invoked care to justify how they dealt with and broached topics related to immigration policies, migratory trajectory, detention, and trauma. They cared about students' experiences from *now on*, in the present and future. But the past was a burden migrant students brought into the classroom that needed to be compartmentalized. At home, parents' gratitude for the opportunity represented by a U.S. education also pushed children and youth into a solitary space to process what schooling was for. I have cowritten elsewhere about these dynamics of "cruel optimism" with Dominican young adults in New York City (Bartlett et al., 2018).

These findings show that despite the restrictions imposed by school personnel, migrant children and youth still found ways to communicate their experiences and resist rigid spaces. Similarly, researchers have identified evidence of this practice among students of different ages. Allard (2015) documented how older teenagers used dark humor (e.g., poking fun at peers who would likely attract more attention from ICE officials because they looked more *paisa*) as a means of coping with the fear associated with undocumented status. Other scholars have examined the different media migrant children and youth use to express themselves when prevented from doing so in the classroom, pointing to the importance of studying young people's written, virtual, photographic, and artistic expression as a means of understanding the full scope of their experiences (Becker, 2021; Coleman-King, 2012; Keat et al., 2009; Marsh, 2012; Sepúlveda, 2011; Schultz & Wilf et al., 2022).

The findings in this chapter further demonstrate the importance of having space to talk about the serious concerns faced by many members of immigrant communities. By providing opportunities for students to express themselves through different activities (e.g., journaling, art, and music), teachers can help create opportunities for them to use classroom resources to express different aspects of their experiences (Schultz & Coleman-King, 2012).

> "It is for them that I wake up in the morning. So, they can have a shot at a better life." (Ms. Andrade, Brazilian elementary teacher)

"I feel so deeply what they are going through. I sometimes cry after I leave because I want to help them." (Ms. Gutierrez, Puerto Rican elementary teacher)

"My dream was to have a documentary or a film showcasing the amazing work so many immigrant parents are doing already with their kids. Show them that there is possibility. I just don't have the time." (Ms. Brito, Brazilian elementary teacher)

Fighting for time, space, flexibility in the curriculum, and a responsive classroom are not easy tasks. Thus, the responsibility must be shared, including that of a government that causes so much harm and trauma to entire populations through its policies. The work is complex, but it starts with a change in perspective and the active support of educators.

FOUR

COVID-19 and the Breakdown of Care and Schooling

THE COVID-19 PANDEMIC EXACERBATED existing socioeconomic inequalities affecting marginalized communities in the U.S. Early in the pandemic, researchers and public health officials expressed concerns about the disproportionate risks COVID-19 would likely pose to low-income communities of color, including Latinx immigrants. Reports released in the spring and summer of 2020 highlighted factors contributing to medical vulnerability among these communities, such as housing density, lack of access to healthcare, and preexisting medical conditions, among others (Cholera et al., 2020; Clark et al., 2020; Wilson & Stimpson, 2020). Over the months and years that followed, many of these early worries were borne out by emergent data on the inequitable effects of COVID-19 (Allen et al., 2023; Garcini et al., 2023; Greenaway et al., 2020; Mehta et al., 2022; Page & Flores-Miller, 2021; Strully et al., 2021). But health risks were not the only ways that marginalized communities were affected. In this chapter I provide an intimate portrait of migrant parents and their children at the height of the COVID-19 pandemic during 2020 and 2021. Breakdowns in care and disruptions to learning related to the COVID-19 pandemic shaped children's schooling experiences in 2020 and part of 2021 and cast doubt on the promise that educational opportunities would provide a path to a better life.

The data in this chapter focus on 2020 and the beginning of 2021, when the pandemic broke down the networks of care available to immigrant families. By early 2020, many of the families in this study had found their footing in the labor market: they were experiencing steadiness in their jobs and consistently sending remittances to their home countries. Children had been in schools for a year since the families had either been released together or reunited post separation. But when the COVID-19 pandemic hit in early 2020, a complex constellation of disruptions and stressors impacted these families. School closures and remote learning measures intended to curtail the spread of COVID-19 sometimes disadvantaged migrant children. While the pandemic destabilized most of the socioeconomic progress families had made, parents and children found ways through the confusion, uncertainty, and fear as education and schooling remained central to their goals for a better life.

Families in this study relied on daily free or reduced-fee school lunches, lived in small apartments that usually had only one or two bedrooms located in affordable housing in Massachusetts, depended on children being in school from 7:30 am to 3:30 pm every day, and on the school-provided transportation to after-school care. None of these families owned a car, and no one had a valid driver's license during the period of study. Parents worked as house cleaners, restaurant line cooks, mechanics, grocery baggers, construction workers, care workers, and factory workers. Individual parents' monthly incomes ranged from $500 to $2,800. Construction workers and mechanics were the highest paid workers in this study, while cleaners and grocery baggers were the lowest paid. None of the participants in this research reported receiving a government stimulus check during the pandemic.

When schools closed in the district in March of 2020, parents had to figure out how to care for their children during the hours they worked outside the home. Many of these parents' jobs classified them as essential workers, and they had to continue working in person through lockdown to be able to pay rent, buy food, and continue sending remittance money home. While this situation was not particular to immigrant families, these parents and children also experienced the constant stress of their vulnerable immigration status and fear of deportation (Li et al., 2016). Over and over, parents and children repeated *"now we are here"* as they reflected on how the pandemic was affecting their lives. This invocation of the present foregrounded the urgency of doing well in school, keeping a job, earning money, living in a healthy space, and ultimately caring for their family members.

March 12: The Shock

On March 12, 2020, one of the elementary schools that migrant children in this study attended held a shelter in place. Just before noon on that Thursday, one student reportedly had symptoms consistent with COVID-19, and an ambulance was called to the school. Children were told over the loudspeakers in their classrooms to stay put. Typically, in schools across the U.S., shelter-in-place measures are used to prevent anyone from entering classrooms, usually during an emergency medical situation, bomb threat, dog search, or other activity requiring that the hallways be clear of students. That morning, I received a text message from Yanet, a mother from Honduras with three sons who were not at that school, but had heard about the shelter in place from a neighbor:

> YANET: Que pasa Gabi cree que van a cerrar todas las escuelas cerraran de tus niños? [What is happening, Gabi, do you think they will close all of the schools/ did your kids' (schools) close?]
>
> GABRIELLE: Hola, Yanet! Hoy cerraran las escuelas de mis niños. Ahorita dicen que solo por dos semanas, pero quien sabe. Como están ustedes? [Hi Yanet! Today my kids' schools closed. Right now, they say only for two weeks, but who knows. How are you all?]
>
> YANET: Por ahora bien. Pero mira si cerraran las escuelas aqui en Estados Unidos es porque la cosa es muy seria. Bueno que Dios le bendiga mando un mensaje por la noche. [Right now, we are good. But look if they closed schools here in the United States it's because it's very serious. Well, may God bless you, I'll send you a message at night.]

Yanet's texts were followed by phone calls from other families who frantically asked me if I had other information regarding the pandemic and school closures. "Is it true that maybe we are all sick?" Emily, Brazilian mother of Flor (6), asked me on the phone. Flor was at the school that held the shelter in place along with other Brazilian students Davi (9), Vinny (6), and Maria Clara (6). The climate escalated quickly when the school announced an early dismissal, sending all parents into a frenzy. That day I spoke to all of the families in the study, checking in with them one by one. Families revealed the shock they were feeling. "This in the United States? It has to be serious," Dylan, a father from Honduras, told me.

Later that day, I checked in with the teachers, who told me about the fear, surprise, and uncertainty they had experienced earlier. One of the elementary literacy coaches in the building explained to me via a WhatsApp voice message: "You will not believe it. It was like a scene from a movie. Some children did very well, and other children cried and cried. I had a feeling it was coming when I saw the commotion about a little boy that was coughing and had a fever." After the shelter in place, caregivers were contacted, and children were released early to go home. School officials communicated that they would close the school for a few weeks to clean and make sure it was safe to go back. Children also recorded voice messages on their parents' phones describing the events of the day and sent them to me:

> "It was so scary, I sat in the closet, *tia*, I sat there near my backpack. But I think we will go back to school soon, it's my favorite place." (Flor)
>
> "I wasn't afraid, because I saw in the news before that they were going to close, but now I will be on a long vacation [laughter]." (Davi)
>
> "I miss my teacher. When will I see her? Do you think we can send letters?" (Vinny)
>
> "For a minute I thought: are we going to jail?" (Maria Clara)

Maria Clara's mother, Cintia, interrupted her and said, "Is that something that you should say?" (Isso é coisa que se fale?) before taking the phone and continuing the recording, saying that Maria Clara had confused the sounds of an ambulance with those of the police. Cintia's quick *correction* was a protective move by mother to child. She explained to me over a message: "The last thing I need is for her to go back to having nightmares! We have to keep them safe."

In the days after that dramatic last morning of school in March 2020, families continued to get in touch with me to try to understand what schools would do. Julio, Guatemalan father of Luz (5), followed up with a voice message via WhatsApp, saying: "Right now we are OK, but I don't know if they will also stop with all the jobs I have, I hope I can still work, but right now who knows."

The shock of school closures hit all of us in different ways. On that March day, none of us knew that kids would not be back to in-person school for at least six months. In the following weeks, most of the conversations I had with parents had to do with job security, housing conditions, fear of contracting COVID-19, and what would happen with their children's schooling.

An imminent feeling of loss informed many of these conversations. At the end of March, Andrea—a mother from Honduras—explained to me over the phone how she felt and what she feared:

> Feels like nightmare after nightmare. But now we just have to calm down and get through it. I trust this country will help everyone. I just can't get sick. I told Javier [her husband] he can't get sick. Our children need us more now . . . He is concerned about the people in Honduras, our family there. But I told him, we are here now, and now we have to get through this. It will be hard if we can't work and if the children can't go to school . . . we were just feeling a little calmer about our days here in America. We can't lose hope . . . God will protect us.

Andrea was concerned about not falling ill and potentially having to leave her children. She also spoke about her partner's concern about people in Honduras, which she quickly followed up with "we are here now." Grappling with yet another *nightmare* was a concern for parents. Their feelings of guilt and loss from their journey north a couple of years prior surfaced again during this trying time. What if children can't go to school? What if the promise of a better life doesn't materialize? Families' basic living conditions were deeply affected as were conditions for Latinx communities across the U.S.

Exacerbating Inequalities for Latinx Immigrants: The COVID-19 Pandemic

As happened in many school districts across the U.S. and across the world, Massachusetts schools did not transition automatically to online or distance education. The amount of communication between schools and parents immediately following the closures varied. Some educators felt more comfortable reaching out and sending activities for parents to do with their children right away, while others were occupied caring for their own families like most people in the country. March, April, and May were difficult months for these families as they navigated the vulnerabilities of their immigration status, which were now coupled with complicated work conditions and a lack of supervised care for their children at home.

To understand the complexities Latin American immigrant families faced during 2020 and 2021, it is important to first understand the conditions this group faced in the U.S. during that time. Migrants who worked in essential jobs were further exposed to the risk of infection through their employment outside the home (Cantos & Rebolledo, 2021; Garcini et al., 2024; Ross et al., 2020). While some of these jobs could be performed in relative isolation, others put workers at high risk of contracting diseases, including COVID-19. These risks persisted regardless of whether preventative practices like masking and social distancing were strictly adopted (Quandt et al., 2020).

As noted in the book's introduction, the ethnographic data presented here provide a window into the dynamics experienced by this community of migrant families. The findings in this chapter may resemble the experiences of families living in poverty and children of color in the U.S. more generally. Migrant families were at the nexus of draconian immigration policies, vulnerable immigration status, and a pandemic. They navigated all three with limited knowledge of how to access public services—including schools.

Yanet had been in the U.S. since the beginning of 2019. She migrated from Honduras in 2018 with her two sons while pregnant with her third: José was 14 at the time and Jair was 2. As a pregnant single mother of two, Yanet left her home in Honduras because of the violence and lack of financial stability she experienced there. Her mother and siblings lived in Honduras, but she had a cousin who had successfully migrated to the U.S. and lived in Massachusetts. Yanet had been in two long-term relationships. The first one was with José's father. They had been together until he left to try his luck migrating to the U.S. in 2007. While Yanet never learned his fate, she believed that he was killed while en route to the U.S., most likely either by dehydration in the desert near the border or caught in the crossfire of drug cartel violence. "Maybe it was bad luck that took him. He meant well. He was going to send money to us, to help José in school and give us more tranquility," she remembered.

It was not until 2012 that Yanet began a new relationship with a man named Erick. Erick and Yanet lived together with José on the outskirts of Tegucigalpa. She worked cleaning commercial buildings in the city, and he owned a mechanic shop. Yanet became pregnant in 2015 and gave birth to Jair in 2016. According to Yanet, that was when things started to get more complicated with Erick:

> He never hit the kids, but he started to drink, drinking, and not showing up to work. He complained that it was either the government or gangs taking his money or not paying him. He used to say that some police officers would come get their cars cleaned and fixed and never pay him... and he was losing money. We lived in a two-bedroom house with two kids, but we had a space outside where my kids played and rode their little bikes. I had to stop working a lot when I had Jair... I think that also made the situation worst.

As she described the context that led to Erick becoming violent toward her, Yanet blamed financial issues, his drinking, and her lack of work for his new behavior. She continued:

> YANET: I knew I had to leave back in 2017. I was trying to find a way to leave ... I was afraid he would do something bad to me and the kids would end up without any parents.
> GABRIELLE: Did he know you wanted to leave?
> YANET: One day he asked me if I was keeping money from him. And I was saving a little here and there as I sold food that I made at home, but I told him no. My *mamá* also said she would help me. She had worked as a live-in cleaner to a family and they paid her good money. She said, "*Hija*, if you want to go I will help you, don't stay there if he will hurt you."
> GABRIELLE: When were you able to leave?
> YANET: I tried in one year, I think it was the beginning months of 2018. But then I... he knew and got mad, and you know I was scared. So finally when my mom and other family members helped me get the money to make it to Mexico, I told him I was going and I was taking the kids... It makes me sad... because you know... he is or was the father, but I didn't have anything there, and my boys would grow up not to have an education, a future... Gabi, it's because you have no idea... there are hundreds of gangs, that's where they go. So I think Erick maybe was relieved I was taking the kids.

Yanet told me this while placing her hand over her heart multiple times. In other conversations she explained that she felt as though she failed as a wife because she had had two relationships that had not worked out. I asked, "Why all the blame on you?" to which she replied, "I am the mother, I care with all my heart."

In the spring of 2018, Yanet decided to go north. After speaking with her mother and because of the growing fears in her community, she was certain: "I am going for my family, for my kids, to leave this danger behind." She waited a few more months until she had enough money for the first leg of the trip, which would get her and the kids to Mexico. The second leg would bring them all the way to the border. In May 2018, she packed a backpack each for José and Jair, and, using the money she had saved plus money from her mother, she paid $3,000 to hire someone to lead her out of Honduras and to Mexico. Remembering the months leading up to her departure, Yanet described the escalation in urban violence: "You pray that no one will take your children and I thought Erick had debt with some bad people, because they were coming to our house and asking him for more and more." Yanet was alluding to the trouble she suspected Erick had gotten himself into. All the way up to her departure she explained they were living "as husband and wife . . . so I got pregnant again." Yanet described the moment she found out she was pregnant and how she closed her eyes and asked God to guide her: "Where am I facing more threats, dear God, here or there?" Her vision was that she needed to go. She did not tell Erick about the pregnancy, nor did she tell the boys.

While Erick knew about Yanet's departure, she chose to leave when he wasn't around to avoid a last-minute confrontation or potential change of plans. Yanet and her two boys traveled through Guatemala and arrived in Mexico. She then paid another person to take her and the boys to the Mexico-U.S. border. By the time they left in May, she was already three months along. She feared the bus journey north, the lack of adequate places to sleep, food insecurity, and, above all, that something would happen to her when she gave birth. At the end of May 2018, they made it to the U.S. border. Yanet recalled that her belly was showing by that time, and because of that she thought more people helped her throughout the journey: "People would say why don't you rest or some other people would give me their water or a blanket, God was with us." She remembered her older son José asking her if that was the same border where his dad had died. Yanet hoped her son trusted her decision to leave Honduras.

Jair, who was almost 3 at the time, grew attached to Yanet and struggled with sleeping and eating during the trek north. He had multiple bouts of diarrhea and dehydration and often spiked a fever during the weeks of travel. When they arrived at the Ciudad Juárez–El Paso border and surrendered to Border Patrol Yanet recalled:

> They took José because he was older and said that he needed to go with the men . . . they just put him in another group, they line people up . . . but I begged them to let us all be together and they were going to take Jair too and that's when I almost passed out. I thought I was going to die. They had cars ready to take us and I started to cry and say that I was pregnant. So another person . . . one that was in charge just gestured with the hand together, and I heard him say "she is pregnant." After that we went all together. I was crying, Jair was crying, José was in shock. He was like a rock. His body was hard as a rock.

Yanet, José, and Jair were detained together for 11 days. Yanet described the "icebox"—or *hielera*—where they were detained together as cold and offering little support for the kids' health. Because of his age, José was often asked to use the bathrooms with other men and stay away from the women in these spaces. Yanet remembered the number of babies and young children with mothers there. She kept thinking, "What do we do now? Now we all have to move forward, we don't have a choice."

Finally, Yanet and her children were released to a shelter in El Paso, where they stayed for four nights until her cousin was able to send plane tickets to Massachusetts. Yanet remembered the relief of being released to a shelter where people were friendly.

> One day the police or soldiers called us and said we were going on a bus to a shelter. And I didn't know if that was another place to stay or if that was a place we will be able to leave. They helped us there [the shelter], there was even a church priest if you wanted to go to mass. We were all sleeping in a big empty space with little beds one next to the other. They had volunteers to play with the kids and some toys as well. Jair was happy . . . but he had a hard time sleeping, didn't sleep, didn't sleep . . . sometimes I would rock him and then look down and his eyes were open staring at me. He didn't

cry, my boy, he didn't . . . but I think he never slept the same after all we've been through.

Even after being released in the U.S. and traveling to Massachusetts, Yanet kept these details about José and Jair alive in her stories. Those moments held significance since to Yanet the unknown was a real stressor in their everyday lives. Sleeping, playing, and a having a place to stay are basic human needs, and Yanet found herself wondering if she would ever have them in peace.

In Massachusetts, Yanet and her sons settled near her cousin in a split condominium apartment in the affordable housing area of a town. They spent July and August trying to figure out work opportunities and what schooling was available for José and Jair. Yanet enrolled José in 10th grade and Jair in the local Head Start program. Yanet began working in a perfume factory, but only for a few weeks as her due date was fast approaching. In November 2018, Josh was born. During the two days Yanet was in the hospital, Yanet's 17-year-old nephew, Eduardo, and José cared for Jair.

I met Yanet, José, Jair, and Josh in 2019. As I was meeting families for this study, Natalia, a mother from El Salvador, introduced Yanet to me at a local event. The event was at a church, and it brought many service providers together. Many nongovernmental organizations, governmental ones, as well as health, psychological, and education services were participating in the event. I brought my own children and husband with me since it was on a Sunday afternoon. There were stations for coloring, and children had plenty to play with while adults talked to one another. As soon as I met Yanet she wanted to talk about school. She asked me many questions about the differences between schools "here and there" and asked me almost instantly, "How long do you think it will take for the kids to learn English and be able to follow classes in school?" I told her there was a big range and it really depended on the school, the child, the teachers, the programming, but maybe between six months and a couple of years.

Yanet's biggest concern was that José would be a good student: "When do the older kids learn English? I know the young ones will learn fast, but what about when they are adolescents?" she asked. We spoke at length about the different opportunities and services José could access in the district. Her kids were slowly finding their footing in school and daycare. After Josh was born

Yanet started babysitting children in the apartment complex where she lived to make ends meet. It wasn't until Josh was seven or eight months old that Yanet was able to leave him with caretakers and in home daycares to take jobs outside the home. She joined a cleaning crew and kept her babysitting job through the beginning of 2020. Jair enjoyed his preschool, and some of the teachers there spoke Spanish, which helped Yanet trust the school and the system a bit more. José had also been receiving support from the school psychologist, extra reading intervention, and had started playing soccer at recess in school and in the town's league. Then COVID-19 happened.

Schooling and Education

Families felt the effects of COVID-19 and related disruptions in distinct ways. Financial insecurity, health scares, and inconsistent school support added to the disruptions families experienced on a daily basis. All families in this study had vulnerable immigration status. They were in limbo, in waiting. While some had court appointments coming up, many were rescheduled due to COVID-19. While jobs were at risk, many of these parents worked in occupations considered essential. Thus, while they may not have lost their jobs, there were no work-from-home options or consistent paid work. In the weeks and months after the initial shock of closures and public health measures, parents pivoted or kept their jobs to maintain a steady income. Housing costs stabilized, and the probability of eviction decreased because of government intervention.

Dylan and Julio, both fathers from Guatemala, continued to work on construction projects. Their work paused for the first two weeks of public health measures in March but resumed in the beginning of April 2020. While construction work that was performed inside residential homes may have paused, outdoor construction continued. Melanie and Daisy, who worked in factories, were not allowed to go back to work for a little more than a month, but then resumed work. Andrea and Melissa, who worked in restaurants as cooks and cleaners, also could not work for almost six weeks. Diana and Cintia had to stop working all together to be home with their young children when childcare centers closed. Gabriel, Pedro, and Edgar worked in construction and mechanics and pivoted quickly to work delivering groceries. Henrique fixed air conditioners, water pumps, and heaters—work that continued without interruption. Beatriz took a job cleaning a laboratory space, and Natalia took a job bagging groceries at a local supermarket. Mimi and Hector, parents from Guatemala, started delivering meals to neighbors and residencies around town. Karina, a mother of three from Brazil, took a free course during the time she couldn't work to become an administrative assistant at a small Brazilian law firm. The urgency to maintain a source of income was the priority for families. Each family faced different issues, but schooling and how to support their children in school was a unanimous worry during that time.

Across the U.S., recently arrived immigrants faced new challenges, especially those with school-aged children. The pandemic highlighted inequities that shaped children's educational experiences, such as access to technology (Slavin & Storey, 2020). After the onset of the pandemic and the mass school closures that followed, public schools across the U.S. initially struggled to stay in contact with students and families. Schools pivoted to an online modality, adopting platforms and technologies to facilitate distance learning. This shift brought into relief a deep rift within the U.S. student population: vast differences in access to technology (Eruchalu et al., 2021; Masonbrink & Hurley, 2020). While some school-aged children had computers, personal cell phones, tablets, and ready access to internet, many did not.

Public schools in this study recognized this gap and raced to distribute tablets or Chromebooks to students so they could attend virtual classes and complete assignments. However, this did not fully solve the problem. Families reported several problems with school-issued devices, some of which were incompatible with the platforms students were supposed to use to attend school. Other devices functioned properly, but the families did not have access to reliable internet, which made it difficult for their children to log on for class. Schools tried different workarounds for this problem, such as providing hot spots and subsidies for a stronger data plan. Reporting from Chalkbeat showed that these initiatives were rolling out across the country with varying degrees of success, as some users still reported issues with functionality and bandwidth (Asmar, 2020a). Some caregivers in this study and elsewhere also reported that some programs asked them to provide a Social Security number to access technology distribution (Asmar, 2020b). All the issues mentioned in wider national reporting were reflected in the experiences of families in this study.

Technology was not the only school-based resource that families had depended on before the COVID-19 pandemic. Researchers documented notable increases in food insecurity among U.S. households in the months following the onset of the pandemic (Niles et al., 2020; Wolfson & Leung, 2020). With schools closed, families that counted on free and reduced lunch programs lost an important food source (Kinsey et al., 2020; Schanzenback & Pitts, 2020; Steimle et al., 2021). While some schools set up meal distribution programs, these were not consistently available. In addition, caregivers were not always able to get to school buildings in order to collect meal packages because of work responsibilities, lack of transportation options, and/or fear of contracting the virus (Fang et al., 2022). This situation was exemplified by Andrea, Melissa, and Julio, who requested help to retrieve tablets and computers from school. On two different occasions I drove to the school to get hardware to then deliver it to families. In speaking with the district, I learned that they had tried to figure out a delivery method that got the technology closer to families. Parents were afraid of getting sick and having to be in the hospital. It was not the fear of dying, Natalia, a Salvadoran mother explained, but fear of a new type or version of separation.

As has been documented in healthcare, migrants in the U.S. may avoid using benefits like the Supplemental Nutrition Assistance Program (SNAP) because they do not know they are eligible, or are worried about their status being exposed, or are concerned that they will later be labeled a public charge (Page et al., 2020). Even for those who do utilize these programs, their access is limited. Children under the age of 18 are eligible for SNAP regardless of their citizenship status; however, undocumented adults and those with legal permanent resident status must live in the U.S. for five years before they can use the program. These disparities can impact whether families make use of support their children are entitled to (Pelto et al., 2020; Bovell-Ammon et al., 2019). In the context of these barriers immigrant families already faced to accessing SNAP and other benefits, losing access to school-based meals increased the risk of food insecurity among both undocumented and mixed-status immigrant families (Cleaveland et al., 2023). For many families the two to three meals children received at school were crucial to their financial health at home. Migrant families often mentioned the fear of using or accepting any government help or assistance, worrying that it could be an illegal activity. While food pantries were available during the first few months of COVID-19, almost every other service, even the essential ones, came to a halt. Not going to a school building every day destabilized the rhythm families had established in the year prior.

School Matters

Families survived and resisted the pandemic in the context of these multiple disruptions. The closure of in-person schools was one of the main destabilizing issues produced by the pandemic. Sending children to school every morning was a practice that conveyed stability for parents. Children were in a place assumed to be safe and consistent. They had access to food and shelter for those hours of the day and were supervised by caring adults. Above all, children were experiencing a type of schooling that parents believed would positively affect their future mobility. Thus, while some parents worried about so-called learning loss—the lack of academic support and curriculum enrichment for their children (Socal, 2022)—during the pandemic, immigrant parents worried about the everyday destabilizing effect school closures generated for their children. This disruption was also directly in conflict with immigrant parents' understanding of the promise of a U.S. education as explored in chapter 1.

Natalia, a mother from El Salvador, explained:

> I remember every now and then about our whole story, our crossings, our emergencies. So many stops. So many challenges. Yes, school is never perfect, I worry about my little boy making friends, and enjoying his learning. But when Cesar went to school I could breathe. He is in school. Even with all the challenges, Cesar being in school reminded me of why we are here, why when I looked at the clothes and the shoes I wore I have hope for us now. It gave me strength.

As Natalia described, for immigrant parents the COVID-19 pandemic was another disruption in a series of emergencies, and it impacted a central aspect of their life, as well as a goal related to their decision to come to the U.S.: schooling. Leaving home, experiencing trauma, loss, and pain along the way was compounded by the loss of a newfound stability. COVID-19 served as a brutal reminder that emergencies lived around the corner for these families.

So many challenges, Natalia explained, but even with all the challenges, being in school gave them hope. As I have written elsewhere (Oliveira, 2022), school is for hope. And education is a currency of love for migrant families. When schooling and education were weakened, migrant families felt the doubts, the guilt, the fear associated with their decision to migrate creep into their minds.

Fatima, a mother from Guatemala, also mourned the loss of everyday schooling: "Where we are from our schools don't have this space, the classes, all of this. We have many people that care, but here seems like more like serious . . . I think because I don't understand a lot of how it works I sometimes can't complain about what I don't know. But we are missing going to school, because that is where they [children] see friends and play and learn . . . and also how I worked." While Fatima mentioned not knowing much about the U.S. educational system, seeing her three children get on the bus and go to school every morning held a positive meaning for her. She explained that putting them on the bus, while sad sometimes, came with the reward of thinking that they were moving in the right direction. A direction that for Fatima represented a chance, an opportunity, that she herself never had, she explained: "I lie awake some nights thinking and planning and thinking how do I keep my kids moving forward, learning, having opportunities. It means so much to me that they do things right . . . school, learning, studying."

It is important to mention that schools were not always the most comfortable, caring, and loving environment for all kids. They experienced plenty of discrimination and silencing there. However, to remain mired in the dichotomy of whether schools are *good* or *bad* would be a mistake. What schools and education came to mean to parents contributes to understandings of many of their actions and decisions regarding migrating and settling in a new country, regardless of whether the promise of an American education held any truth. In schools, many immigrant children accessed services like counseling, speech therapy, reading remediation, and consistent nutrition. Daisy, a mother from El Salvador, described:

> DAISY: So my son is a what they call . . . one that is learning the English.
> GABRIELLE: English Language Learner.
> DAISY: Yes, that's it . . . so he is that so it's not just one teacher telling him what to do . . . he is only 7, and there were two teachers one for Spanish

and one for English, and even if they were not in the classroom together ... they were in the building, and someone could call them to help Cruz. But now we are more alone in this ... it's not what I hoped for Cruz, I am sending messages to people I know and asking them if they know what we are supposed to do ...

GABRIELLE: It seems like no one knows, right?

DAISY: But that's the problem ... if the ones who teach don't know, imagine me! I just try to discover what to do and try to go online and read the messages, and also everyone has to stay healthy. I know the teachers are doing the best that they can.

Daisy explained her strategies for trying to figure out how to support her son. At the same time, she described feeling alone in her battles even though she thought highly of the educators in charge. For Daisy, Cruz going to the school building and having the resources to support his learning helped structure her days and strengthened her belief that leaving El Salvador had been the right thing to do for her son. She affirmed, "It's not what I hoped for Cruz"— meaning *losing* school. School was indeed for hope.

The concepts of education and schooling sometimes are conflated in the U.S. educational system. For migrant parents that is also true. An extensive literature analyzes the differentiation of education (*educação, educación*) and schooling across contexts. *Educación* is not just the acquisition of knowledge and skills, but also the development of moral and ethical values, as well as social responsibility (Valenzuela, 1999). During the pandemic, migrant parents were more concerned with *educación* than with schooling. Parents' sense of loss when it came to school buildings closing or the transition to online learning was deeply connected to ideas of care and how education could cultivate these values and responsibilities: school was a site of care and hope. This is not to say that schools were always fair, just, and equitable spaces for migrant children, or that parents believed them to be so all of the time. However, the meaning parents assigned to school as a space of everyday care meant that closures signified a loss that parents mourned.

Beatriz, a mother from Honduras who had a third grader at the start of the pandemic, wondered about the structures that were no longer in place from March to July 2020. "It's that a person, a family, the children go through so much, and then we are feeling OK with our jobs and then *las cosas desmoronan* [things fall apart]," she said. "And I thought how can I make sure my daughter continues to get support, support that she needed . . . you know we came all the way here." The idea that something would again "disappear" or "fall apart" brought Beatriz's thoughts closer to the past—something she was avoiding. "In school they study, think about their future and good things, with adults that take care," she said. "Now here at home she has too much time to think about what happened in the past, the terrible things." That school held the promise of breaking with the traumas and complications of the past deepened parents' feeling of loss when school buildings closed. School was a space that allowed for education as a care practice to happen, and it symbolized the promise of migration to the U.S.

Parents were preoccupied with the loss of school-based services early in the pandemic and found it difficult to access government assistance that might fill the gap, even when it was offered directly. Food insecurity, for instance, was exacerbated by both school closures and the opacity of government assistance programs. Julio, a father from Guatemala, had received a card from the school district, through which he could access $200 to buy groceries, but he struggled to use it. In a WhatsApp message, Julio sent me a picture of the card and asked, "Does it say I have to call somewhere to use it?" I responded yes and indicated the phone number. Yanet and Melanie were also nervous about having to call to activate the card. Calling an office to ask about government-sent assistance was stressful for parents, and the customer service lines were often busy or there were long waits, and in some instances the representatives did not speak Spanish or Portuguese. Julio asked me multiple times if the office he was calling would know that he had the card because of his daughter, not for himself. Yanet and Melanie had heard from neighbors that if you did not use the card in time, the funds would be gone.

The card was from the Pandemic Electronic Benefits Transfer (P-EBT) program, which the federal government created to temporarily replace school meals during the pandemic while schools were closed to in-person learning. Parents sent me picture after picture of the cards they received (figure 4.1). They wanted to understand what the text on the back meant, especially the words "unlawful" and "fraud," which made them feel uneasy. While those sentences are common features of official documents, the words felt personal. Parents wondered how and when to use the card, if there were limits on what could be purchased, and if they would receive another one the following month. After a few tries and communication with the district, immigrant parents were able to use their cards at their local grocery stores, but these barriers to accessing benefits were not inconsequential.

In 2020, none of the families had a car or a valid driver's license. Thus, when the district distributed computers and hot spots to families, many struggled to get to the school to retrieve these material resources. Schools had set up drive-throughs so cars could pull up and receive the materials. Since many families could not travel to schools, the district also mailed one

FIGURE 4.1   Image of P-EBT Cards Distributed.

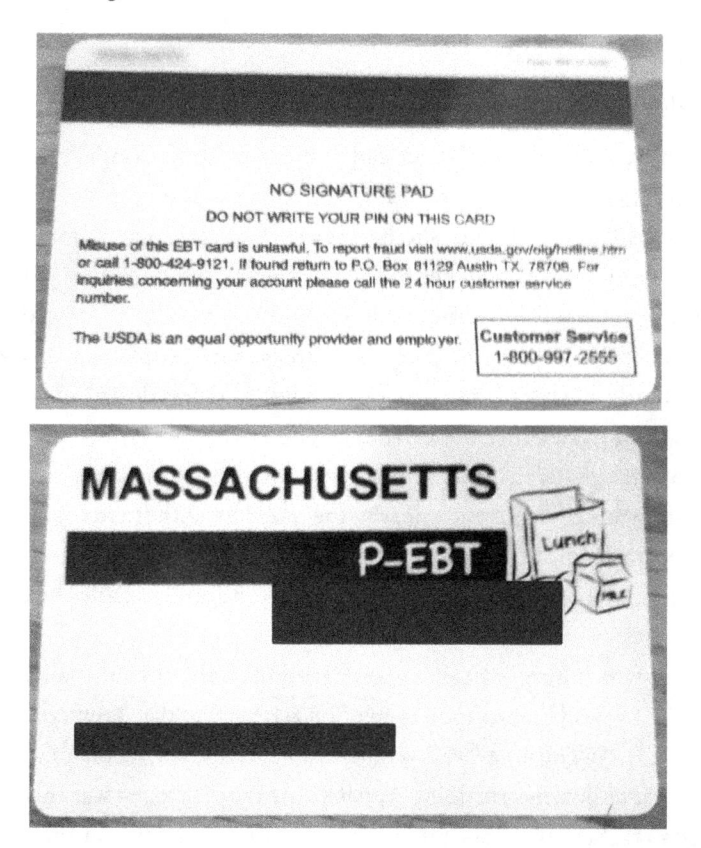

Source: Author.

computer per family in need initially, but later increased that to one per student in need. For families that had not been able to get internet through the local provider, the district distributed hundreds of T-Mobile hot spots so that students could participate in online learning when it began in April 2020. Of course, the logistics of the transition to online learning were complicated for many districts and schools across the U.S. and the world. While some schools or districts communicated with families in multiple languages, many long, detailed messages were sent in English. The months of March, April, May, and June of 2020 were challenging for the families as they figured out how to pay rent, keep food on the table, and keep up with important instructions from schools—all against the backdrop of a raging pandemic that was taking lives in high numbers every day. It was not long before members of these families became sick.

What (Dis)Appears Online

One evening in May 2020, Yanet called me, sounding exasperated. "It's because I have an emergency," she said. "I'm going to the hospital." One of her biggest fears had come true: she had severe COVID-19 symptoms and had asked her neighbor to drive her to the emergency room. At that point in the pandemic, patients were admitted alone, and no one was allowed to accompany them inside emergency rooms or clinics. Yanet explained that she was having a hard time breathing—"siento la muerte" (I feel death) she repeated a few times. She passed the phone to her neighbor who told me they were headed to the hospital, that Yanet's children—Jair and Josh—were with José, and that her cousin would come from a nearby town to stay with them that night. The fear of contracting COVID-19, transmitting it, and dying haunted most people at that time, when the virus was poorly understood, and vaccines had yet to be developed.

I asked which hospital Yanet was headed to so that I could call and check in and said I would deliver food to her house later that day. I remained in contact with Yanet's cousin as well, who was able to update me on Yanet's health and how her children were doing. Yanet's only request to me was that I tell her children's teachers that José might not be online that day and that Jair, who only had a couple of sessions of online preschool during the day, would also be absent: "Diles que los niños no estarán en linea hoy, yo creo" (Tell them that the kids will not be online today, I think), she told me. I assured her that I would let them know and emailed the teachers right away. That same night I had a migraine and could not drive, so my partner drove to Yanet's house to drop off food for her children and cousin.

Yanet received medical care for COVID-19 in the hospital and was released after a four-day stay. It was the longest she had ever been separated from her sons. None of her children contracted COVID-19 from her—a big relief for Yanet. I did not have direct contact with Yanet while she was hospitalized, but on the second day her cousin texted me and said she had been able to speak by phone to a nurse who assured her that Yanet was going to recover. On the third day of Yanet's hospital stay, I dropped off some groceries at her house for the family. From outside, I saw José playing with Jair who was jumping from the couch to the floor. I waved to them and gave a thumbs up. José rushed to the door and opened it. I stood at a distance, masked, and asked how they were feeling. Josh responded, "It's OK, it's just that another friend is also sick, and he is in the hospital." I asked José if he could get in touch with the friend or his family to check in, and he told me "sometimes." I told them I would come back in a few days in case they needed more groceries. I had also put some children's books and coloring pads in with the groceries. Jair and Josh rushed to the door waving and jumping, and Yanet's cousin Eva joined them at the door. We waved to each other, and Eva put her hands together as if she were praying and looked up to the sky. I did the same.

When Yanet was released from the hospital she sent me a text message: "Already at home and will make boys be in their classes [prayer hands emoji]." Without missing a beat, Yanet was focused on her children's schooling. In the first few weeks after March 13, teachers and schools scrambled to figure out how to have virtual face time with their students, which meant there was some variation in terms of which children saw their teachers online and which ones did not. In this moment of transition and instability, however, Yanet's commitment to her sons—especially José—showing up online was relentless. She explained:

> Every morning I ask José: "Do you know where you need to be? You need to show for your classes, *hijo*." But sometimes he tells me he is in class but he

is not . . . and he has friends that are sick, and I was in the hospital, we need to take care of the health of our minds. José's friend is in a hospital with a psychiatrist because he had some bad ideas . . . you know? And that teachers can't see on the computer, it doesn't appear on the computer.

Showing up to class was a big deal to Yanet. She was concerned about the teachers not *seeing* her kids there. Invisibility was the opposite of what Yanet hoped for her children once they were in the U.S. Teachers were used to cameras being turned off. It happened a lot for different reasons, like students feeling nervous about showing their surroundings, but also because some students were not at their computers during class sessions.

Yanet was not the only parent concerned about what was visible or invisible online. Julio, a father from Guatemala, was worried about his daughter Luz's well-being. Luz was in first grade, so Julio would prop up his phone or an old tablet in front of her at the kitchen table for "school time" until they received the new hardware. He relied on neighbors in his building to watch Luz when he was working outside of the home. But before he left for work every day, Julio made sure Luz had headphones and that the device was working. After district schools distributed Chromebooks, Julio was able to set up Google Meet on the computer for Luz to participate in classes. He sent me weekly messages or voice recordings on WhatsApp, often expressing concerns about Luz: "It's that the little girl sleeps, she is always sleepy, tired, I think she is depressed. She is asking about her *mamá* more now. The other day I saw her on the phone with her mom during a class. I can't be mad at her, but I am worried that all of the work . . . like how far we came . . . I am always praying she does well."

Julio was referring to the multiple times Luz would take the device (phone, tablet, or computer) and use it to connect with her mother in Guatemala. Luz learned quickly how to make calls and use video chats. She read the commands on the computer and felt proud of herself: "See here where it says c-all, you press here, then you can choose video if you want to see the person. I want to see the person." It didn't take long for Luz's teacher to contact Julio about Luz being "disconnected" or overly "distracted" during her blocks of online instruction. Near the end of June, Julio told the teacher, "I will keep trying, but I'm not home, I'm not home and there are other children in the background. She needs a quiet place to listen." In those first months of the pandemic, parents like Julio and Yanet juggled work and care in an increasingly precarious situation in which health, education, income, and any hard-won stability felt fragile once again.

Andrea, a mother from Honduras, was also concerned about her children's attendance to online lessons or that, when they did attend, they kept their cameras off. As a parent of a middle schooler, Andrea was concerned that making children be on the computer all day would make their brains tired, and that they would feel sad. Like Julio's concerns about Luz, Andrea explained that her daughter, Felipa, was more irritable, angry, and was lashing out at her parents more. "The teachers don't always see this in the computer online, but I think their heads need a rest." For Andrea the physical aspect of being at school had a clear benefit: "At least in their school there are a lot of people for them to play and talk, that's good . . . and they are safe." Schools were a stabilizing force, a predictable routine, and a recompense for the sacrifices of leaving one's home. Before the pandemic, migrant kids had plenty to say about what they liked and didn't like about school. However, the pandemic reinforced the positivity of the promise of an American education precisely because of its absence.

If parents were home during online instruction, they tried to listen to the lessons and enforce their children's visible presence online. Andrea showed up on her children's video backgrounds every now and then. She would wave to the teachers and bring snacks to her children—Daphne (11) and Francisco (8)—when they had been sitting in front of a device for a while. Francisco's teacher described those appearances as demonstrations of care: "You can see that the mom is trying, she is watching them, yelling at them, making sure they stay on task. It's hard, but it warms my heart" (Miss Jonas, white elementary teacher, U.S.-born). While sometimes teachers' perceptions of immigrant students tend to be lower (Papalazarou & Triliva, 2019), these visible "acts of care" helped some teachers reframe their opinion of immigrant families. What appeared onscreen mattered to parents and informed teachers' perceptions of parental care and their commitment to education. However, what remained invisible on camera were the breakdowns in work, health, food needs, and emotional support that remained a feature of these families' lives during those months of online instruction.

Care and Education

Daisy, a Salvadoran mother, worried about how her son Cruz spent his days. Because she had to keep working outside the home while in-person school was closed, she made a deal with a neighbor whom she paid to keep an eye on Cruz while she was working. The neighbor, a middle-aged woman from El Salvador, watched a group of six kids between 9 am and 2 pm every day, making sure they were all connected online and attending school sessions. One June afternoon right before the end of the school year, I met Daisy where she worked at a small supermarket, bagging groceries, cleaning bathrooms, and restocking shelves. I gave her a ride from the supermarket to her house since her husband was not able to pick her up that day. On the 25-minute car ride, Daisy expressed her frustration, guilt, and fear of not being able to, in her words, "be there for Cruz." She explained that when Cruz was physically in school, he had not been able to make many friends, because while the class was in Spanish, during recess kids spoke in English. Daisy reflected:

> I'm so thankful we are here, I'm so thankful Cruz was able to go to school in Spanish! See how wonderful this is ... but I am thinking here to myself, maybe they [school staff] didn't think about recess and other parts of the day for the children who don't speak English. When they play at school is all in English. So now he is with this group of children, who cause a lot of trouble at someone's house, and I get nervous about his education, you know ... because I know he needs to learn the math and the reading, but he needs to know how to behave and make friends ... and I don't know, be part of the school.

When caregivers explained feeling uneasy and nervous about their children's education they focused on social-emotional dynamics like "making friends" and being present. For Daisy, school was a place to stay out of trouble and learn to "be part" of a larger societal system. She expressed unwavering gratitude for schooling and being *here now*. Her gratitude didn't stop her from pointing to so-called *nonacademic* skills that she wanted Cruz to develop and gain. Daisy worried about the experience of belonging for Cruz, how accepted and happy he felt in school. Thus, online learning directly impacted her hopes for Cruz in terms of inclusion in everyday schooling as well as his well-being.

One early afternoon in June 2020, Daisy and I arrived at her apartment complex with our masks on. Cruz was supposed to be in a neighbor's apartment connected online and attending classes. Her neighbor had three children, all elementary age, who were also supposed to be online learning. We climbed the stairs to the fourth floor to avoid using the elevator. Daisy knocked on the door of her neighbor's apartment, but no one answered. It was 1:30 pm so she knew the elementary-aged children had at least another hour of school. Daisy got her phone out and called her neighbor. No answer. We ran up another flight of stairs to her own apartment to see if Cruz was there. Nothing. She called her husband, Luis, who was working as a mechanic that day. He had no idea where Cruz could be. Daisy then called every other parent of the children in the neighbor's care; two answered and were worried that their children were not at the neighbor's apartment. Daisy's shift at her other job, a restaurant, would start in one hour. She was allowed to bring Cruz with her to that job if he stayed in the back with his school device or watching television. She was worried about Cruz as she looked at her phone to check the time.

Daisy started to panic: "They took him! They took them!" I asked, "Who took them?" and she replied, "I don't know, Gabi, the police?" I asked her if we should knock on some other doors, maybe the kids were all playing in someone else's home. Tears ran down Daisy's cheeks. "They are supposed to be online," she said. She then remembered that there was a small playground behind the apartment complex on the ground floor. We ran down the stairs to the playground to find the children running and playing, spraying water at each other, and eating popsicles another neighbor had brought for them. Daisy ran to Cruz, hugged him, kissed him, squeezed him: "Where were you? I didn't find you," she said to him. Her neighbor approached her and said, "The teachers finished early today so I brought them down." Daisy found out later that this was not true when Cruz's teacher sent her a WhatsApp message regarding his absence in the last block of instruction.

On the playground, Daisy told me that she felt nauseous, and Cruz asked her why she seemed so upset. Daisy turned to me and exhaled: "This is what makes me nervous, is that he is not in school, I'm not with him, he is there, here. In God's name . . ." During another conversation later in the summer Daisy remembered this moment in June and offered another reflection: "I think I always remember everything that happened to my little boy. When we crossed, when for four days we stayed in the place, the cold place, and they took our documents, sometimes I think about the days we didn't see Luis [her husband], and my little boy just sleeping there on the floor, and it's that I don't think of this for a long time, but now it's here again [her memories]." Even as narratives of immediatism were extant in Daisy's accounts, the memories of separation, loss, and fear permeated her present. Both caregivers and children commonly combined *now* and *then* events. The pandemic exacerbated feelings of uncertainty and brought back the sense of a lack of stability. The break in school meant so much more than missing a math lesson or a decrease in standardized testing performance. The pandemic came as a reminder of what a disruption can cause.

Parents cared deeply about their children's education, which they understood as a path to socioeconomic mobility, but also as a way for them to develop socioemotionally. They rarely used specific frameworks like grades or test scores to measure or discuss their children's schooling. Their biggest concern was losing education—one of the cornerstones of how they constructed what a better life would look like for their kids.

The recurring breakdowns associated with health issues, work schedules, the difficulties of accessing income supplements, and distrust in people who cared for their children amid the early pandemic dislocations in care and schooling destabilized part of the better life imagined. The promise of U.S. schooling as a site of possibilities became contested, strained, and unclear. While journalists and scholars have focused on pandemic academic learning loss, these anxieties are inconsistent with how immigrant parents articulated the meaning of schools. Of course, they worried about how their children were doing academically, but they also mourned the loss of the most structured, predictable part of their children's lives: schools. Between 2021 and 2023 a lot was published on youth mental health and its association with the pandemic (Alvis et al., 2022). Scholars have reported higher levels of youth anxiety and depression developed over the pandemic in 2020 (Panda et al., 2021). The compounded nature of the disruptions Daisy described further contributed to immigrant parents' anxiety regarding what school loss meant for their children.

Pedro and Mila were parents to Dario, an 11-year-old fifth grader. They had two older sons, ages 18 and 21, in Guatemala to whom they sent monthly remittances. Pedro and Mila's biggest dream was to enable their sons to attend university or at least enroll in some vocational schooling in Guatemala. From March to June 2020, the family was able to send very little money home, sometimes just 20 dollars a month. During the same period, Mila experienced two instances of accelerated heart rate that resulted in her going to the emergency room during the time when patients had to enter alone. Pedro became ill with COVID-19 in early April but did not go to the hospital. Sometimes he would sleep in the bathroom of their small one-bedroom apartment in order to avoid transmitting the disease to the rest of the family. Mila explained: "We are here, right? We came here, you know . . . but now we can't help there and we can't help here. Tenemos que cuidar a nuestros hijos, entiendes [We need to take of our sons, understand], all of them. And my mother, too. Para que puedan sobresalir [So they can excel]." The precarity of those months once again brought the present tense of the lived experience to the forefront: "We are here." The stakes of having migrated, having been detained and/or separated, feeling as though they had a chance at a better life, were deeply impacted by the pandemic. This multidirectional care (Bruhn & Oliveira, 2022) was also interrupted as remittances became harder to send. Fortunately, the months that followed offered more possibilities.

Summer Dreaming

The months of July and August were a school break for many students. While all elementary-age children in this research attended bilingual classrooms, these were not available during the summer, and they were instead enrolled in online summer school to continue their English language learning. Middle and high school youth in this study were also enrolled in tutoring sessions in disciplines like math and social studies. Public parks and playgrounds began to reopen in summer 2020, and children and youth were looking forward to being outside and enjoying the warm weather. By July, some jobs that had not been available for many parents during the previous months began hiring again. As Dylan, a father from Guatemala, explained, "Slowly we will make it back to before, but not the before before, just the before"—indicating the period between leaving his country and the COVID-19 pandemic. Now, the ideal present meant going back to before 2020.

Adriana, a 16-year-old youth from Brazil, sent me a text message through her mother's phone in mid-July: "I'm in summer school. How boring." I responded that I was sorry it was boring but asked if she was learning anything new. Adriana replied that the repetition was hard for her. Since she was not an advanced English speaker, she spent a lot of time in introductory-level English instruction. She wrote: "It's like the world is on fire and they are here like 'use the *th* for something.'" Adriana was conscious of her surroundings and juxtaposed the context of learning phonics in English with a rampant global pandemic. Adriana had always been a critical thinker, witty, and fast on her feet. She was also creative and enjoyed writing.

During the summer, I asked children and youth if they could write or draw something brief about how they felt about migrating to the U.S. and how their lives were going amid the changes brought by COVID-19. Adriana wrote a short paragraph and sent it to me via text message through her mother's phone:

O meu poema para você. [My poem for you]

Eu não sou daqui, eu não sou mais de lá. Eles me mandam para lá para e cá. Na fronteira não foi tão ruim, mas na escola agora não sobrou o mais importante. Eu tenho saudades de ver meus amigos, sair de casa, ir em lugares. Eu não sou daqui, eu não sou mais de lá. Para o meu futuro eu quero: paz, amor, e que esse virus acabe logo. Eu quero aprender e ir para o College. Eu quero um futuro sem tanta pausa.

[I am not from here; I am not from there. They sent me there and here. At the border, it wasn't so bad, but at school, the most important thing is now missing. I miss seeing my friends, going out, going to places. I'm not from here, I'm not from there anymore. For my future, I want peace, love, and for this virus to end soon. I want to learn and go to college. I want a future without so many pauses.]

Adriana's hope of a future without so many pauses, intermissions, and breakdowns felt more attainable to her during the summer. The summer, for a moment, offered a glimpse into the possibilities of a future of peace and love, as Adriana explained, even as bored as she was.

Since my prompt involved migration (past) and their current lives (present), the responses I received from children and youth put these perspectives into conversation with one another. However, the future took center stage in their responses. Maria Clara (8) recorded a voice memo on her mother's phone through WhatsApp, telling me:

> Eu quero logo voltar para a escola porque eu tenho saudade dos meus amigos, das minhas professoras e do playground. A minha mãe diz que não fica pior daqui para frente, tia. Daqui para frente, a gente melhora! Eu nem lembro mais que a gente ficou com medo lá na fronteira, com fome e com frio e saindo do Brasil. O meu medo já passou, e agora o sonho é do futuro, se deus quiser.

> [I want to go back to school soon because I miss my friends, my teachers, and the playground. My mom says it won't get worse from here on, Auntie. From now on, things will get better! I don't even remember being scared at the border, being hungry, and being cold, or leaving Brazil. My fear is gone now, and my dream is for the future, God willing.]

I could almost hear Maria Clara's mother's voice through the voice memo she sent me, her focus on the future and naming all the things she had supposedly forgotten about. *It only gets better from now on.* One of the main thoughts guiding migrant families' decision to leave was that leaving home and moving to another place would mean less suffering and better lives.

Luz and William were attending online summer school to continue working on their English language development. They both found it draining. Luz, who was 7 at the time, explained: "It's that the person becomes very tired of being on the computer when the sun is there." William, who was 9 at the time, rationalized: "I don't like it, I get bored and sleepy, I want to go play outside or video games." Santo, who was 6 years old in 2020, worried that no one would remember him when he went back to school: "¿Crees que los profesores me recordarán? Quiero ver mi nueva sala en la escuela" (Do you think the teachers will remember me? I want to see my new classroom at school). Reflections from children and youth illustrated the excitement, fear, nervousness, and hopefulness for their future. Time had been suspended for migrant families at different moments in their journey. Leaving their homes made their memories of their houses, schools, and communities static, while they remembered detention and/or separation at the border as marking a specific period, a moment, that they carried with them still. Now, the emergency of the pandemic had interrupted schooling—the symbol of a stable and consistent path toward mobility and healing—thus suspending access to the benefit that made migration seem worth the pain. The summer offered a breather but was also a precursor of what was to come.

In the state of Massachusetts, July and August 2020 brought a slight reprieve from the restrictions that had been in place since March. During the summer, the schooling schedule for some kids was even manageable for parents who had to work outside the home and find supervision or care for their children. Many families were nervous about what school and work would look like in the fall and voiced their concerns.

One hot afternoon I was with Beatriz and her daughter, Paloma, at a splash pad near their house. The children were in bathing suits running across the pad as the water sprayed them from every direction. Some children wore sandals and others were barefoot, giggling, running, and screaming when water unexpectedly hit their faces. Just two years before (2018), Beatriz had been detained and separated from Paloma, age 11 in 2020, on their journey from Honduras to the U.S. That day at the splash pad we sat on the bench together. I asked Beatriz if she had thought we'd be here now, at the park, outside playing given the pandemic. In her answer she reflected on her life since that time:

> I give you a whole story, OK? It's that two years ago we arrived at the border ... me and my little girl. Together ... the two of us. After they caught us and put one in each place I thought, through God, I am never going to see her again. I thought about her in her uniform going to school, learning in my country, in my country ... But then those 13 days I was so sick I thought I was not going to make it. My doctor says that because so many things happened in our lives we just live very nervous, very nervous life. After we were together [reunified] I made a promise to support my little daughter, support her in everything she does. Being here now ... look how she is happy, she will go to school in two months, we will do it ... mira mira como lo hago respire asi ... hace tu? [look, look how I do it breathe like this ... you do it?].

Beatriz took multiple deep breaths. She attributed this technique to Paloma's pediatrician who had encouraged her to take deep breaths when she felt anxious about the future. Living a nervous life, a life of uncertainty, was nothing new to Beatriz. Back in Honduras they had both had their share of scares, witnessing violence, losing jobs, feeling hopeless. They also had love for home and a longing for the moments that were positive, like seeing Paloma going to school in her uniform.

Beatriz and Paloma were reunified thanks to pro-bono lawyers working with a nongovernmental organization. Typically, children and parents were taken to U.S. Customs and Border Protection (CBP) processing centers when they were arrested. Participants described these as jail-like facilities where sleeping, eating, and showering were precarious opportunities. After passing through CBP custody, however, Beatriz and Paloma were separated. Beatriz cannot speak about this moment without being overcome with emotion. Paloma was 9 years old at the time, and Beatriz remembered when two uniformed women escorted Paloma toward a different area of the facility. At the time, it was not clear to Beatriz what was happening until another parent told her, "They are taking her." Beatriz was convinced that the officers had only taken Paloma for a wellness check since she had been complaining about an earache. When she didn't come back, Beatriz had a sinking feeling of loss.

According to Beatriz, while she was detained in Texas, Paloma was sent to a government-run facility that operated like a shelter for children in the same state. Paloma remembered the moment when she was separated from her mother: "They just told us you will go play with more children, there will be more children there or something. I thought I was going somewhere to play more, and then at night I slept in a place with more children like me . . . no dad no mom there, just the Mrs. that gave us things like food and clothes." I asked Paloma how she felt then, and she explained: "Every night I used to think: my mom will arrive right here! But I just knew one day, one day." Paloma remembered counting on her fingers how many nights she slept without her *mamá*: "After I finished my two hands, I started to get nervous, when is she going to come?" As soon as Beatriz understood that the separation could in fact be permanent, she started to ask others how to get help. Different organizations tried to help detained migrants, and Beatriz explained her case to a lawyer who visited her detention center and he agreed to take her on. Beatriz said in the group she was detained with there were other women who knew their children had been taken to other states, but in her case, she felt she was lucky and protected by God, because Paloma had remained in Texas.

For Beatriz, imagining a bright future in which Paloma's education would mean stability, safety, and a possible path to a better life worked as a counternarrative to all the trauma they had experienced at the border. Every time I visited Beatriz and Paloma, who rented a small room in a three-bedroom apartment, Beatriz made sure to show me all the homework Paloma completed and the books she read. "You think you can find more books that could be a challenge for her? She could try to read more advanced, *maestra*, what do you think?" For Beatriz, the school closures and other disruptions of the COVID-19 pandemic were a financial stressor. "Now I almost have to choose to work or to take care of her . . . and I think I can never leave my baby again. My mission on this planet is to make sure she studies and is successful. We will not be with this virus for too long." Beatriz was concerned with giving her daughter stability. As Paloma said, "No more separated times, OK?" to which Beatriz would say, "Never again, *hijita*."

Education was the currency of love. Planning, counting on, and discussing education as both theory and practice-based experience established and brokered relationships between parents and their children. While every family in this research talked about family separation or detention at the border openly and in community, every now and then these conversations about leaving home, the border, and separation became unbearable. Thus, while parents centered their need for work and a stable income, the path forward they imagined for their children depended on a good education. As the summer came to an end, families looked forward to receiving guidance regarding what school would look like in fall 2020. Maria Clara, age 8 in 2020, seemed hopeful: "I want to buy all the new material for my school, *mamãe*, like the backpack that has glitter, like water glitter for me to take it to school and see my friends. I am very excited!" Her mother replied, "It's what we can hope for . . . right now we just want the minimum that you have a good place to go and learn a lot, because that's all you have to do. Learn learn learn . . . we didn't come here for anyone to lose opportunities."

Muted Identities

In fall 2020, schools around the U.S. used different models of instruction: all online, all in person, in person but with restricted hours, masked, socially distanced, hybrid formats with some in-person and some online instruction, or phased plans that brought the youngest or most vulnerable students to in-person school first. In the schools where my observations took place, school leaders decided on an online start followed by a phased approach in which different groups of students were brought to in-person school according to their needs. For example, children with individualized education plans were candidates to join physical classrooms earlier in the year. By the spring of 2021, most children were back at school with varying numbers of hours of in-person schooling.

While my observations of schooling between September 2020 and early spring 2021 were online, after vaccinations were rolled out in 2021, I was able to resume in-person classroom observations. Through these observations I was able to witness how children and youth participated in schooling activities and how parents supported their efforts. For most children and youth in this research, the main issues with virtual schooling were unreliable infrastructure, parental illness or work responsibilities, and interpersonal dynamics with teachers who sometimes supported them, and other times did not.

When children and youth joined their online classroom, each student's default status was to enter the virtual classroom muted. In many ways, students' muted status online reminded me of the dynamics I have called pedagogies of silence in the previous chapter. While the muted status—indicated by the small symbol of a microphone with a red line through it—was an important tool for teachers trying to maintain order with 20 to 30 students in a virtual classroom, its use also meant less spontaneous communication among students and between students and teachers. While participants used chat boxes, younger children in kindergarten and first grade primarily used emojis to communicate. Children starting in second grade were more likely than younger children to write notes to friends and try to make connections with peers during class.

Elementary age students longed for social connection. Paloma, age 9 from Honduras, wrote in Spanish on the chat: "Alguién quiere jugar despues de la escuela?" (Someone want to play after school?) Her teacher quickly intervened. "Paloma, not the time to do that OK. Another time when we go on a break. OK, let's look at this," she said as a slide went up on the screen. This was one of multiple instances when students attempted to connect with one another. Teachers sometimes deactivated the chat option altogether to try to maintain focus.

Online classes became increasingly more lecture based even for the earlier grades. Teachers used slide presentations, which made the tiles showing students' faces very small. Davi, age 11 in 2020, complained to me: "Everyone is muted, and I can't see anyone. And my internet is bad." His parents worried about his younger sibling, Vinny, who already had an individualized education plan in school (or an IEP) and needed more accommodations. Gabriel, Vinny and Davi's father, explained: "É trauma atrás de trauma para esses meninos. O pior mesmo é para Vinny que tinha um monte de serviço e coisa na escola. Agora ele quer mais é ver mais tela, mais tela" (It's trauma after trauma for these boys. The worst is for Vinny that had a lot of services and things at school. Now he wants to watch screens the most, more screens). Many parents shared this concern: that screens beget screens and children would normalize being in front of them all day. Prior to the pandemic kids already had plenty of access to screens, but at different points in the day.

Most of the virtual elementary classrooms I observed followed a rigid protocol in which students stayed connected from 9 am until after 3 pm. Teachers enforced attendance and reported absent children in the same way they did with in-person activities. Despite these attempts to replicate the school day, not all routines readily transferred online. Teachers struggled through the first few attempts at circle time for children in kindergarten, first, second, and third grade. Practices that included saying good morning to someone in your class by chanting, "Good morning [name of student], how are you today?" required quick responses from young students who had to find the unmute button and start speaking only when that action was completed. "Não dá para ouvir você!" or "No te escuchamos" (We can't hear you) were common refrains from students and teachers during those activities, becoming almost a comical spectacle of (mis)communication. These morning routines were some of the most common activities in early elementary education: talking about the weather, naming the day of the week, month, and year, and greeting one another.

Online, however, children and teachers talked over one another, which resulted in more rules of engagement—which sometimes in turn gave teachers a window into their migrant students' realities. "From now on everyone is on mute until I say you can unmute," Ms. Gutierrez, a third-grade bilingual Spanish-English teacher, explained. Immediately after she finished speaking, Augusto, a 7-year-old migrant child from Guatemala, asked, "But what if it's emergency, like someone comes here to my door and I need help." Ms. Gutierrez responded, "Augusto, please stay on after we finish this lesson so I can talk to you, OK?" I was in the same online classroom, and Ms. Gutierrez sent me a text message via phone and told me she was concerned. Since Ms. Gutierrez and I were not sure what Augusto wanted to disclose, I left the online meeting so they could speak privately. After a few minutes Ms. Gutierrez sent me a text message inviting me to reenter the meeting. I reconnected and Augusto continued to explain: "It's like I told you Miss . . . happened to my neighbors that the police came and maybe they take a father or a mother." Ms. Gutierrez asked why Augusto thought the police would come and take anyone in his home, to which he responded: "It's because we are missing different papers and they decide who stays." Ms. Gutierrez sought support from the school psychologist and the principal to find out what to do next. She ended up speaking to Augusto's mother, Mimi, who relayed that she thought there had been an immigration raid near where they lived and maybe Augusto had heard about it. Raids were not completely uncommon but seemed to happen less often during COVID. It was unclear if it had been an immigration raid or if the police had been called and then immigration officers became involved or if it was an ambulance with sirens. In any case, Augusto was aware and nervous about the possibility that it could happen to his family. Similar to what I observed in in-person classrooms before the pandemic, children brought their knowledges and fears into online learning spaces. In this case Ms. Gutierrez followed up individually with Augusto, which seemed like a good use of the online teaching feature.

Windows into Realities

While elementary students had a confusing start to online learning—problems accessing online materials, passwords, stable internet, background noise—for many teachers the new modality offered a window into children's realities. Ms. Gutierrez, Augusto's first grade teacher, had been on the job for five years. She was born in Puerto Rico but moved to the U.S. as a baby. Ms. Gutierrez adored her students. When school was in person, she was affectionate with them, brought them food and clothes, and would often comb the girls' hair and style it in neat braids or ponytails. She was 28 years old and described herself as answering a calling to become a teacher: "If I don't advocate for them, who will?" However, the information Augusto shared with her about his fears and documentation was new to her, as she later debriefed with me: "I had no idea this was a fear of his. Now I know. Baby steps with these kids, they've been through so much."

During the height of the COVID-19 pandemic, I held a monthly zoom meeting with six elementary teachers from three different schools. These meetings were often like group venting sessions in Portuguese, Spanish, and English: each one of us with a beverage, sitting in front of our computers, and talking about teaching online, parenting, and all the funny online situations that had been occurring. In one meeting during December 2020, the consensus was that while the past few months had been the most challenging of their careers—COVID-19, their personal and family lives, the lack of consistent support from districts, and worrying about their students—they had also gained a window into their students' home lives.

> MRS. MATOS: I wish we could do home visits, even before the pandemic, like go there to their homes...
>
> MRS. DIAZ: We used to do it remember... when it was, I think in 2018.
>
> MRS. ANDRADE: I don't think she was there yet [referencing how Mrs. Matos was not at their school then]
>
> MRS. DIAZ: Well, I think when we know more about what is happening to our students we can be more responsive. It doesn't mean it will be perfect, but I am always shocked at how we don't discuss this enough in graduate school and when we are at the job...
>
> GABRIELLE: Discuss what specifically?
>
> MRS. DIAZ: Strategies to get to know your students deeply, not their favorite food or color, but the real stuff: what have you left behind? What is happening in your home? Makes sense... to... I don't know...
>
> MRS. BRITO: True, true... the other day I was on Google Meets with my class and one of my students—you know Gabi, Cesar—kept getting up and leaving his chair over and over, when finally I asked him to show me what he kept getting up for. He picked up the computer and took it to the living room and I saw at least three babies or toddlers playing with a woman watching over them. I was taken aback, because Cesar doesn't

have siblings—or not that I know—so I assume it was him and his mom at home. Which I found out it is, but his mom needs someone watching him during the day sometimes and the neighbor has three children and brings them to play while Cesar is connected. Do you get the complexity?

MRS. MATOS: Yeah, I feel like I have a lot of stories like that too. Who appears on camera, the noises, the chair, table, lunch, environment that kids are living in, makes me feel bad sometimes.

GABRIELLE: What do you think of their home environment?

MRS. MATOS: It's not ideal. Not a lot of space to do homework, no quiet space...

MRS. DIAZ: But that's how a lot of children live, it's not just the kids that are immigrants.

MS. ANDRADE: But you have to agree that there are elements that make their experience uniquely complicated and it's helpful for us to understand... so hard.

GABRIELLE: Will you tell me what these elements are?

MS. ANDRADE: I'm going to be blunt...

MS. BRITO: Here we go [laughter]

MS. ANDRADE: Not being a citizen puts a forever stress in their hearts and brains. Your life is on the move. You left your home country, maybe you had to stay in Mexico a while, then there is the border, then they are here. Now they are here, but their papers are not in order, it's not up to them. And did you know this: for these families to plead for their case in front of a judge—and guys I mean not to be sent back! That's what is a stake—they have to retell the whole story of what happened.

MRS. SOUZA: Trauma on trauma.

This conversation persisted for another hour as teachers made sense of the specificities of their students' life experiences. According to teachers, these reflections came out of teaching online—seeing interactions such as more extended family on screen, or the lighting and environmental conditions, as well as the care of parents—provided teachers with a window into children's realities. "O que eu acho é que quem já tinha pouco tem menos ainda" (What I think is that whoever had a little, now has even less), Mrs. Matos explained. "The parents can't be there, sometimes they are... we can't help them in person, give them a hug, some snacks, it's like the order of who and how children are cared for disappeared," said Ms. Souza, a second grade teacher.

Teachers alluded to how COVID-19 had exacerbated and exposed the inequality their students experienced, discussed seeing the complexity of their lives close up, and reflected on how to best care for their students. The idea of learning loss or "learning lag" (Pier et al., 2021) is used "in order to underscore that a lag in learning can occur relative to expected progress, even as students continue to learn and gain new knowledge and skills, and also that learning that has been delayed during the pandemic can be recouped through deliberate intervention" (p. 1). The focus of new knowledge and skills is usually connected to academics. But at the height of the pandemic in 2020, parents, children, and teachers were concerned about both mental health and socioemotional learning. Later, as children went back to school full time, some educators, policymakers, and some parents turned their full attention to academic lags and losses. Migrant families, however, continued to be concerned about how their children's well-being was being impacted in school.

Conclusion

In early 2020, the COVID-19 pandemic brought yet another disruption for families that had endured a combination of traumatic experiences and hope for the future on their journey to the U.S. Migrant parents faced job losses and financial hardships due to the pandemic, particularly those in low-wage and essential sectors such as hospitality, restaurants, and retail, who experienced high rates of unemployment as businesses shut down or reduced their operations. Without a safety net or access to unemployment benefits, many faced difficulties in meeting their basic needs. Fear of immigration enforcement and limited access to healthcare made it difficult for some to seek medical attention when needed. This situation was particularly vulnerable because many immigrants work in essential sectors where the risk of viral exposure was higher.

The pandemic also affected immigration policies and procedures. Travel restrictions, border closures, and reduced consular services made it challenging for immigrants to reunite with their families or complete immigration processes. Many immigration courts had to postpone hearings, leading to delays in legal proceedings and uncertainties for those awaiting immigration decisions. As Cruz, a 7-year-old from El Salvador explained as he moved his hand up and down like a roller coaster: "Uno se va pensando que será mejor, luego ... realmente malo, y hay muchas personas malas, luego es bueno con muchas personas amables, y ahora este virus malo que no me deja ir a la escuela" (A person leaves thinking that it will be better, then it's really bad, and a lot of bad people, then it's good with a lot of nice people, and now this bad virus that makes me not go to school). This chapter has illustrated how families lived through the height of the pandemic and specifically the educational and employment disruptions that affected them so fundamentally: from issues related to health and jobs, to how care was structured in the home, to consequences for education and schooling.

These stories are concentrated in the months of disrupted schooling between March and September 2020, during which immigrant parents experienced breakdowns in care, health, and employment, and through fall 2020 when children began their formal online education. In these stories, education was the thread that tied together immigrant parents' narratives of breakdowns in care, health, and schooling. Parents remained determined to see their children through their educational achievements even as networks of care and support became less readily available. From taking children to work to making sure they were connected online in the care of a neighbor, parents prioritized attending school. At the same time, the switch to virtual learning gave teachers a new window into their students' lives, and they worked to make sense of their experiences with families and students. This "window into student realities"—as some teachers described it—allowed them to gain more insight into how students spent their time at home, as well as the pressures and stresses they were under.

Not only was 2020 shaped by the COVID-19 pandemic, but also by a contentious presidential election. In November 2020, we witnessed the election of President Joe Biden to the U.S. presidency, defeating incumbent President Donald Trump. While it would be a mistake to lump all immigrants from countries across Latin America into a single, monolithic voting bloc (or any single narrative for that matter), these families had all experienced detention and/or separation under the Trump Administration's zero tolerance and Migrant Protection Protocols (MPP) immigration policies. They were also released and reunified during the Trump administration. Julio, a father from

Guatemala explained his perception: "It's complicated to say that it's because of one person that my daughter was taken from me. It's hard. But I am hopeful for the future because this ... [the administration] talked about not doing this to more families ever. Right now, I have to be grateful." The change in U.S. leadership resulted in changes for immigrant families, but also continuities. Gabriel, an immigrant father from Brazil explained: "We were given a second, and now a third chance. Second when we could leave our country and survived the border. Third, when we didn't die of COVID and can continue giving our children a better life." When I asked families if there was something about the election that gave them hope or fear, they expressed that they felt both. There was hope when then–candidate Joe Biden promised sweeping immigration reforms on the campaign trail. Some families hoped for a type of complete amnesty. Others were more realistic and described American politics as confusing and distant from their realities.

FIVE
Lost and Found

> Siempre hay tantas cosas, guantes, sudaderas y botellas de agua en las escuelas. Cosas que la gente pierde y que otras personas encuentran. Lo llaman... sabe que... lost y found.
>
> [There are always so many jackets, gloves, sweatshirts, water bottles at the schools. Things people lost and other people found. They call it... you know... lost and found.]
> —FATIMA, Guatemalan immigrant mother of three children.

FATIMA WAS ALWAYS AMAZED by the number of lost items that piled up on tables at the schools her children attended. Students often forgot items like jackets, gloves, sweatshirts, lunch boxes, water bottles, pencil cases, sometimes entire backpacks. She commented that in Guatemala, she didn't think so many youth would forget or lose so many things mainly because there was less to lose. She explained:

> Simplemente yo pienso que estábamos en una situación donde había menos que... perder. La escuela en mi país se preocupaban por los niños, aquí también se preocupan en la escuela, pero es un cuidado diferente. Aquí se trata más de la oportunidad de ser alguien, allá se trataba de que una persona pudiera vivir.
>
> [I simply think that we were in a situation where there was less to lose. In the school in my country, they cared about the children, and here in the

school, they also care, but it's a different kind of care. Here, it's more about the opportunity to become someone, whereas there, it was about a person being able to survive.]

Fatima reflected on several issues that pertained to her life. While the lost and found area of the school was a mundane everyday fixture of schooling in the U.S., in our conversation about leaving a country, schooling, and care, the metaphor of losing and finding things triggered a deeper reflection—mainly, the hope that being in the U.S. offered to her and her family. For Fatima, the U.S. was about breaking with lack of opportunity, carving out space for mobility. Schools and the promise of an education were ingredients for that. In Guatemala, surviving and existing every day were her goals. While Fatima and other families explained the differences between "here" and "there," they also acknowledged what was in between the two locations. In the U.S., migrant families lived at or below the poverty line. In addition, families' immigration statuses were fragile as they waited for their fate to be decided by a judge. Employment was vulnerable since their work permits were often delayed. Health, food, and transportation were all dependent on the stability of that vulnerable employment or on charity from organizations. But these were also newfound, hopeful spaces where schooling and education were central to the possibilities for mobility and hope for the future.

This chapter is about families' articulations of their hopeful trajectories during the three years they had been in the U.S. As newcomers who hoped to thrive and provide a better life for their children, they seemed to face constant hurdles. Immigration case backlogs meant that it could be years until they learned their fate in the U.S. The unstable economy, a pandemic, and breakdowns in caregiving structures deeply influenced how they perceived their ability to care for the family members who were with them in the U.S., as well as those who had stayed behind. Remittances were interrupted, and they made fewer calls to their family members in their home countries. Participants feared that family members in El Salvador, Guatemala, Honduras, and Brazil would die of COVID-19 and that they would not be able to help them, see them, say good-byes. However, mothers, fathers, children, and youth repeated the affirmation "now we are here" as they articulated the paradoxical feelings of gratitude for being alive and together, and the fear of removal, separation, and loss.

In this chapter, I discuss "lives lived in relief" (Feldman, 2018), emergency, and disruption, as well as migrant families' hopes for their future in the U.S. Will things get better? Have we made the right decision? Has the promise of a good education materialized for our children? This chapter is dedicated to narratives of recovery in the face of a global pandemic, but also of grief for the losses experienced along the way. Fatima's observations of what was lost and found, or even what was lost by one person but could be found by another, serves as a metaphor for the different narratives these families developed.

Fatima, Fernando, Rosa, Daniel, Vivi

Fatima worked at a lettuce factory when we first met in April 2019. She and her family had arrived in the U.S. six weeks earlier. The family had left a small town in Guatemala early in January of that year and finally arrived in Ciudad Juárez, Mexico, on February 22. Fatima described her reality in Guatemala as *muy dura*. Fatima, Fernando, Rosa, and Daniel spoke at length about how they had feared for their safety there. While it was a small town outside of Guatemala City, Rosa and Daniel encountered several issues as they went to school, went out with friends, or simply went to the market to buy food. Daniel recalled: "My soccer ball was taken, or some people would ask my friends for their money, or sometimes they said we had to work for them." Rosa, their then-17-year-old, had been robbed multiple times on her way to work in Guatemala City. One of the times, Rosa explained that she was nervous they would do something like sexually assault her: "It was the same group that came after me, because they thought someone I knew had their money, but it was a mistake."

Fernando, her father, explained that he had accumulated debt by borrowing money from informal groups so he could build his house. In exchange for the money he borrowed, besides having to pay it back with interest, Fernando was to tell other people to borrow money from the group. Fatima described the group as criminals who were involved in drug trafficking. She also thought they may have bought and sold weapons. Fatima could never confirm those claims, but she explained that on multiple occasions she heard members of the group discuss weapons and drugs.

Fatima had feared that their children would experience interrupted schooling because of lack of safety. In Guatemala, Fatima took care of her children while her husband worked in landscaping, construction, and gardening.

Fatima described her goal as a mother in Guatemala as "luchando para que estudien" (fighting for them to study). When the family decided to leave Guatemala, Rosa was 17, Daniel was 15, and Vivi was 6. Since Fatima knew friends who had gone to the U.S., she proposed the idea to Fernando at the end of 2018. Fernando was nervous about the news of families being separated at the border, and he particularly worried about Vivi being only 6 years old. However, Fatima convinced him that anything that could happen to them on the way to the U.S. could not be worse than staying put in Guatemala. She explained: "When someone thinks no, we can't go, like Fernando did, I told him, and stay here and wait for the judgment day? Wait for when it's our turn for something to happen to our children? We know so many people that something bad happened to them. We don't need the worst case of violence for us to leave . . . we leave so the worst doesn't happen, understand?"

The family started to think about how to raise money to migrate north. A total of $9,300 U.S. dollars was necessary to cover the whole family and half of the total amount had to be paid in advance. They sold their house, animals, and other belongings like an old motorcycle and two bicycles. Additionally, they were able to borrow money from friends who were already in the U.S. and came up with almost $4,500 to pay two men who would take turns guiding them in a group across Mexico. Fernando explained to the two men that they wanted to surrender themselves to U.S. Border Patrol and not be smuggled into the country. That decision made the price slightly cheaper. When the time came, Fernando had a hard time leaving the house he worked so hard to build: "The person works, sacrifices to build a home and we lose it, leave it. A person goes without knowing if they will find home again." When asked about his hopes for his children, Fernando shared, "I love my country and my people. These are good people and God's people too. My children they deserve a good life, not this [situation in Guatemala], not now."

The family's route included an initial 12-hour bus ride to the Guatemala-Mexico border. "It was fast, and it was OK," recalled Rosa about crossing into Mexico. The trip through Mexico proved to be more complicated. Lack of places to sleep, fear of the Mexican police and other people who might extort or kidnap them, as well as fears of getting sick and being robbed were constant. The family relied on the goodwill of volunteer organizations that had shelters along the route to the Mexico-U.S. border and provided one to two free meals a day. The two men in charge of guiding the group split their assignments. The first one was responsible for the Guatemala-Mexico route. The second individual took the families through Mexico and made sure they arrived at the border. Once at the border many of the individuals known as "coyotes" or smugglers left families to fend for themselves, to find shelters, and to figure out how to enter the U.S. This was the case for Fatima and her family.

Fatima and her family stayed at a Catholic Church–run shelter in Ciudad Juárez, and they learned from others when the best time of the day would be to try to cross and surrender. "Not when it was too hot, not a good time to cross," Fatima relayed. Daniel (15) also recalled being told by other men at the shelter that there were some Border Patrol officers that would "shock" you upon crossing, but others that were "kind." Daniel concluded, "We needed to count on our luck." They stayed at this shelter for one week. At the shelter, as the family discussed when to cross, Vivi (6) explained, "It's that I couldn't sleep, I couldn't eat. I was so nervous. Is it going to work? I was so nervous." At the shelter Vivi and Daniel described that a small space had been set up for small children to color, read, and play. Vivi called it *la escuelita* (the little school). Vivi explained how the little school was a place where she enjoyed spending time since it meant a break from the daily discussions of when to cross and surrender to Border Patrol.

It was confusing for families to understand what could happen to them once they crossed. Fernando was concerned: "I was thinking if they take my children from me, if I go to jail, if I am deported." This was a common reflection among families as they received conflicting information from different people at the border. Daniel had heard from a teenager at the shelter that women with young children had higher chances of getting through to the U.S. He was apprehensive about a potential separation and deportation: "I remember thinking that my dad and I could be sent back and that... thinking about that made me feel lost and nervous."

After six days at the shelter, the family packed their belongings into small backpacks and prepared to cross into the U.S. That day they crossed the border and surrendered to Border Patrol. Several hours passed from when they left the shelter and when they were apprehended by Border Patrol. Fatima described having finished every bottle of water they had but not remembering to urinate. She felt pain on her right side and felt like it could be a urinary tract infection or dehydration. At the same time, Fatima remembered feeling hopeful; she could almost see their future. "Just a little bit more," she rationalized to me.

Once in U.S. territory and upon encountering a Border Patrol agent, the family asked for protection because they were escaping violence and persecution in their town in Guatemala. When the family was taken to the ICE processing site, Fatima, Rosa, and Vivi were put together on one side of the facility that looked like a large cell with other women and children, and Fernando and Daniel on another side with only men and boys. On the Immigration and Customs Enforcement website there are definitions of what they call "hold rooms in detention facilities." There are many guidelines including: "3. Males and females shall be confined separately. 4. Minors (persons under 18) shall be held apart from adults, except for documented related adults or legal guardians, provided this arrangement incites no safety or security concerns" (U.S. Immigration and Customs Enforcement, 2011). This was Daniel's fear. That the separation would be different for him and his dad. Fernando explained: "People think it's a small problem, but you lose your country to find another opportunity, you risk losing your family, because you want to find a way out . . ." Fernando was emotional as he spoke about this experience, his voice cracking when he mentioned the moment they were separated at the border.

Fernando told me this as his children sat around their small living room listening to him speak about this moment. A long silence followed. Fernando stood up from the couch and walked to the kitchen. Fatima whispered to me, "It's that it's too soon after all of that . . . it's hard for him to see that now we are here and we passed that part of our lives." Fatima picked up the story where Fernando left off and described the feeling of being sent to a jail and having your phone, your documents, anything that connected a person to the world taken away: "When everything was taken . . . they take all, everything that is yours . . . but my kids I couldn't lose my kids, and hope, God willing." For Fatima it was not an option to lose her children, her family, or as she explained, her hope. Fernando and Fatima both explained that the unknown was the worst part of the detention. Not knowing who you could trust or what was true.

Fernando was convinced that it was because they were a complete family that they were allowed to leave: "We were one of the only families that didn't need all the lawyers, they [ICE] knew we were a good family trying to do what is right. We are not criminals . . . no law was broken, we just want to work hard and provide for our families." After two days in a processing facility and three days in a government-run space, the family was released to a shelter in Texas. A few days later they were on an airplane headed to Massachusetts.

"First thing we have to do is find school," Fatima told me when I asked her what were some of the first few things she did when she arrived. Vivi was excited about school and that Fatima had been able to enroll her in first grade. "I had to get shots, and see three doctors," Vivi explained while pointing to her arms. Daniel and Rosa were not as enthusiastic, at least not in the beginning. They both told me that they would rather just work at that point and not go to a brand-new school. Fatima overheard them telling me that and interrupted, "Listen, it's hard, but it's why we came, you will make choices, just not now." I asked Fatima if she thought maybe the two of them—Daniel and Rosa—were still shaken by the border crossing experience and a conversation among the four of us started.

> FATIMA: You know when they separated us women and men my heart hurt for Daniel. I just wanted him with me . . . not because Fernando, but the boy needed his *mamá* . . . me. I thought I lost him . . . and I still had Rosa and Vivi to take care of . . . but those days were long, long, and sometimes you don't know what will happen there.
>
> GABRIELLE: How long were you in the ICE facility?
>
> FATIMA: I don't know . . . five nights maybe or . . . then they sent us to another place in Texas, looked like a prison, then another shelter . . . and from there we were able to get tickets with help from my cousin in Massachusetts and we went airport . . . airplane, and they got us from the airport.
>
> GABRIELLE: And Fernando and Daniel?
>
> FATIMA: For them was a little longer, they stayed longer at the prison place and then from there just one night at one shelter . . . they took a bus somewhere first, maybe to Dallas or how do you say . . . to Houston, slept in the airport . . . Fernando had the [points to the ankle] thing on his leg, the police put it and can't take it off until a judge I think . . . right Fernando?
>
> DANIEL: We ate frozen food . . . one day I took a bite to a frozen burrito and I thought my tooth would fall out [laughter]. It was not good.
>
> ROSA: The problem with all those days from one place to another was that

you didn't know if you will be in the U.S. or Guatemala or Mexico the next day. *Mamá*, remember the family we met? They were there for one night and then disappeared.

GABRIELLE: How did you feel, Vivi?

VIVI: I was just a little bit afraid . . . but a little not much . . . I played and I did drawings, but I was with my *mamá* and that was good, because she said, "don't be afraid we are almost there . . . I mean here [laughter]." The food at my school is not good [laughter]. There are two other girls in my class from Guatemala and speak in Spanish. The food sometimes at my school is cold.

ROSA: I think it's easier for Vivi.

GABRIELLE: Why do you think that?

ROSA: She is little and maybe she will not remember the stress, leaving, going, arriving. She gets to dream and hope that her school is good, teachers are nice, she has her whole life to learn English. I am older, I have to think about working here, learning English, going to school . . . and it hurts when I think about how we one day left everything behind.

FATIMA: *Hija*, think about what you will find here . . . it will be better for us. Nadie quiere dejar su hogar y pasar por todo eso [No one wants to leave their home and go through all of this].

DANIEL: It's that sometimes no one understands . . . No me desperté y dije, "quiero ir a otro país, ir a la cárcel, hacer que mi papá use un de eso . . . como se dice . . . la cosa electrónico, y ahora, como por arte de magia, necesito ir bien en la escuela." [I didn't wake up and say, "I want to go to a different country, go to jail, make my dad wear one of those . . . how do you say . . . the electronic thing (ankle monitor) . . . and now like magic I have to do well in school"].

Our conversation continued a while longer. Both Rosa and Daniel expressed that this sometimes linear expectation that leaving a place that was constructed—by facts and imagination—as bad, and arriving to another place that was also constructed—by facts and imagination—as good, would automatically provide families with a better life was not the whole story. Fatima pressed the children to talk about what they thought they would find in their *new* home, and not dwell on what they had lost. The contrast between present and future tense that both parents and teachers (as shown in chapter 3) emphasized for children and youth assumed a form of linearity that has also long dominated the field of immigration studies. The emphasis on the sacrifice, on the ruptures of leaving, on the torturous journey to arrive in the U.S., all for a hopeful future, serves as backdrop for stories, movies, and novels alike. While much of it is accurate to the experiences of these families, it is not the complete story. Centering education as both a means and an end to the traumas experienced in migratory paths offers a counternarrative to one that centers loss.

While many conversations, meals, and play took place in their home, Fernando remained the member of the family who spoke the most about guilt. He explained to me during a conversation when no other family member was present that he thought that he was the main reason they were here in the U.S. He was the one who had put the family in danger. He was the one who had made them vulnerable. When I asked him about the socioeconomic structures in Guatemala and in the U.S. that contributed to violence, poverty, and unemployment, Fernando was categorical: "It's still my responsibility. I can't blame it on bad government or bad leaders. I made decisions. I hope this time I made the right one too. And I will make sure I work every hour of every day to do what is right for my children. We can find our lives here."

During this interview Fernando exited the living room without warning and came back a minute later. He had something to show me. It was a letter he had written to his own father more than 20 years ago. For many migrant families, personal belongings that you or I may have tucked away in our homes—heirlooms from our grandparents, a child's first drawing, a picture, a framed painting, or a diploma—were likely to have been left behind or lost. Thus, I wondered how Fernando had been able to hold on to a letter he had written to his father decades prior. Fernando's dad had passed away a few years before and in the process of clearing his father's things from the house, Fernando had found the letter and kept it. The letter was written on the front and back of a lined piece of notebook paper. In it, Fernando explained that he was headed to the U.S. to earn money and change their lives: "I promise you, *papá*, that I will make you proud when I find a job and when I am able to send money home." Fernando had not migrated to the U.S. back then, but now it was his time. Now he was here.

My Right to Feel

Articulations of what was lost and found and the experiences of recovery also took place at schools. Young children and youth debated, discussed, contested, regretted, and justified their migration at cafeteria tables for whoever wanted to listen to them. In many instances, the perceived lack of space to externalize feelings of rage, hope, and belonging meant that youth and children found room to express themselves in unexpected times and places. While for parents it was important to contextualize the past (what they had left behind) to explain the present (why they were in the U.S.) and their hope for the future (centering education and opportunity), children and youth artfully interwove multiple points in time, factors, and descriptions to explain how they felt about their place in the world.

During lunch in the cafeteria of one school, I sat at a table with Diego (13) and nine other Brazilian middle schoolers while they carried on a lively and loud conversation. When Diego introduced me to the group at the table as "the teacher that is writing about us coming to America," students quickly peppered me with questions: "Why are you writing about coming to the U.S.?" "Are you a college professor?" "Do you have kids? What are their names?" "Do you like living here?" "Do you want to go back to Brazil?" I tried to answer as many questions as I could. Yes, I am a college professor. Yes, I have two children, their names are Jack and Noah. I do like living here. But I choked on the question about wanting to go back to Brazil. I tried something like, "In my mind yes, but in reality, no." They all giggled, and Anabelle (13), from the state of Goiás in Brazil who had been in the U.S. for two months, followed up: "Teacher, if you had the safety you have here, if you could guarantee your children would be in a good school, and with all things being equal . . . yes or no?" I let out, "Yes." I told Anabelle that she had hit every single point that tugs on my heartstrings. I turned the question back to the group: "What about you all, would you want to go to Brazil?"

"Me!," "Not me," "Maybe!," "No way no way" were some of the answers I was able to document. Diego, the 13-year-old whose family's stories we learned about in the last few chapters explained to me,

> No Brasil a gente era pobre mas era feliz, aqui a gente é pobre e nem sabe o que é ser feliz. Mas aqui tem um propósito né? Aqui para a gente ter um futuro estudando, mas será que ele chega?

[In Brazil we were poor but we were happy, here we are poor and we don't even know what it is to be happy. But here there is a purpose right? Here is for us to have a future studying, but do you think it [future] arrives?]

Opinions diverged at the table, and the middle schoolers became more animated. Another boy, Carlos, yelled out: "Cala a boca! Aqui você tem mais dinheiro sim. Não sabe fazer conta?" (Shut up! Here you do have more money. Can't you do math?). Diego quickly responded to him: "É o meu direito de sentir assim, ué não posso? Você agora é quem decide como eu sinto que foi sair do Brasil e morar aqui? Eu queria muito voltar para a minha casa e morar lá, mas aqui é a terra de oportunidade né não?" (It is my right to feel this way, I can't? You now decide how I feel about leaving Brazil and living here? I really wanted to go back to my house and live there, but here is the land of opportunity, is it not?)

Chatter continued, and other students started to make jokes. Flavia (13) had been in the U.S. for six months and offered, "Yes, opportunity, but they don't like us here, they don't like us so much that they give us this disgusting food. Frozen corn, dried out beans, they are trying to kill us, poison us!" The table laughed together. That school food was bad was a common complaint among middle and high schoolers in general, not just newly arrived migrant students. However, migrant children and youth spent time telling me about the food they ate when they were traveling through Mexico, at the border, in detention facilities, and now in public schools. Diego followed up: "I definitely think that food makes us sad . . . like it reminds us of what we are not to have anymore. And I know our parents are going to be like, 'I can't believe you have this opportunity and now you complain about food!' but it's always telling us what we will find here in America, and not letting us complain ever about anything. So unfair!"

Rita (14) had started school only a few days before and was the newest arrival at the school. She was sitting quietly amid the rowdy group. She had a book on her lap, a Portuguese version of Harry Potter. I nudged Rita to see if she wanted to share her thoughts about being at a school in the U.S. Rita told the group, "I don't know . . . I mean I am thankful [*estou agradecida*] we are in America. Like, I am in America now. I can't believe it. But I think my parents think it's automatic that we will find a better life here. They think: it will happen." "What about you?" I inquired. Rita responded: "Nothing is ever automatic in life. Why would coming to America be? We will have so many challenges to fight. People don't want us here, this is not where we are from, we are learning the language, we don't have family here, we live in a small apartment, there is inequality here too."

Most scholars of immigration, including myself, have written about parental sacrifice as intrinsically connected to migration. However, when youth and children articulate their perspectives and views of what it means to leave, they add nuance and complexity and disrupt the assumed linearity of the life improvement project. As Diego offered earlier, "It is my right to feel," and Rita reiterated, "Nothing is ever automatic in life"—not even migrating north could guarantee a better life. Articulating what it meant to lose and find hope, to persevere, but also to maintain the right to feel was paramount for youth.

Mental Health and Moving Forward

By the fall of 2021 and early 2022, most families had regained some of the financial stability they had established before COVID-19 disrupted their lives. Jobs in construction picked up again for most men, and parents were able to send on average more than $200 home every month. Schooling, while uneven in terms of modality (in person versus hybrid), was also becoming more predictable as parents and children could trust they would be able to hop on the bus and get to school every morning. With that stable expectation, parents started to pick up more shifts in factories, more construction jobs in towns that were farther away, and count on schools to keep their children safe during the day. This situation came closer to the original expectations they had had of living in the U.S. back in 2018 and 2019. But one key difference for families was how disconnected their children felt from teachers, schools, and education in general. The support that many children had had back in 2019 from reading specialists and for socioemotional learning was still being reassembled in schools, and thus, for some families, the feelings of loss were real.

Families were concerned about how their children and youth would move forward in school. Could the promise of an American education ever become actualized? In the year after the pandemic, Dylan, a father from Guatemala who had migrated in 2018, worried about how its potential consequences could manifest for his now-10-year-old son, William:

Before we left there was so much violence and *delinquencia* in Guatemala, I used to work in agriculture there, and now I look at where we are, we live in a small apartment, we went through the border crossing, fifteen, sixteen days . . . we get here and all the things at the border, hunger, fear, cold, hot weather . . . but thanks to God the church here accepted me, but for William when he was home with the pandemic learning in the computer he was stressed . . . and anything distracted him. I paid a babysitter to just sit with him but he was depressed . . . missed people in Guatemala. Sometimes I think I gave him an illness of depression because of my decision to bring him.

Dylan continued to speak about how much he worried that his son's mental health had been compromised by his actions. The tendency to blame oneself for the complications of their children's present and future was a common practice for migrant parents. As discussed in chapters 1 and 2, parents rarely spoke negatively about the U.S. government or immigration policies as external factors that had impacted their families' well-being. Instead, they directed their gaze inward, positioning themselves as the primary decision makers and bearing sole responsibility for the predicaments their families faced. He continued: "The teachers have so much work now that the children are back . . . and there are so many more problems now that didn't exist before . . . I don't think teachers know about the *transcursos* [course] we have experienced between leaving my country and entering the school. It's like we lived many lives. One works hard here in America, that I will tell you. We come here to work hard."

William was struggling in school. He was in fourth grade now, and there were repeated instances of other boys teasing him. He was involved in arguments and was routinely sent to the principal's office. Dylan explained that he thought his son was depressed and sad, that all the hope he had had as a younger boy a couple of years prior was leaving his body. William's school experience was not unique to him. Teachers reported children struggling to be together with others in classrooms for several reasons. First, in 2021 many schools required the use of masks to prevent the spread of COVID-19. The tables in the classrooms were rearranged to seat students individually instead of at round or community tables. This collective isolation proved harder on some children than on others. William was shy to begin with and participated very little in classroom discussions in both in-person and online modalities. He was a great soccer player and loved recess. But without the communal scaffolding in class and opportunities to work and talk in groups, William felt distant from his peers. "It's that I can't talk to anyone in class and it's hard . . . because then if I don't have a friend to defend me, I lose." When I asked why he needed to be defended William answered, "Everyone finds a friend that can defend you if you need. Like if you are in trouble."

Schools were scrambling to support students at all levels. It was not just William who was feeling this sense of loss even as he was finally back at school; other elementary students and middle and high schoolers did as well. Felipa, now a 14-year-old from Honduras, started cutting classes. Her mother Andrea was concerned because Felipa had always been a great student. When I spoke to Felipa in the summer of 2021, she told me that she had a boyfriend, and he was going to be a senior. She was excited. Felipa told me that she was bored at school because it felt very repetitive to her: "We already learned it online before." And while Felipa reported not feeling challenged, her teachers had spoken to Andrea about their concerns about Felipa, who they said was presenting as an anxious student. Andrea said she was biting her nails more often and was generally feeling sad and staying in her bedroom for long periods of time.

Felipa did get support at school. Her teachers were quick to have her speak to the school psychologist and social worker who held weekly sessions with Felipa. She was reluctant in the beginning: "Why do I have to talk to people about this, don't I talk to you already [laughter, referring to me]?" I told her the difference was that the educator at school was going to have everyday strategies for her to feel better at school. Felipa's school responded to her needs in a coordinated way. Her teachers, the school psychologist, the family liaison, and people in leadership were involved in devising a plan with Felipa and her parents. The key measure that changed things for Felipa at school was accountability. She had multiple meetings a week in which she talked about how she was feeling, but she also became a helper in other classrooms, she picked up journaling again, and within months her family could see changes. The school psychologist explained: "It makes a world of a difference when we have language and common ground with kids. Knowing what Felipa and her family had gone through, being able to tap into that knowledge together and then think together about loss, fear, was liberating for her and all of the involved."

For parents and educators, it was hard to distinguish what was a mental health concern versus a socioemotional issue in light of a global pandemic that had stopped young people from cultivating relationships. Ms. Andrade, a first-grade teacher, explained: "We have to figure out a way of understanding what is added in terms of layers for these kids. What should be the layers we are considering when teaching? Migration, violence, loss, but also hope, gratitude? The tough part is that you can't just make a decision, that because a kid had a tragic or complicated last couple of years that will determine everything about their mental health." For migrant families, their children's experiences unfolded against the backdrop of a complex past in which their schooling experience was a central counterbalance to their complicated experiences.

Hope and Education

Prior experiences of migration had consequences for families' outlook on life and education once in the U.S. Natalia, a mother from El Salvador, had migrated to the U.S. at the end of 2019. When I met Natalia, she and her son Cesar were at school waiting to meet with the principal. I was on my way out when I said hello to her and introduced myself. We ended up speaking for several minutes and agreed to continue our conversation at another time. Cesar was going to start kindergarten, and she was excited about the prospects for his education. Before arriving in the U.S., Natalia had left what she described as an "unsafe" home in El Salvador. As a single mother of a young child, she had trekked on her own with Cesar through Guatemala and Mexico.

When they had arrived in Ciudad Juarez in Mexico, Natalia stayed in a shelter that was only for women and children. There were about 12 women and 14 children living at the shelter. There, they made bags, earrings, purses, and bracelets and sold them to help fund the shelter. Natalia stayed there for four months while she waited to try to cross into the U.S. She was afraid of drowning in the Rio Grande and that something would happen to Cesar. In our first conversation together at a playground, Natalia shared with me about her journey from El Salvador to the border:

NATALIA: Sometimes I think God will not forgive me. There was one moment in Mexico when I saw the train going fast and . . . and . . . we had to get on the train so we could keep moving forward in our trip. I screamed for Cesar to walk faster, run with me because I couldn't carry him long enough . . . he couldn't run fast enough . . . [tears start to come down her face]. He couldn't run quick enough, so I held his arm and his hand, and I dragged him . . . my baby I dragged him so hard . . . I pulled his arm . . . his shoes fell off. I was desperate [crying] I was desperate and dragging him I hurt him. His little legs were dragging on the ground, and I just kept running and pulling him with me.

GABRIELLE: I am so sorry this happened to you and Cesar, Natalia. [I handed a tissue to Natalia.]

NATALIA: Thank you. It's so sad when I think about it. And then we finally made it to Juárez my little boy only wanted to sleep with me in the same bed. He had earache and diarrhea and pain. So much pain. I did this to him. I feel like I made him suffer when I dragged him and hurt him . . . And I still get sad about it, and I wonder if he gets sad.

GABRIELLE: What do you think?

NATALIA: I think yes, but he holds it in for me. For his *mami*. He is my baby boy. And look at him, he is my life. I will do anything for him to have a better life. Si no tienes esperanza, más te vale estar muerto [If you don't have hope that you might as well be dead].

The pain in Natalia's story gave her both hope and guilt. The dilemma of what was lost and found. She needed hope to stay alive and to move forward; however, she felt as though she had hurt her child to try to provide him with a better life.

Cesar spoke about the train incident only once in the almost three years I knew him. We were sitting on his rug in the living room in 2021 playing with Beyblades, a popular toy that spins and can be played in a battle. "Do you remember if you played with these in El Salvador?" I asked him. "No no no, they don't have these there . . . I had a big big backpack with many toys before but I lost them." Natalia was making food in the kitchen and stretched her neck almost into the living room as she whispered to me, "He lost things in the trip." I nodded yes to her. Cesar quickly caught the interaction and said, "I heard you *mami*! You still are afraid of the train because of my knee." Natalia was surprised as Cesar continued, "I hurt my knee because we had to run fast." Natalia put her hand on her heart and turned back to making food. Cesar and I continued to play with the Beyblades on the floor. "What happened to your knee?" I asked Cesar. He explained: "The train was leaving and my mamá told me let's run so we can catch it . . . but I lost my shoe as I was running with her . . . she held my hand so so tight, and I was too slow so we didn't get in the train. She was sad I hurt my knee." After finishing the sentence Cesar started explaining the different Beyblades and their meanings.

The three of us had a meal together after that interaction. At the table, Natalia told us both, "I just need Cesar to remember, everything is for him. Everything he does now will mean a better life, so keep studying a lot! Study, study, because education is your future. You are so smart!" Cesar responded, "I know mamá, I am reading to you right? I learn and I read to you and teacher [talking to me] I can do big math problems. Ask me anything!" Somewhere caught between the most difficult memories parents could unearth from their past and their hopeful feelings for the future lived their present. Even before they left their home countries, parents had a clear view of the centrality of a quality education for their children. Their narratives and experiences show the multiplicity of their identities, the urgency of their quest, and the depths of their care. Children and youth, on the other hand—the assumed beneficiaries of parental sacrifice—remembered, resisted, and re-told those stories from their own perspectives showing both love for their parents and hope for an unknown future.

Karina, a Brazilian mother of three girls, Giselly (14), Daiany (7), and Carly (4), was a fierce advocate for her children's education in the U.S. She migrated with her daughters at the end of 2018, and she was part of a group of Brazilian migrants who were detained and released together at the border. Karina left her job as an administrative assistant in the city of São Paulo to try to ask for asylum in the U.S. She described an increasingly unsafe neighborhood, lack of hope for the future, and possibilities for her daughters as reasons to leave Brazil. Her husband at the time was also working as a maintenance worker in an office building. Karina's father had been sick with Parkinson's disease and passed away a few months before she left for the U.S. She explained: "After I lost my father, I thought to myself I need to find hope, find a better life for my girls. They can't have an OK future; it needs to be a bright hopeful future."

The hopeful framing Karina described was linked to the educational possibilities for her daughters. Upon arriving at the border, the family was detained together. Karina described still having nightmares about the process. In her words,

> We arrived in Mexico City by plane. We were able to buy tickets after we sold everything we had, and we flew through Panama. In Mexico City there was a person we paid to take us to the border with Texas, I think. I mix up a lot. Then we crossed and we looked for the police and said we wanted to apply for asylum. They took all of us. My husband had a temper, and I thought he was being rude to the police officer, you can't do that. Be rude to the police. So I remember just crying and thanking them so they would know I was grateful and I wasn't breaking the law . . . I remember the girls crying too because they were nervous, their dad was yelling. I can't explain these moments . . . it feels like you went far . . . far into a dream. You have to move forward. Then when I think about them in school now, doing so well I take a deep breath. *Alívio* [relief].

Karina went on to explain that in her mind the only thing no one will ever take from her is how much she will fight for her children. She continued: "For you to leave home and try your life somewhere else with no guarantees, it requires a lot of strength. I want my girls to know that, their mom has strength. We are not *just* immigrants." After arriving in Massachusetts Karina proudly enrolled her daughters in school. She was excited for them to be in bilingual programs and was an active participant in school events.

After one year of being in the U.S., Karina divorced her husband. She described him as a verbally abusive person, especially toward her middle child, Daiany. Daiany had severe anxiety in school, which impacted her academics. According to both Daiany and Karina, the girls' dad would call Daiany "stupid" or "dumb" and often criticize her reading skills. In one instance at their house, we were reading a book together in Portuguese when Daiany's dad arrived from work. He caught the last sentence of Daiany reading with me and quickly told us, "You see how slow this girl is. When is she going to learn?" Karina could not stand anyone, and especially her husband at the time, criticizing a child's process of learning. The hope of a better life was intertwined with the opportunity to learn more and receive a formal education. Daiany explained: "My mom knows I try my best and I want to make her proud, she knows it . . . sometimes I don't know if my dad cares as much or knows how much I try." Giselly, the older sister continued: "When I go to college and I do all the things, he will see why we are good, why we do good here. He will see, Daiany, and he will regret what he told you." The three girls and their mom were united in their quest to honor their migration to the U.S.

Karina felt she had to report her ex-husband to officials because of the persistent verbal abuse. She also described moments when he would break things around his family and in the house without hurting them directly. Karina felt like she was on the brink of getting physically assaulted by her ex-husband and according to her, "You can't wait to get hurt or your kids getting hurt to do something." After she reported him to authorities, Karina enrolled herself in an English course. She asked for help from her siblings in the U.S. and in Brazil to borrow money, and she was able to petition and change her status to a student in the U.S. After that, with the help of an immigration lawyer, Karina started her process to apply for permanent residency. Her status as a student and the reported domestic abuse she suffered contributed to her case. Karina thought her ex-husband had been deported, as she had not heard from him in a long time.

Karina continued to focus on her daughters' education. She moved homes to be closer to schools that would be better for one of her daughters. She described herself as someone who did not rest until she could find the solution for a problem related to her girls. As Carly, the 4-year-old, explained to me as we played with dolls in her living room, "I'll be a teacher when I grow up! My mom loves that I am a teacher, right *mamãe*?" To which Karina responded, "That's right! We found an opportunity and we don't abandon an opportunity, do we?"

Conclusion

In 2021 and 2022 families were finding their bearings once again. They were no strangers to the destabilizing force of the COVID-19 pandemic. However, parents' commitment to the education and schooling of their children was resolute. The hope of what was found came on the heels of the possibilities of work opportunities and education for children. When I asked parents "What are your hopes for your children's future once they get this education?," the resounding answer I received was, "So they can *choose* a path that will bring them success and happiness" (Melanie, Guatemalan mother of three).

I emphasize the word "choose" to foreground the idea of choice. Up until now, parents discussed their migration to the U.S. as a *decision* they made. As Edgar explained to me, "There is a difference in choice and decision. Decision you have to make and it could be something like life or death. You have to decide. Choice comes with freedom." But the idea of being able to choose a path that could bring success did not mean that parents were flexible regarding what career their children might choose. In most answers, parents identified occupations that would provide stability, like an accountant, a manager at a company, a teacher, a doctor, a *licensiado* (someone with a bachelor's degree).

The narratives presented in this chapter show how deeply trying to *find* a better life runs through parental decisions. Parents equated the constructed promise of a U.S. education for their children with the ideals of better opportunities for work and mobility for adults. To separate these is to misunderstand family migration patterns. Children and youth are active participants in these migratory trajectories, even if parents made the decision to leave. This chapter brings to bear intimate portraits of leaving, losing, and finding a space and a place to thrive. This is not the end of the story, but it is a display of what it means to lose and find home. In many of these interviews, parents, children, and teachers alike pondered what it takes for someone to leave their home. Families described some sort of complicated setting they were escaping. However, that their previous experiences were filled with violence, poverty, and corruption did not take away their love for their home. When one youth asked me if—with all things being equal—would I stay or go, they implied exactly this: if the conditions allowed us to live a life of dignity, would we *have* to leave? As Edgar put it, would it be a decision or a choice?

Conclusion

WHO GETS A CHANCE to live a life of dignity? That was the initial question Adriana posed to me in the introduction of this book. The year is 2025, and Adriana is now enrolled in a local community college and wants to pursue a degree in nursing. She told me over the phone, "I want to help, and I want to have a job that we will always need: nurses!" Her mother, Melissa, was proud of her and often sent me pictures of Adriana going to school, studying, and learning. The painful question her mother entertained after migrating to the U.S.—"was it worth it?"—pops up from time to time, especially when Melissa reflects on the differences between her children's experiences. Adriana's siblings, Juliana and Diego, are still finishing school and sometimes struggle with the routine and the varying degrees of support they receive.

However, it seems unfair to leave the question of whether or not migration was worth it to individuals to carry alone. After all, structural conditions that include colonialism, neoliberal policies aimed at Latin American countries, a history of U.S. interventions during the Cold War and beyond, draconian border and immigration policies, political instability, and the continuous rise of authoritarian regimes in the region deeply influence the *decisions* families make every day. In the U.S., however, the discourse of pulling oneself up by the bootstraps and showing so-called resilience conceals the larger macro structures under which decisions are made. In her book, *Migrant Aesthetics* (2023), Glenda Carpio argues for a change in paradigms of telling migrant stories. Through an analysis of fiction literature that centers on stories of immigration,

Carpio shows how the acculturation plot and the use of migrant narrators as cultural guides who must appeal to readerly empathy ignore and deny these larger structural forces.

In this book I have shown how migrant family stories are situated within complex contexts of regional and global dispossession. Throughout the book, I resisted the urge to track children's paths of *assimilation* and thus succumb to the idea that there is indeed any linearity to migrant children's paths. Just like any other children, migrant youth bring their knowledge, their challenges, and their strengths to classrooms and schools. Unlike many children though, they and their parents have vulnerable immigration status that could be taken away at any moment. But in the last few decades most work in the immigrant education literature has tried to answer the question of why migrant children are performing in the way that they are in schools. Work addressing that question has focused almost exclusively on the nation-state (or country of origin) as the foundational determinant of a migrant child's performance in school. Frameworks like the model minority, for example, emerge exactly in these academic productions that further emphasize single-story stereotypes. My question, then, is how has this type of work contributed to teachers' and educators' ability to provide a better educational experience for migrant children in schools?

One of the main questions I am asked when I talk about my work is: "Well, are the migrant children better off here?" The easiest answer for me to give is yes. They are better off because they are not in imminent danger from urban violence, they live in homes, they attend schools, their parents have jobs, they are mostly healthy, and they have friends. Academically there is huge variation. Children in elementary school learned English faster than their teenage counterparts, and many now prefer to communicate in English instead of in Portuguese or Spanish. Thus, sometimes that means that when taking a standardized test in English they may score higher than their teenage siblings. Even though elementary-aged children in this study were in bilingual programs, the hegemonic power of English shaped how they chose to communicate at home and in school. There are some examples of children and youth who get the highest grades and advance in specialized classes, while there are also other examples of children and youth who need more support in school. There are cases of children who have gotten meaningful support from their teachers and others who have not. Thirty-one children and youth were enrolled between pre-K and grade 12 when I first met them between 2018 and 2020. Since then, all five eligible teens have graduated from high school. Three are enrolled in community colleges, and two have started and changed full time jobs including working as servers, cashiers, mechanics, and secretaries. Younger children continue to move up the grades, play soccer, take dance lessons, learn to ice-skate, and join little league sports.

However, the other side of the answer is that children and youth continue to deal with their pasts—pasts that influence their present. None of these families have gained any formal immigration status as of this writing. They have spent money on lawyers, have sent money back home, and some continue to suffer from the effects of long COVID. Economically, parents agree that they are better off living in the U.S. As Karina, a Brazilian mother of three, explained: "It's always bittersweet because since I have been here I have been able to save money, I was able to take my kids to a water park in a different state, they are safer here . . . I was able to send money back to my mom. But the cost is high. The cost of our emotional state is high because we don't know our future. We simply don't know if we can stay or if we have to go." These conclusions will feel unsatisfactory to most. But showing both the ordinary and the extraordinary contexts and experiences of migrant families in the U.S. serves a purpose: to show how specific, unique, and important their experiences are, but also to challenge the perspective that these must always be stories of either suffering or of success. Entire lives are lived *in between* such dichotomies.

The Single-Story Stereotype

What happens when we only show stories of resilience or of suffering? By dichotomizing the migrant experience as solely success or suffering we reduce it to single stories that fit one stereotype or another. Anthropologist Andrea Flores (2021) explains how "exclusionary terms of belonging" influence the lives of Latino/a/x in the U.S. Flores argues that Latino youth's educational achievements were viewed "as positive moral proof against deficit constructions of Latinos while also maintaining a link to *educación*'s [emphasis in original] personal, cultural, and familial value" (p. 16). Migrant families have complex and unique stories that are both grounded in their past experiences of mobility and border crossing, but also in their present. The push to answer the simplistic question of "Are they better off?" defeats the purpose of understanding all people as equally deserving and human. If we follow Adriana's lead—who asked, "Wanting a good school, good education, having a chance ... is that a crime?"—our frameworks for educational, immigration, and social policy change, freeing us from the quest to find a single theoretical model to *explain* migrant students' success and failure.

Nigerian writer Chimamanda Adichie described the effects that labels can have on how we think about ourselves and others. According to Adichie (2009), "The single story creates stereotypes, and the problem with stereotypes is not that they are untrue, but that they are incomplete. They make one story become the only story." In this book 16 families so kindly opened their lives to me, built, lost, rebuilt, resisted, thrived, struggled, and were joyful during the three years I was lucky enough to witness their experiences. When teachers, social workers, school psychologists, policymakers, politicians, volunteers, and educators understand how and why families make decisions to uproot their lives and travel to the U.S., they increase their chances of connecting with students and families. But not only that. They also defeat the single-story stereotype by connecting on a deeper level with not just families' struggles but also with their everyday lives. For teachers, when families and students trust them, their teaching expands, strengthens. For families, when teachers don't see them as a single-story narrative, families appreciate the work in schools and support teachers in their children's learning.

For children and youth, being treated fairly is key. They want to belong, exist, and thrive in the community they now live in. In chapters 1 and 2, I demonstrated how parents and children in the same family units hold different analysis and perspectives of their migration journey. Children and youth were considerably more critical of the structures that contributed to their predicament than their parents were. They looked at immigration policy, the government, and schools as institutional actors and spaces that could either help or hurt them. Parents tended to put the blame on themselves, on their individual decisions to leave their home country. The individual focus left parents wondering about regrets and grappling with guilt.

Children and youth showed us that when we move away from individualizing blame for one's life to understanding the interactions between structure and agency, our perspectives on pedagogical practices and policies may change. The structure mentioned across the chapters includes immigration policy, schools, institutions, laws, a history of U.S. interventions, a global pandemic, as well as authoritarian and corrupt governments. The chapters also showed how even after uprooting and migrating, parents and children rearrange and continue to *do* family.

Contested Care Spaces

Critiques of U.S. public schools and the education structure in America are endless. As Flores (2021) asserts, "Educational institutions are key sites of socialization, or where we learn how to behave in formal organizations and how to engage with unrelated others. They are also where the existing hierarchies of class, race, gender, sexuality, and ability are reproduced for the next generation through educators' and students' own efforts" (pp. 12–13). Education, *educación*, or *educação* continues to top the list of priorities for migrant populations as both a goal and an aspiration in the U.S. Schools matter for migrant families and students, but not only for the reasons some may think. Of course, schools matter for parents and students seeking to advance academically, learn to read, write, and numeracy. In their book, *Immigrant Stories: Ethnicity and Academics in Middle School*, Cynthia García Coll and Amy Kerivan Marks (2009) contend, "Schools, in particular, have the potential to become great equalizers—institutions that increasingly open or close the doors for personal and group advancement in the social stratification system of our country" (p. 174).

But migrant parents also see schools in the U.S. as a stable counternarrative to the traumas experienced in the past. For families, schools are for hope, for future building. Scholars Sarah Dryden-Peterson and Cindy Horst (2023) have argued that to address "the disconnects between aspirations for education and realities we must move beyond temporal and spatial binaries. These are: present vs. future, here vs. there—that are so common in refugee education discourse and policy" (p. 1). While the authors were referring to protracted refugee crises around the globe, there are important lessons across contexts. Parents stressed that the *present* offered respite from the past. However, the past—realities in their home countries and border experiences—entered classrooms, schools, cafeterias, and playgrounds and interwove with the present. The future served as a beacon of hope, regardless of its material chances of realization. Thus, Dryden-Peterson and Horst call attention to the artificial temporal divisions that may inform education policy. When educators can't see each student through the past, present and future, they miss the chance to establish a connection, develop trust, and change their expectations of the child. Instead, schools become contested spaces where students *should* feel safe, happy, and grateful, but cannot do so and also be their whole selves.

So much of my own work in the past several years has been dedicated to training educators to understand that what happens at the border, federally, and locally in immigration policy impacts their classrooms. When Brazilians were not able to secure as many tourist visas to travel to the U.S. because of changes in policies and a backlog, more of them arrived through the U.S.-Mexico border. When Mexico implemented the "Expansion of the Frontera Sur" in 2014 under pressure from the U.S., it meant that the country enacted a border control strategy aimed at curbing the flow of undocumented Central Americans transiting through Mexico to the U.S. This involved using checkpoints and raids to restrict migrant mobility. For the migrants who were able to survive Mexico's militarized border with Guatemala and Belize and arrive in the U.S., the trauma of the violence persisted. When the states of Georgia and Florida passed restrictive immigration laws, causing many migrant families to leave and relocate to New York City, for example, children carried these disruptions with them as they enrolled in and entered schools elsewhere. When governors of different states loaded migrant families onto buses and *shipped* them to cities they had no connection to, schools would be many parents' first stop in their new community. Thus, knowing these dynamics matters.

In chapter 3, I showed how school became a contested care space overly focused on *keeping a lid on* any particular issue involving immigration, border crossing, or detention. In many instances teachers did not feel that they could enter directly into conversations about these issues because of the potential spillover to kids in the classroom who had not had similar experiences. By practicing select care, the classroom and school as a care space was compromised. Children tried over and over to burst the bubble of the classroom space and lead with their knowledge, make connections, and expand on intimate thoughts regarding migration. While children and youth were met with displays of care, these often excluded their experiences.

Politically, the U.S. will continue to shift and change its immigration policy landscape; because of that, many more families and children will enter U.S. educational spaces having been impacted by such policies. In the last several years I have spent hours delivering professional development training for teachers and educators regarding immigration policy in the U.S., but also explaining how education works in each of the countries of origin I study. Educators are hungry for information and data that will make their work better, more streamlined, more meaningful. It is not by leaving these stories on the margins that we will improve the education experiences of immigrant children in the U.S.; it is by working alongside them.

Political Landscape

As I write this book the U.S. has elected former President Donald Trump to the highest office in the American government. What will it mean for millions of migrants in the U.S. who are waiting to learn their fate? What kinds of immigration policies will be enacted, and will they further complicate or support the lives of people escaping violence, poverty, and looking for a better life? Historically, what we know is that while some changes will depend on who the next leader of the country is, most decisions regarding large-scale immigration policy reform will remain the same. The sameness owes to the lack of resolve from politicians in Congress and the House of Representatives to reform immigration policies in the U.S., at the border, and with other countries.

In his book *Migrating to Prison: America's Obsession with Locking Up Immigrants* (2023), César Cuauhtémoc García Hernández argues that over the past few decades, the U.S. has increasingly used immigration detention and deportation as a response to undocumented immigration. This "migrating to prison" phenomenon mirrors the criminal justice system's expansion of mass incarceration. Detaining and deporting immigrants is now a multibillion-dollar industry in which private prison companies profit from the incarceration of people. This has incentivized more stringent immigration enforcement. Detention harms immigrants both physically and mentally and disrupts families and communities. Mandatory detention laws passed in the 1990s have led to the routine imprisonment of migrants, even those who pose no threat. This undermines principles of due process and proportional punishment.

This problem is bigger than any president elected. As political scientist Elizabeth Cohen (2020) explained, "Undocumented immigrants do not pose a grave danger to anyone, they do not deprive US citizens of jobs, and they do not burden the collective resources of the country" (p. 13). She continued by explaining that the majority of ICE detainees do not have a criminal record and that the vast majority of them have only a minor offense like "a traffic violation" (p. 14). Yet the path from migration to detention is well trodden in every administration. Deterrence is a key principle underlying many immigration enforcement policies. In this context, deterrence refers to efforts to discourage undocumented immigration by establishing policies intended to convince potential migrants that the risks and costs of unauthorized entry or stay in a country outweigh any perceived benefits. But as Yanet, a Honduran mother of three, told me: "They can build as big of a wall they want, we still do what is right for our children. We are not victims, we are not in a movie, we want to live, and provide a good life for our children."

Migrant Children's Perspectives

Listening to children and youth and centering their experiences and words bring depth to studies of migration. For too long migrant children have been discussed as luggage with expressions like "left behind" or "brought over"—framing that does not fully recognize their humanity and agency (Catalano & Musolff, 2019). Bhabha (2006) in her article entitled "Not a Sack of Potatoes: Moving and Removing Children Across Borders" examines how migrant children are often treated as passive objects in immigration policies, akin to inanimate items like luggage. Some analyses framed children primarily in relation to their migrating caregivers, as passive dependents who were either "left behind" in the country of origin or "accompanied" the adult migrant. This perspective risked treating children more as burdens than as individuals with their own experiences, needs, and perspectives. More recent approaches have rightly sought to place migrant children at the center of research in their own right, exploring how migration impacts their lives and development from their point of view. This shift recognizes children's capacity for resilience as well as their right to have their voices heard on issues that deeply affect them (Dobson, 2009; Orellana et al., 2001).

In a similar vein, when we relate children to a particular label that implies a lack of agency or role in family migration, we develop incomplete policy in both education and immigration. The data gathered for this book focus on what children say and do inside and outside of the classroom. Migrant children are astute observers who are critical of the systems of oppression they inhabit. When Daphne, an 11-year-old from Honduras, asserted "somos MPPs," she provided a sharp analysis of what it meant to embody policy as a young teen. Daphne's statement explained how her identity was intertwined with a policy that was intended to hurt her and her family. It was almost as if she had *absorbed* the policy to diminish its impact on her family by claiming it as her own. Her brother Francisco made a drawing of a zone of surveillance that he characterized as "the border." At the tender age of 5 he astutely drew clear divisions between El Paso and Ciudad Juárez by drawing an airplane flying above. On the Mexico side he drew children playing near the border, a house, and a tree. On the El Paso side, mountains and tall buildings awaited. Children see it clearly; we, adults, are the ones in need of assistance.

In school the story is similar. Children and youth articulate their fears, their critiques, their hopes for the future. They are fearless and determined to share pieces of their lives with educators. But children and youth remain in between spaces: parents put their hopes for a better life on their children, which creates a somewhat isolated individual experience. Parents in this research had made the decision to migrate to the U.S.; children and youth trusted their parents and came along with them. The paradox for children and youth is that they were uprooted and went through detention and sometimes separation in order to have a better life. The good future offered by migration is deeply associated with a disruptive past. In fact, there is no future in the U.S. without the past experience of border crossing. As we home in on children and youth as the experts of their lives—without pushing for any sort of triangulation with adults to check for accuracy—we can reconstruct the types of support needed for children inside and outside schools. But only if we listen.

Who Cares?

In the spring of 2024, I received a call from Julio. He was concerned that his daughter was not getting picked up by the school bus in the mornings. "How can I make sure my daughter makes it to school every day if there is no bus stopping for her?" After phone calls with the town, I figured out that their apartment was just on the cusp of ineligibility for priority school bus transportation. They had recently moved for the third time. Luz, now in fourth grade, had missed a few days of school because of the problem with the bus. I called the school district to inquire, and they told me that there was a shortage of drivers, so they were prioritizing busing for the children who lived the farthest from school. I explained the situation to Julio. We went through a few scenarios together, including the idea of asking a neighbor or asking the teacher to ask all the parents in her class if she could carpool with them. Julio explained that his court date was coming up and he didn't have a driver's license yet, so he didn't want to get in trouble. He said: "I have to have my paperwork in order." Finally, we worked out a way for Luz to get to school with a boy in her class who lived near them whose mom offered to bring her in the mornings. Julio told me: "Every day I pack her bag with her ... her backpack, I try to make some lunch, the girl always forgets a sweater, I tell her it's cold here, put the sweater on ... every day I want her to go to school and learn. It's her life, her precious life."

The backpack, lunches, school bus, drawings, journals, letters, passports, documents, food cards, computers delivered by the school—all of these pieces composed the story of the 16 families in this book. When Julio mentioned packing lunch and Luz's backpack it occurred to me that those were some of the first actions I had seen him do for his daughter almost six years ago. The objects "appeared" yet again, and it reminded me of the concept of Chekhov's gun: the narrative principle that every element in a story must be necessary and relevant to the plot. It is a guiding principle for many writers, reminding them to only introduce essential elements into their stories. These elements later provide dramatic tension and payoff. The care that Julio and other migrant parents display every day toward their kids often relates to schooling and education. These "objects" appeared in every chapter of this book. Throughout this journey, parents and teachers struggled and succeeded in caring for migrant children inside and outside schools. They pondered their guilt, their knowledge, and their own capabilities to make a difference in kids' lives.

So, who cares? We should all care. Not because one in four children in U.S. public schools are children of immigrants. Not because over 36 million children are on the move worldwide and will end up in a classroom sooner or later. Not because it is good for children and youth to experience inclusion and multilingualism in their classrooms. But because we shouldn't need to explain caring for migrant children and youth. Diana, a Guatemalan mother of three, explained her conflicted feelings about migrating to care and the role of education in 2023 when she called me to ask about the news she was hearing about university campuses. I picked up the phone and she asked me, "Are you OK? Hopefully you are!" I told her I was OK and asked how she was doing. Diana said things were good and that they were going to move again because they needed more space. She was pregnant. Amidst her excitement and fear, Diana told me it was another boy. We celebrated together.

> You know . . . so much time has gone by since I left Guatemala . . . sometimes I want to think and imagine my home a lot, so I don't forget. I don't want to forget; I know now I am here. We are here. But I need to care for all my four babies now, and my job is to make sure they make a future different than mine. No one should pity us. Maybe more people could think of us as strong, brave, courageous, family people. We care, you know. Others should care too.

APPENDIX: HISTORICAL ANTECEDENTS

In this appendix I aim to briefly supplement the historical discussion started in the introduction. My goal is to provide more references and data points regarding U.S.-related immigration policy to further contextualize the particular moment in time this book references. This appendix is not meant to be exhaustive, and it only scratches the surface of the country's deep historical roots with restrictive immigration policy. Restrictive, draconian, and potentially cruel immigration policies are not the work of any single government, party, leader, or moment in time.

The U.S. has a long history of immigration policy that has evoked much criticism from advocates, scholars, migrants, and politicians. Scholars have documented the history of immigration policy in the U.S., examining the shortcomings and the consequences policies have had for migrant populations (Anzaldúa, 1999; Daniels, 2004; Mangual Figueroa, 2024; Ngai, 2004; Oliveira & Segel, 2022; Zolberg, 2006). In the seminal work by Mae Ngai (2004), the author examines how the category of "illegal alien" was constructed through the implementation of immigration restriction in the U.S. beginning in the late 19th century. The restrictions first appeared in 1790 with the Naturalization Act: a law passed by the newly formed U.S. Congress to establish rules for acquiring American citizenship. It limited naturalization to "free white persons" of "good moral character" who had lived in the U.S. for two years (later amended to five years in 1795). This excluded Native Americans and enslaved or free Blacks from citizenship (Ngai, 2004). Through such policies, immigration and nationality law were racialized from the very founding of the U.S., establishing whiteness as a prerequisite for full membership in the nation and the rights of citizenship (Ignatiev, 1995; Ngai, 2004).

The Page Act of 1875 and the Chinese Exclusion Act of 1882 set precedents for defining certain immigrant groups as "illegal" and restricting their entry and citizenship rights. Ngai argues that "the illegal alien as a new legal and political subject emerged through the intersection of immigration restriction, nationality law, and race in the early twentieth century" (2004, p. 2). The 1917 Immigration Act established a system of immigration control based on national-origin quotas that privileged northern and western European immigrants. It also "created a new legal category—the illegal alien—through its prohibition of entry and deportation provisions" (p. 66). As Ngai states, "The illegal alien is a creature of law—or, more precisely, of specific immigration laws and the particular ways they have been administered and enforced" (p. 8). She explored how immigration enforcement targeted Mexican migrants in the 1920s–1940s through Border Patrol activities and deportation campaigns. For example, she quotes a Border Patrol report of that time stating the goal was to "encourage the Mexican to stay in Mexico" (p. 71). This last quote resembles the type of policies we witnessed in the last decade, such as the implementation of the Migrant Protection Protocols, which came to be known as the "remain in Mexico" policy.

The U.S. has historically legislated and passed restrictive and discriminatory immigration policy, regardless of the political party in power. For example, the Chinese Exclusion Act (1882) was the first significant law restricting immigration into the U.S. It specifically banned Chinese laborers from entering the country (Lee, 2002). The Immigration Act of 1917 (Asiatic Barred Zone Act), which expanded the ban on immigration to include a vast region known as the "Asiatic Barred Zone," also introduced a literacy test for immigrants over 16 years old (Lee, 2015). The Immigration Act of 1924 (Johnson-Reed Act) limited the number of immigrants allowed entry into the U.S. through a national origins quota. The quota provided visas to 2 percent of the total number of people of each nationality in the U.S. as of the 1890 national census. Later, the Immigration and Nationality Act of 1965 (Hart-Celler Act) abolished the national origins quota system that had been in place since 1924. It prioritized family reunification and so-called skilled immigrants, which significantly changed the demographic makeup of immigration in the U.S (Tichenor, 2009). In the 1980s under Ronald Reagan, the Immigration Reform and Control Act of 1986 granted amnesty to nearly 3 million undocumented immigrants, while also sanctioning employers who knowingly hired individuals without the legal right to work in the U.S (Massey et al., 2002). This was perhaps the last real piece of legislation to provide a path for undocumented migrants to remain in the U.S. Still, in the 1980s, the landmark U.S. Supreme Court case *Plyler v. Doe*, 457 U.S. 202 (1982) ruled that undocumented immigrant children have the same right to public primary and secondary education as U.S. citizen children under the Equal Protection Clause of the 14th Amendment.

In the 1990s, the Illegal Immigration Reform and Immigrant Responsibility Act of 1996 focused on strict enforcement measures, such as border control strategies and return-to-sender policies for noncitizens (Bosniak, 2006). Also in the 1990s, the U.S. continued the process of border militarization. The U.S. government launched operations like Operation Hold the Line (1993) and Operation Gatekeeper (1994) to deter what it considered to be unauthorized immigration at the U.S.-Mexico border. These operations involved the deployment of large numbers of Border Patrol agents and the construction of physical barriers, which effectively militarized the border (Andreas, 2000). At the end of the 1990s, the Flores Settlement Agreement set standards for the detention, release, and treatment of undocumented minors detained by the U.S. government. The settlement arose from the 1985 *Flores v. Reno* class action lawsuit, which challenged the detention conditions of unaccompanied minors by the former Immigration and Naturalization Service (INS) (Menjívar & Perreira, 2019). It included provisions like not holding children in unlicensed facilities for more than 20 days and providing education, medical care, recreation, supervision, and contact with family members.

In 2001 as a response to the 9/11 terrorist attacks, the U.S. Congress passed the Uniting and Strengthening America by Providing Appropriate Tools Required to Intercept and Obstruct Terrorism Act, commonly known as the USA Patriot Act. It expanded the authority of U.S. law enforcement agencies for the stated purpose of fighting terrorism, including the surveillance and detention of immigrants suspected of terrorism-related activities (Cole, 2003). One year later the Homeland Security Act (2002) established the Department of Homeland Security (DHS), which absorbed the Immigration and Naturalization Service and assumed its duties. Within the DHS, the responsibilities of immigration enforcement and services were divided into separate agencies: U.S. Immigration and Customs Enforcement (ICE) and U.S. Citizenship and Immigration Services (USCIS) (Alden, 2008). In the early 2000s, other policies like the Real ID Act of 2005 came into effect, which set new standards for state-issued driver's licenses and ID cards to be accepted by federal agencies for official purposes, including boarding commercial flights. It also tightened asylum laws and provided additional funding for border security (D. A. Martin, 2005; P. Martin, 2006). In 2006, the Secure Fence Act authorized and partially funded the construction of 700 miles of fencing along the U.S.-Mexico border. It also mandated the use of advanced technology such as drones, satellites, and radar to reinforce border security, continuing the government's commitment to border militarization (Secure Fence Act of 2006 Public Law 109-367)).

In 2012, the Deferred Action for Childhood Arrivals (DACA), enacted by President Obama, allowed some individuals who were brought to the U.S. as children to receive a renewable two-year period of deferred action from deportation and become eligible for a work permit in the U.S. (Gonzales & Bautista-Chavez, 2014). Over his tenure, President Obama earned the nickname "Deporter in Chief" due to the high number of deportations that occurred during his presidency. According to data from the Department of Homeland Security, over 2.5 million people were deported from the U.S. between 2009 and 2015. This was a significant increase compared to previous administrations. It is important to note that the increase in deportations was partly due to a change in how deportations were counted. Before the Obama administration, individuals caught at the border and quickly returned were not counted in the total number of deportations. Under Obama, these were classified as deportations, which contributed to the higher numbers.

The U.S. also has a long history of legislation regulating refugee entry as well as procedures for asylum seekers. In the last 100 years some of the milestones in refugee policy coincided with the immigration policies reviewed above. According to the American Immigration Council (2022), the U.S. became a signatory of the United Nations 1951 Convention and 1967 Protocols relating to the Status of Refugees. Prior to that the Displaced Persons Act of 1948 was the first specific refugee act passed by Congress with the goal of addressing the displaced population after World War II. Different versions of migration and refugee assistance and parole programs have been in place since then (examples are the Hungarian Escape Program, Azorean Refugee Act of 1958, Cuban Refugees, Hong Kong Parole Program, Indochinese Immigration and Refugee Act, Mariel Boatlift, Nicaraguan Adjustment and Central American Relief Act of 1997, and Haitian Refugee Immigrant Fairness Act of 1998).

At the time I write this book, President Joe Biden is about to finish his mandate and pass the torch to President-Elect Donald Trump. Biden's legacy of governing between 2021 and 2024 has impacted some immigration policies. While during his administration Congress was unable to pass any significant bills reforming the immigration system in the U.S., and ultimately failed to offer paths to changing immigration status for millions of people in the U.S., the Biden administration extended Temporary Protective Status and advanced hundreds of immigration executive actions over his presidency. He also doubled down on some of Trump's previous policies, for example by keeping Title 42 in place. Immigration was a hotly debated topic during the 2024 U.S. election, and we can expect the incoming administration to act on its promises.

APPENDIX: NOTES ON METHODS

As an ethnographer I have always looked for the details in books and articles that showed how scholars conducted their research. I wanted to know where they were, how long they spent in each place, and what kind of relationship they had with participants. In the introduction I laid down the foundation of the data sources I used, how data were collected, and discussed who I am as a researcher. This appendix is meant to complement and extend the methodological reflection started in the introduction. Thus, here I repeat what I did in my first book, to which I added a methods appendix, and I follow the lead of Annette Lareau (2003), Joanna Dreby (2010, 2015, 2025), and Derron Wallace (2023) and so many others who have expertly provided in-depth methodological discussions of their work in their respective books. This appendix is not enough, but it is a start.

A common question in qualitative and ethnographic research is how you know and assess the quality of the work. My answer usually hinges on the quality of the methods implemented in order to collect data. What goes in heavily determines what comes out. Elsewhere in the literature, scholars like Small and Calarco (2022) propose five components to evaluate *good* qualitative research, including ethnography. The main points they propose are cognitive empathy, heterogeneity, palpability, follow-up, and self-awareness. Briefly, cognitive empathy refers to the researcher's ability to understand participants' perspectives and experiences, their motivations, and how they make meaning out of situations. Heterogeneity means acknowledging diversity within groups and avoiding overgeneralizations. Palpability denotes presenting findings in a vivid, concrete manner through thick description and well-chosen examples/excerpts from data. Follow-up means asking additional questions as needed during interviews/observations to probe responses more deeply and get clarification. Finally, self-awareness means to engage in reflexivity about how the researcher's own background, assumptions, and biases could potentially shape the research process and findings.

However, these components are only relevant in what the authors call "high exposure" contexts, which refers to the number of hours, days, months, and years researchers are in the field, or the data researchers are able to collect in the first place. This ethnographic project took over three years to be completed. Thus, not all of the data collected are reflected in this book. As researchers and writers, we make choices beginning with the initial research design and then at every step along the way through data collection. My goal from the beginning was to maximize "exposure," meaning that I planned my data collection around the availability of participants and made sure to create a schedule—albeit a flexible one—specific to the families I was visiting and spending time with.

Weekly and monthly organization were key to conducting solo ethnographic research with a high number of participants (22 parents, 35 children and youth, 18 educators, community members, and additional youth and children). In order to recruit such a high number of participants and keep them for three years, I had to put in work up front. For example, for months leading up to the start of my research I had multiple conversations in person and over the phone with participants. At least five families I contacted in the beginning wanted to stay in touch and talk but were nervous about being recorded and participating in a research study. All this is to say that I initiated contact with more families than ultimately participated. Thus, what you read in articles and books is the result of data collected with participants who were willing to share their stories and their time. There were two families who wanted to participate but ended up moving to another state to be closer to family members. I had already been working with immigrant communities for a different project when I started meeting families who were detained and/or separated at the border for this research. Thus, it helped that I was a known person in schools. Still, it was weeks or even months, in some cases, of talking and explaining the research, going through consent forms, before the official date of data collection started.

I collected data across a multitude of spaces: home, work, park, school, church, restaurants, cafes, walking down the street, picking up children from school. I didn't go where I wasn't wanted or invited, and most of the time when I asked to accompany a member of the family somewhere the answer was yes. Going to work with parents was not always possible. I wasn't allowed into factories or some residences where migrant parents cleaned homes. So instead, I took public transportation with families when they went to work in locations where I could not enter. We talked on the way, and I debriefed with parents after a day of work, for example. Throughout the book I signal where the conversations took place as much as I can. Most of them were in homes, schools, and parks.

I consider participant observation to be the main tool of conducting ethnographic research because it allowed me to ask questions, engage in conversations, and help with minor tasks in real time with families and teachers. To be in so many places during the week, I used a scheduling planner to book the blocks of time I'd be spending with each of the 16 families. I tried to spend equal time with each family unit, but ultimately their schedules determined when I could accompany them to different activities. According to Small and Calarco (2022), "Participant observation is also a reactive interaction, as even the most passive researcher, merely by being present, inevitably shapes what is observed. And given that the ethnographer writes every one of the hundreds of thousands of words that constitute a typical set of field notes, the observer is inescapably embedded in the data themselves" (p. 21). I often put my notebook down to help around the house, hold a baby, draw and color with younger kids, or even to get on the phone and translate for families. Thus, my presence was felt to different degrees throughout my work.

To offer a sample of what the engagement looked like with each family, at a minimum I collected about 150 hours of participant observation, 25 hours of interview data (unstructured and semistructured), six drawings and narratives, 72 hours of school observation, weekly text messages, 20 hours of WhatsApp voice recordings, and 30 pages of copied conversations over text message, in addition to kinship maps and descriptions of home, school, and workspaces. I did this for each family, thus accumulating more than 2,500 hours of observations over the years. Interview data and participant observation data hours sometimes overlapped. I also conducted at least 5 interviews and a maximum of 12 with each teacher whose classroom included one or more of the children observed. These interviews lasted between 10 minutes and two hours. Principals, specialists, and other administrators were also interviewed at least twice over the period of research. I also held several group conversations with teachers, parents, and students. These were often planned, but many happened spontaneously depending on where I was with the families. For example, when I accompanied a family to their daughter's recital at school, I ended up in a circle talking to teachers and parents together.

I had to make sure I was available some nights and weekends as well. Nights were easier for parents who worked full days at factories and as mechanics or builders. Weekends also meant I could spend less-structured time with the families. I carried a notebook and two recorders with me in case one stopped working. While I was able to record many interactions and interviews, I also took detailed fieldnotes in different spaces. I also resorted to recording myself on my way home to catch any specific questions or follow-ups while they were fresh in my mind. My transcriptions were done within 48 hours from the time I took those notes, but I made a habit of listening to the recordings on the same day and jotting down additional notes. I organized the notes within family folders, and then during the analysis I reorganized them thematically into categories like "policy embodiment" or "pedagogies of silence."

The unstructured interviews with children were more like multiple informal conversations lasting 5 to 45 minutes. They focused on separation and/or detention experiences, educational experiences, attitudes toward school, support for education from their community, perceptions of the role of education in realizing future aspirations, and support from teachers and their parents. They were also about food, toys, books, boredom, fears, coloring, and TV shows, among other things. We drew together, and youth wrote their own narratives about experiences that mattered to them. Thus, I never asked children directly "How was the border experience?" but instead made conscious space for them to bring up whatever it was they wanted to talk about with me. Time is the strength of ethnographic work, in my view. Because I was in families' homes or talking to them every other day, children, youth, and families offered me insight into their experiences of migration on their own time. One thing I learned was that, even years after detention and/or separation at the border, families continued to talk about their experience; it was very much present in their everyday. Ethnographic approaches allowed me to witness these moments and follow up in real time.

Being in schools was a simpler task because I knew children and youth would be there, and the schedule was predictable and set. During my school visits, I often sat in class with the children and youth, observing instruction or during a special like art or physical education. With youth in middle and high school, I sometimes spent more time in the cafeteria during lunch or outside for breaks. It was important that the teachers welcomed me into their classrooms and felt somewhat comfortable with my presence. Researchers always affect the spaces they are in. No matter how close a relationship I had with each teacher, child, or youth, coming into a classroom or a home always shifted participants' attention. The way to address this imperative was to do it for a long time, so that my presence became expected. I tried, as much as I could, to switch up the days of the week I went into schools. However, I also had scheduling conflicts with my own children who were 5 and 2 when I started this research, so I ended up sticking to somewhat more predictable time frames of visits.

When school buildings and broader social life shut down in March 2020, I adapted my methods of data collection and continued the research. While I conducted interviews over the phone, I also focused on communicating with participants via different social networks. I often received videos or pieces from the news about the pandemic, school closure, and toilet paper shortage. I responded and reacted to these links and had conversations over the different social networks. For observations and interviews I received WhatsApp written or audio messages detailing families' days. At different parts of the day, family members would share snippets in videos, voice recordings, or photos with text. I also connected with families by video call during meals or outings—like a walk around the block when I would hold my phone on my end and show my street, for example, and kids or parents would show their spaces. I continued to have one-on-one conversations online with children and parents. Younger children enjoyed engaging in drawings and narratives of how they were feeling and sending those to me, while adolescents recorded messages on their parents' phones and tagged me in their posts on Facebook and Instagram. I was also able to conduct online observations in children's virtual classrooms. I was often looped in as a translator for school- or health-related issues via phone.

Communication with the 16 families during the COVID-19 pandemic took different forms but remained consistent, which had been my goal. I had daily interactions with all families that varied from a five-minute phone call to a two-hour video call. In many ways these families had been using these modes of communication for a long time to communicate with relatives in their home countries. Thus, while many of us worried about what the pandemic would mean for human connection and displays of care and love, these families had it figured out and taught me how to continue to be in touch with loved ones.

Since I continued my research during COVID, I was able to capture important shifts as family members became sick, went to the hospital, lost their jobs, started new jobs, taught their children at home, and survived during a pandemic. From July to November 2020, in addition to collecting data digitally, I resumed observations and in-person conversations with the families, but outside, masked, and at a distance. In November, when cold weather disrupted this strategy, I resumed speaking to participants over the phone or video, and waited for a sunny day and higher temperatures to meet in parks or outside on families' porches. By March 2021, I was back to being in close physical proximity to families and children, but masked as many of us had not yet received the vaccine.

In April 2021, when schools in the district fully opened and vaccines became more readily available, I was able to resume in-person observations and meet with families in parks, playgrounds, and their homes until December 2021. While my formal weekly commitment with families finished in December 2021, I did some follow-up interviews and conversations during 2022 and 2023. In fact, as I write this appendix in 2025, I continue to receive updates from all families as well as pictures of how fast the children and youth are growing. Some have gotten their driver's licenses, others are dating, new babies and grandbabies have been born, and a few have graduated high school. I say this because the idea of "exiting the field" has always bothered me. The concept of a bounded "field" has received critique for not adequately capturing how social phenomena diffuse across space. As Gupta and Ferguson note, "the idea of 'the field' as a clearly demarcated site is a fiction that has been and continues to be produced through the practices of anthropologists" (1997, p. 35). Social processes are often not contained within geographic locales but rather cut across them (Gupta & Ferguson, 1997). Fifteen years after collecting data for my first book, I continue to speak to the families that participated in that study. If there are things I can do to support them by pointing them to resources, assisting with translation, or serving as an expert witness in their cases, I continue to do so. I think about this as a reciprocity principle in my work: one should not expect to take time from people and not be reciprocal in the relationships. I think with and learn from Silvia Cusicanqui's work (2019) where she critiques the way academics from the Global North often appropriate the ideas of Indigenous scholars without acknowledging the power dynamics and relations of force that define their relationships. Thus, the principle of reciprocity is important (Weddle & Oliveira, 2024).

All of the interviews and participant observation with families were done in either Portuguese or Spanish. I have translated the quotes, journal entries, and recordings to English. At times in the book, I keep some words or sentences in the original language, but because of space constraints most of the data are presented in English.

Designing ethnographic research takes time in both the planning, data collection, and analysis phases. However, the two most important features of my ethnographic work were time—almost three years—and the variety of data collected from parents, children, youth, and educators. This rigorous, expansive undertaking resulted in large amounts of data that can be overwhelming to analyze and code. The practice of consistently transcribing fieldnotes and voice memo notes to myself every week allowed me to enter the data analysis portion of this work with a figurative map in hand. I toggled between analog modes of data representation—posters on my walls, white boards covered with themes and families' pseudonyms, sticky notes, and index cards that could be moved around—to digital modes using text documents and spreadsheets to organize the data into themes, categories, and codes.

I found the data analysis for the book to be different than that for an academic article, for example. For the book I was able to focus on the arc of the story for each of the families; thus most of my data analysis time was spent reading and rereading fieldnotes and listening to recordings across all participants. My goal was not to force a convergence of themes across all the families, but to understand how leaving their homes, traveling to the U.S., facing detention and/or separation, starting their lives in Massachusetts, enrolling children in schools, surviving the pandemic, and simply existing influenced their experiences. From the very beginning the theme of the promise of an American education was salient in their responses, followed by the affirmation that is also the title of this book: *now we are here*. Each chapter of this book is a theme found in the data analysis, and I move through these chapters or themes chronologically because that is how families told me their stories. As Karina, a mother from Brazil with three daughters, told me, "We have to start from the very beginning to know where we are now ... I know now we are here, but there is always a story."

REFERENCES

Abrego, L. J. (2014a). Latino immigrants' diverse experiences of illegality. In C. Menjívar & D. Kanstroom (Eds.), *Constructing immigrant "illegality": Critiques, experiences, and responses* (pp. 139–160). Cambridge University Press.

Abrego, L. J. (2014b). *Sacrificing families: Navigating laws, labor, and love across borders.* Stanford University Press.

Abrego, L. J. (2019). Relational legal consciousness of U.S. citizenship: Privilege, responsibility, guilt, and love in Latino mixed-status families. *Law & Society Review, 53*(3), 641–670. http://www.jstor.org/stable/45217740

Abrego, L. J., & Gonzales, R. G. (2010). Blocked paths, uncertain futures: the postsecondary education and labor market prospects of undocumented Latino youth. *Journal of Education for Students Placed at Risk (JESPAR), 15*(1–2), 144–157. https://doi.org/10.1080/10824661003635168

Abu El-Haj, T. R. (2015). Unsettled belonging. In *Unsettled belonging: Educating Palestinian American youth after 9/11.* University of Chicago Press.

Abu-Lughod, L. (1991). Writing against culture. In R. G. Fox (Ed.), *Recapturing anthropology: Working in the present* (pp. 137–162). School of American Research Press.

Abu-Lughod, L. (2000). Locating Ethnography. *Ethnography, 1*(2), 261–267. https://doi.org/10.1177/14661380022230778

Adichie, C. N. (2009, October 7). *Chimamanda Ngozi Adichie: The danger of a single story* [Video]. TED Talk. YouTube. https://www.youtube.com/watch?v=D9Ihs241zeg.

A.I.I.L. v. Sessions, No. 4:19-cv-00481 (D. Ariz. Oct. 3, 2019). https://clearinghouse.net/doc/103587/

Alden, E. (2008). *The closing of the American border: Terrorism, immigration, and security since 9/11.* HarperCollins

Alegría, M., Álvarez, K., & DiMarzio, K. (2017). Immigration and mental health. *Current Epidemiology Reports*, 4(2), 145–155. https://doi.org/10.1007/s40471-017-0111-2

Allard, E. C. (2015). Undocumented status and schooling for newcomer teens. *Harvard Educational Review*, 85(3), 478–501. https://doi.org/10.17763/0017-8055.85.3.478

Allen, R., Pacas, J. D., & Martens, Z. (2023). Immigrant legal status among essential frontline workers in the United States during the COVID-19 pandemic era. *International Migration Review*, 57(2), 521–556. https://doi.org/10.1177/01979183221114712

Alvis, L. M., Douglas, R. D., Shook, N. J., & Oosterhoff, B. (2022). Associations between adolescents' prosocial experiences and mental health during the COVID-19 pandemic. *Current Psychology*, 42(15), 12347–12358. https://doi.org/10.1007/s12144-022-03018-0

American Immigration Council. (2020). Immigrants in Massachusetts. www.americanimmigrationcouncil.org/sites/default/files/research/immigrants_in_massachusetts.pdf

American Immigration Council. (2022, modified 2024). The "migrant protection protocols" fact sheet. https://www.americanimmigrationcouncil.org/research/migrant-protection-protocols

American Immigration Council. (2025). Fact sheet: The "migrant protection protocols": An explanation of the Remain in Mexico Program. https://www.americanimmigrationcouncil.org/research/migrant-protection-protocols

Andreas, P. (2000). *Border games: Policing the U.S.-Mexico divide.* Cornell University Press

Anzaldúa, G. (1999). *Borderlands/La Frontera: The New Mestiza.* San Francisco: Aunt Lute.

Arnold, L. (2021). Communication as care across borders: Forging and co-opting relationships of obligation in transnational Salvadoran families. *American Anthropologist*, 123(1), 137–149. https://doi.org/10.1111/aman.13504

Asmar, M. (2020a). Why hotspots and internet deals still leave thousands of Colorado students disconnected from school. *Chalkbeat.* https://co.chalkbeat.org/2020/8/28/21406056/colorado-digital-divide-remote-learning

Asmar, M. (2020b). Wi-fi holdup: Social Security question still a barrier, Colorado teachers say. *Chalkbeat.* https://co.chalkbeat.org/2020/4/29/21241839/wi-fi-social-security-question-a-barrier-colorado

Bajaj, M., & Bartlett, L. (2020). Critical transnational curriculum for immigrant and refugee students. In E. Toukan, R. Gaztambide-Fernández, & S. Anwaruddin (Eds.), *Curriculum of global migration and transnationalism* (pp. 25–35). Routledge

Bajaj, M., & Suresh, S. (2018). The "warm embrace" of a new-comer school for immigrant and refugee youth. *Theory Into Practice*, 57(2), 91–98. https://doi.org/10.1080/00405841.2018.1425815

Bajaj, M., Walsh, D., Bartlett, L., & Martínez, G. (2022). *Humanizing education for immigrant and refugee youth: 20 strategies for the classroom and beyond*. Teachers College Press.

Bakewell, O. (2008). "Keeping them in their place": The ambivalent relationship between development and migration in Africa. *Third World Quarterly, 29*(7), 1341–1358. https://doi.org/10.1080/01436590802386492

Baldassar, L., & Merla, L. (2014). Locating transnational care circulation in migration and family studies. In L. Baldassar & L. Merla (Eds.), *Transnational families, migration and the circulation of care: Understanding mobility and absence in family life* (pp. 25–58). Routledge.

Banks, J. A. (2008). Diversity, group identity, and citizenship education in a global age. *Educational Researcher, 37*(3), 129–139. https://doi.org/10.3102/0013189X08317501

Baraldi, C., & Cockburn, T. (Eds.). (2018). *Theorising childhood: Citizenship, rights and participation*. Springer.

Barker, C. (2012). *Cultural studies: Theory and practice* (4th ed.). SAGE Publications.

Bartlett, L., & García, O. (2011). *Additive schooling in subtractive times: Bilingual education and Dominican immigrant youth in the Heights*. Vanderbilt University Press.

Bartlett, L., Oliveira, G., & Ungemah, L. (2018). Cruel optimism: Migration and schooling for Dominican newcomer immigrant youth. *Anthropology & Education Quarterly, 49*(4), 444–461. https://doi.org/10.1111/aeq.12335

Barrucho L. (2021). 57 Mil detidos: Número de Brasileiros cruzando fronteira do México para EUA aumenta 8 vezes em um ano e bate recorde (57 thousand arrested: number of Brazilians crossing the border increases 8 times in a year and shatters records). *BBC News Brazil*. https://www.bbc.com/portuguese/internacional-59018135

Batista Willman, N. (2017). Reaping whirlwind: How U.S. interventionist foreign policies created our immigration crisis. *Public Interest Law Reporter, 23*(1), 36–49. https://lawecommons.luc.edu/pilr/vol23/iss1/8

Bean, F. D., Brown, S. K., Bachmeier, J. D., & Bachmeier, J. (2015). *Parents without papers: The progress and pitfalls of Mexican American integration*. Russell Sage Foundation.

Beck, U. (2006). *Cosmopolitan vision*. Polity Press: Cambridge, UK.

Becker, M. L. (2021). Unboxing care: Constructions of happiness and gratitude in a Brazilian transnational family's video production in the United States. *Journal of Early Childhood Literacy, 23*(4). https://doi.org/10.1177/14687984211030668

Bejarano, C. A., Juárez, L. L., García, M. A. M., & Goldstein, D. M. (2019). *Decolonizing ethnography: Undocumented immigrants and new directions in social science*. Duke University Press.

Bellino, M. J., & Gluckman, M. (2024). Learning in transit: Crossing borders, waiting, and waiting to cross. *Social Sciences, 13*(2), 121. https://doi.org/10.3390/socsci13020121

Bemak, F., & Chung, R. C. Y. (2017). Refugee trauma: Culturally responsive counseling interventions. *Journal of Counseling & Development, 95*(3), 299–308. https://doi.org/10.1002/jcad.12144

Bermeo, S., & Leblang, D. (2021, March). *Honduras migration: Climate change, violence, and assistance* (Policy Brief). Duke University Center for International Development. https://dcid.sanford.duke.edu/wp-content/uploads/sites/7/2021/03/Honduras-Migration-Policy-Brief-Final.pdf

Bhabha, J. (2006). Not a sack of potatoes: Moving and removing children across borders. *Boston University Public Interest Law Journal, 15*(2), 197–218. https://www.bu.edu/pilj/files/2024/04/Bhabha.pdf

Blitzer, J. (2024). *Everyone who is gone is here: The United States, Central America, and the making of a crisis.* Penguin.

Blommaert, J., & Jie, D. (2020). *Ethnographic fieldwork: A beginner's guide.* Multilingual Matters.

Bluebond-Langner, M., & Korbin, J. E. (2007). Challenges and opportunities in the anthropology of childhoods: An introduction to "Children, Childhoods, and Childhood Studies." *American Anthropologist, 109*(2), 241–246. https://doi.org/10.1525/aa.2007.109.2.241

Boehm, D. A. (2008). "For my children": Constructing family and navigating the state in the U.S.-Mexico transnation. *Anthropological Quarterly, 81*(4), 777–802. http://www.jstor.org/stable/25488242

Boehm, D. (2012). *Intimate migrations: Gender, family, and illegality among transnational Mexicans.* New York University Press.

Bosniak, L. (2006). *The citizen and the alien: Dilemmas of contemporary membership.* Princeton University Press.

Bovell-Ammon, A., Ettinger de Cuba, S., Coleman, S., Ahmad, N., Black, M. M., Frank, D. A., . . . & Cutts, D. B. (2019). Trends in food insecurity and SNAP participation among immigrant families of US-born young children. *Children, 6*(4), 55. https://doi.org/10.3390/children6040055

Brennan, D. (2018). Undocumented people (en)counter border policing: Near and far from the US border. *Migration and Society, 1*(1), 156–163. https://doi.org/10.3167/arms.2018.010114

Brettell, C. (2003). *Anthropology and migration: Essays on transnationalism, ethnicity, and identity.* Rowman Altamira.

Brettell, C. B., & Hollifield, J. F. (Eds.). (2023). *Migration theory: Talking across disciplines.* Routledge.

Briggs, L. (2021). *Taking children: A history of American terror.* University of California Press.

Bruhn, S., & Oliveira, G. (2022). Multidirectional carework across borders: Latina immigrant women negotiating motherhood and daughterhood. *Journal of Marriage and Family, 84*(3), 691–712. https://doi.org/10.1111/jomf.12814

Buch, E. D. (2015). Anthropology of aging and care. *Annual Review of Anthropology, 44*(1), 277–293. https://doi.org/10.1146/annurev-anthro-102214-014254

Burnett, J. (2021). Why people are fleeing Honduras for the U.S.: "All that's left here is misery." NPR. https://www.npr.org/2021/05/10/994065661/why-people-are-fleeing-honduras-for-the-u-s-all-thats-left-here-is-misery

Burrell, J. (2009). The field site as a network: A strategy for locating ethnographic research. *Field Methods, 21*(2), 181–199. https://doi.org/10.1177/1525822X08329699

Cantos, V. D., & Rebolledo, P. A. (2021). Structural vulnerability to Coronavirus disease 2019 (COVID-19) among Latinx communities in the United States. *Clinical Infectious Diseases, 73*(Suppl 2), S136–S137. https://doi.org/10.1093/cid/ciaa1378

Cardoza, K. (2021, February 21). *Pandemic leaves undocumented students more vulnerable*. NPR. https://www.publicradioeast.org/post/pandemic-leaves-undocumented-students-more-vulnerable

Carpio, G. R. (2023). *Migrant aesthetics: Contemporary fiction, global migration, and the limits of empathy*. Columbia University Press.

Castles, S., de Haas, H., & Miller, M. J. (2014). *The age of migration: International population movements in the modern world*. 5th ed. Guilford Press.

Catalano, T., & Musolff, A. (2019). "Taking the shackles off": Metaphor and metonymy of migrant children and border officials in the US. *Metaphorik.de, 29*, 11–46.

Cavanagh, S. E., & Fomby, P. (2012). Family instability, school context, and the academic careers of adolescents. *Sociology of Education, 85*(1), 81–97. https://doi.org/10.1177/0038040711427312

Cervantes-Soon, C. G. (2014). A critical look at dual language immersion in the new Latin@ diaspora. *Bilingual Research Journal, 37*(1), 64–82. https://doi.org/10.1080/15235882.2014.893267

Chao, R. K., & Kaeochinda, K. F. (2010). Parental sacrifice and acceptance as distinct dimensions of parental support among Chinese and Filipino American adolescents. In S. T. Russell, L. J. Crockett, & R. K. Chao (Eds.), *Asian American parenting and parent-adolescent relationships* (pp. 61–77). Springer Science + Business Media. https://doi.org/10.1007/978-1-4419-5728-3_4

Chernilo, D. (2006). Methodological nationalism and its critique. In Delanty, R., & Kumar, K. (Eds.), *The Sage handbook of nations and nationalism* (pp. 129–40). Sage Publications.

Chernilo, D. (2011). The critique of methodological nationalism: Theory and history. *Thesis Eleven, 106*(1), 98–117.

Cholera, R., Falusi, O. O., & Linton, J. M. (2020). Sheltering in place in a xenophobic climate: COVID-19 and children in immigrant families. *Pediatrics, 146*(1). https://doi.org/10.1542/peds.2020-1094

Clark, E., Fredricks, K., Woc-Colburn, L., Bottazzi, M. E., & Weatherhead, J. (2020). Disproportionate impact of the COVID-19 pandemic on immigrant communities in the United States. *PLoS Neglected Tropical Diseases, 14*(7). https://doi.org/10.1371/journal.pntd.0008484

Cleaveland, C., Lee, M., & Gewa, C. (2023). "I thought I was going to die there:" Socio-political contexts and the plight of undocumented Latinx in the COVID-19 pandemic. *SSM–Qualitative Research in Health, 3.* https://doi.org/10.1016/j.ssmqr.2023.100242

Coatsworth, J. H. (2005). Structures, endowments, and institutions in the economic history of Latin America. *Latin American Research Review, 40*(3), 126–144. https://doi.org/10.1353/lar.2005.0040

Cockburn, T. (2005). Children and the feminist ethic of care. *Childhood, 12*(1), 71–89. https://doi.org/10.1177/0907568205049893

Coe, C. (2011). What is love? The materiality of care in Ghanaian transnational families. *International Migration, 49*(6), 7–24. https://doi.org/10.1111/j.1468-2435.2011.00704.x

Coe, C., Reynolds, R. R., Boehm, D. A., Hess, J. M., & Rae-Espinoza, H. (Eds.). (2011). *Everyday ruptures: Children, youth, and migration in global perspective.* Vanderbilt University Press.

Cohen, A. K., Littenberg-Tobias, J., Ridley-Kerr, A., Pope, A., Stolte, L. C., & Wong, K. K. (2018). Action civics education and civic outcomes for urban youth: An evaluation of the impact of Generation Citizen. *Citizenship Teaching & Learning, 13*(3), 351–368. https://doi.org/10.1386/ctl.13.3.351_1

Cohen, E. F. (2020). *Illegal: How America's lawless immigration regime threatens us all.* Basic Books.

Cole, D. (2003). *Enemy aliens: Double standards and constitutional freedoms in the war on terrorism.* The New Press.

Coll, C. G., & Marks, A. K. (Eds.). (2009). *Immigrant stories: Ethnicity and academics in middle childhood.* Oxford University Press.

Collins, B. A., & Toppelberg, C. O. (2020). The role of socioeconomic and sociocultural predictors of Spanish and English proficiencies of young Latino children of immigrants. *Journal of Child Language, 48*(1), 129–156.

Coritz, A., Peña, J. E., Jacobs, P., Rico, B., Hahn, J. K., & Lowe, R. H., Jr. (2023, September 21). 2023 Census Bureau releases 2020 Census population for more than 200 new detailed race and ethnicity groups. U.S. Census Bureau. https://www.census.gov/library/stories/2023/09/2020-census-dhc-a-race-overview.html

Corsaro, W. A. (2015). *The sociology of childhood* (4th ed.). Sage Publications.

Creative Associates International (2019). *Saliendo adelante: Why migrants risk it all.* https://www.creativeassociatesinternational.com/story/saliendo-adelante/

Cuevas, S. (2019). "Con mucho sacrificio, we give them everything we can": The strategic day-to-day sacrifices of undocumented Latina/o parents. *Harvard Educational Review, 89*(3): 473–518. https://meridian.allenpress.com/her/article-abstract/89/3/473/425862/con-Mucho-Sacrificio-We-Give-Them-Everything-We?redirectedFrom=fulltext

Cusicanqui, S. R. (2012). *Ch'ixinakax utxiwa:* A reflection on the practices and discourses of decolonization. *South Atlantic Quarterly, 111*(1), 95–109. https://doi.org/10.1215/00382876-1472612

da Silva Iddings, A. C., & Reyes, I. (2017). Learning with immigrant children, families and communities: The imperative of early childhood teacher education. *Early Years, 37*(1), 34–46. https://doi.org/10.1080/09575146.2016.1273202

Dabach, D. B. (2011). Teachers as agents of reception: An analysis of teacher preference for immigrant-origin second language learners. *The New Educator, 7*(1), 66–86. https://doi.org/10.1080/1547688X.2011.551736

Dabach, D. B. (2014). "I am not a shelter!": Stigma and social boundaries in teachers' accounts of students' experience in separate "sheltered" English learner classrooms. *Journal of Education for Students Placed at Risk (JESPAR), 19*(2), 98–124. https://doi.org/10.1080/10824669.2014.954044

Dabach, D. B., & Fones, A. (2016). Beyond the "English learner" frame: Transnational funds of knowledge in social studies. *International Journal of Multicultural Education, 18*(1), 7–27. https://doi.org/10.18251/ijme.v18i1.1092

Damaschke-Deitrick, L., Galegher, E., Davidson, P. M., & Wiseman, A. W. (2023). Teaching refugee and forced immigrant youth: Lessons from the United States. *Teachers and Teaching: Theory and Practice, 29*(5), 465–478. https://doi.org/10.1080/13540602.2022.2062720

Daniels, R. (2004). *Guarding the golden door: American immigration policy and immigrants since 1882.* Hill and Wang.

Darlington, S. (2018). A year of violence sees Brazil's murder rate hit record high. *New York Times*, August 10, 2018. https://www.nytimes.com/2018/08/10/world/americas/brazil-murder-rate-record.html

De Genova, N., & Peutz, N. (Eds.). (2010). *The deportation regime: Sovereignty, space, and the freedom of movement.* Duke University Press.

De León, J. (2024). *Soldiers and kings: Survival and hope in the world of human smuggling.* Penguin Random House.

DeNicolo, C. P., Yu, M., Crowley, C. B., & Gabel, S. L. (2017). Reimagining critical care and problematizing sense of school belonging as a response to inequality for immigrants and children of immigrants. *Review of Research in Education, 41*(1), 500–530. https://doi.org/10.3102/0091732X16689045

Dicks, B., Soyinka, B., & Coffey, A. (2006). Multimodal ethnography. *Qualitative Research, 6*(1), 77–96. https://doi.org/10.1177/1468794106058876

Dobson, M. E. (2009). Unpacking children in migration research. *Children's Geographies, 7*(3), 355–360. https://doi.org/10.1080/14733280903024514

Dreby, J. (2010). *Divided by borders: Mexican migrants and their children.* University of California Press.

Dreby, J. (2015). *Everyday illegal: When policies undermine immigrant families.* University of California Press.

Dreby, J., & Schmalzbauer, L. (2013, March). The relational contexts of migration: Mexican women in new destination sites. *Sociological Forum*, 28(1), 1–26. https://doi.org/10.1111/socf.12000

Dreby, J., & Stutz, L. (2012). Making something of the sacrifice: Gender, migration and Mexican children's educational aspirations. *Global Networks*, 12(1), 71–90. https://doi.org/10.1111/j.1471-0374.2011.00342.x

Dryden-Peterson, S., & Horst, C. (2023). Education for refugees: Building durable futures? *Journal of Refugee Studies*, 36(4), 587–603. https://doi.org/10.1093/jrs/feac078

Dyrness, A., & Abu El-Haj, T. R. (2020). Reflections on the field: The democratic citizenship formation of transnational youth. *Anthropology & Education Quarterly*, 51(2), 165–177. https://doi.org/10.1111/aeq.12324

Dyrness, A., & Sepúlveda III, E. (2020). *Border thinking: Latinx youth decolonizing citizenship*. University of Minnesota Press.

Edozie, R. K., Lewis, B., Lo, S., Mattos, T., Melnik, M., Rivera, L., ... & Woods, J. C. (2016). *Changing faces of Greater Boston*. Boston Indicators, The Boston Foundation, University of Massachusetts–Boston, and University of Massachusetts–Donahue Institute.

Ehrenreich, B., & Hochschild, A. R. (Eds.). (2003). *Global woman: Nannies, maids and sex workers in the new economy*. Granta Books.

Emery, R. (2018). WhatsApp voice messaging as an emergent digital practice: A multimethod analysis. *Cahiers du Centre de Linguistique et des Sciences du Langage* (55), 135–157.

Engster, D. (2020). A public ethics of care for policy implementation. *American Journal of Political Science*, 64(3), 621–633. https://doi.org/10.1111/ajps.12497

Enriquez, L. (2011). " Because we feel the pressure and we also feel the support": Examining the educational success of undocumented immigrant Latina/o students. *Harvard Educational Review*, 81(3), 476–500. https://doi.org/10.17763/haer.81.3.w7k703h71010r210

Eruchalu, C. N., Pichardo, M. S., Bharadwaj, M., Rodriguez, C. B., Rodriguez, J. A., Bergmark, R. W., ... & Ortega, G. (2021). The expanding digital divide: Digital health access inequities during the COVID-19 pandemic in New York City. *Journal of Urban Health*, 98, 183–186. https://doi.org/10.1007/s11524-020-00488-5

European Central Bank. (2016). Box 1: What is driving Brazil's economic downturn? *ECB Economic Bulletin*, Issue 1. https://www.ecb.europa.eu/pub/pdf/other/eb201601_focus01.en.pdf

Evans, M., & Liu, Y. (2018). The unfamiliar and the indeterminate: Language, identity and social integration in the school experience of newly-arrived migrant children in England. *Journal of Language, Identity & Education*, 17(3), 152–167. https://doi.org/10.1080/15348458.2018.1433043

Expósito, S., & Favela, A. (2003). Reflective voices: Valuing immigrant students and teaching with ideological clarity. *The Urban Review, 35,* 73–91. https://doi.org/10.1023/A:1021783524301

Fang, D., Thomsen, M. R., Nayga, R. M., & Yang, W. (2022). Food insecurity during the COVID-19 pandemic: Evidence from a survey of low-income Americans. *Food Security, 14,* 77–95. https://doi.org/10.1007/s12571-021-01212-5

Feldman, I. (2018). *Life lived in relief: Humanitarian predicaments and Palestinian refugee politics.* University of California Press.

Feliciano, C. (2020). Immigrant selectivity effects on health, labor market, and educational outcomes. *Annual Review of Sociology, 46*(1), 315–334. https://doi.org/10.1146/annurev-soc-121919-054639

Flores, A. (2021). *The succeeders: How immigrant youth are transforming what it means to belong in America.* University of California Press.

Foner, N. (2005). *In a new land: A comparative view of immigration.* New York University Press.

Frankel, K. K., Brabeck, K. M., & Rendón García, S. A. (2022). Understanding unaccompanied immigrant youth's experiences in US schools: An interdisciplinary perspective. *Journal of Education for Students Placed at Risk (JESPAR), 27*(1), 27–58. https://doi.org/10.1080/10824669.2021.2015124

Freire, P. (1970). *Pedagogy of the oppressed* (M. B. Ramos, trans.). Herder and Herder.

Gallo, S. (2017). *Mi padre: Mexican immigrant fathers and their children's education.* Teachers College Press.

Gallo, S. (2021). Transborder pedagogies of the home in contexts of forced repatriation. *Ethnography and Education, 16*(4), 491–506. https://doi.org/10.1080/17457823.2020.1860418

Gallo, S., & Dabkowski, M. (2018). The permanence of departure: Young Mexican immigrant students' discursive negotiations of imagined childhoods allá. *Linguistics and Education, 45,* 92–100. https://doi.org/10.1016/j.linged.2018.05.002

Gallo, S., & Link, H. (2015). "Diles la verdad": Deportation policies, politicized funds of knowledge, and schooling in middle childhood. *Harvard Educational Review, 85*(3), 357–382. doi:10.17763/0017-8055.85.3.357

Gallo, S., & Link, H. (2016). Exploring the borderlands: Elementary school teachers' navigation of immigration practices in a new Latino diaspora community. *Journal of Latinos and Education, 15*(3), 180–196. https://doi.org/10.1080/15348431.2015.1134530

Gálvez, A. (2011). *Patient citizens, immigrant mothers: Mexican women, public prenatal care, and the birth weight paradox.* Rutgers University Press.

Gálvez A. (2019). Transnational mother blame: Protecting and caring in a globalized context. *Medical Anthropology, 38*(7), 574–587. https://doi.org/10.1080/01459740.2019.1653866

Gándara, P., & Ee, J. (2021). *Schools under siege: The impact of immigration enforcement on educational equity.* Harvard Educational Press.

García, O., Woodley, H. H., Flores, N., & Chu, H. (2013). Latino emergent bilingual youth in high schools: Transcaring strategies for academic success. *Urban Education, 48*(6), 798–827. https://doi.org/10.1177/0042085912462708

García-Mateus, S., & Palmer, D. (2017). Translanguaging pedagogies for positive identities in two-way dual language bilingual education. *Journal of Language, Identity & Education, 16*(4), 245–255. https://doi.org/10.1080/15348458.2017.1329016

García-Sánchez, Inmaculada M. (2018). Children as interactional brokers of care. *Annual Review of Anthropology, 47*, 167–184, 2018. https://ssrn.com/abstract=3272720 or http://dx.doi.org/10.1146/annurev-anthro-102317-050050

Garcini, L. M., Vázquez, A. L., Abraham, C., Abraham, C., Sarabu, V., & Cruz, P. L. (2024). Implications of undocumented status for Latinx families during the COVID-19 pandemic: A call to action. *Journal of Clinical Child and Adolescent Psychology, 53*(1), 10–23. https://doi.org/10.1080/15374416.2022.2158837

Garver, R., & Hopkins, M. (2020). Segregation and integration in the education of English learners: Leadership and policy dilemmas. *Leadership and Policy in Schools, 19*(1), 1–5. https://doi.org/10.1080/15700763.2019.1711133

Gibson, M. A. (1988). *Accommodation without assimilation: Sikh immigrants in an American high school*. Cornell University Press.

Gilligan, C. (1982). *In a different voice: Psychological theory and women's development*. Harvard University Press.

Gitlin, A., Buendía, E., Crosland, K., & Doumbia, F. (2003). The production of margin and center: Welcoming–unwelcoming of immigrant students. *American Educational Research Journal, 40*(1), 91–122. https://doi.org/10.3102/00028312040001091

Gombata, M., & Fagundes, A. (2022, April 8). Taxa de brasileiros que saem do país e não voltam é a maior em 11 anos. *Valor Econômico*. https://valor.globo.com/brasil/noticia/2022/04/08/brasileiro-volta-a-buscar-no-exterior-uma-vida-melhor.ghtml

González, N., Moll, L. C., & Amanti, C. (Eds.). (2006). *Funds of knowledge: Theorizing practices in households, communities, and classrooms*. Routledge.

Gonzales, R. G. (2016). *Lives in limbo: Undocumented and coming of age in America*. University of California Press.

Gonzalez, R. G., & Bautista-Chavez, A. M. (2014). *Two years and counting: Assessing the growing power of DACA*. American Immigration Council.

Gonzales, R. G., Heredia, L. L., & Negrón-Gonzales, G. (2015). Untangling Plyler's legacy: Undocumented students, schools, and citizenship. *Harvard Educational Review, 85*(3), 318–341. https://doi.org/10.17763/0017-8055.85.3.318

Goodman, R. D., Vesely, C. K., Letiecq, B., & Cleaveland, C. L. (2017). Trauma and resilience among refugee and undocumented immigrant women. *Journal of Counseling & Development, 95*(3), 309–321. https://doi.org/10.1002/jcad.12145

Goodwin, A. L. (2017). Who is in the classroom now? Teacher preparation and the education of immigrant children. *Educational Studies, 53*(5), 433–449. https://doi.org/10.1080/00131946.2016.1261028

Gramlich, J. (2022). Key facts about Title 42, the pandemic policy that has reshaped immigration enforcement at U.S.-Mexico border. Pew Research Center. https://www.pewresearch.org/fact-tank/2022/04/27/key-facts-about-title-42-the-pandemic-policy-that-has-reshaped-immigration-enforcement-at-u-s-mexico-border/

Greenaway, C., Hargreaves, S., Barkati, S., Coyle, C. M., Gobbi, F., Veizis, A., & Douglas, P. (2020). COVID-19: Exposing and addressing health disparities among ethnic minorities and migrants. *Journal of Travel Medicine, 27*(7). https://doi.org/10.1093/jtm/taaa113

Gu, X. (2021). Sacrifice and indebtedness: The intergenerational contract in Chinese rural migrant families. *Journal of Family Issues, 43*(2), 509–533. https://doi.org/10.1177/0192513X21993890

Guo, K., & Dalli, C. (2016). Belonging as a force of agency: An exploration of immigrant children's everyday life in early childhood settings. *Global Studies of Childhood, 6*(3), 254–267. https://doi.org/10.1177/2043610616665036

Gupta, A., & Ferguson, J. (Eds.). (1997). *Culture, power, place: Explorations in critical anthropology*. Duke University Press.

Häggström, F., Borsch, A. S., & Skovdal, M. (2020). Caring alone: The boundaries of teachers' ethics of care for newly arrived immigrant and refugee learners in Denmark. *Children and Youth Services Review, 117*, article 105248. https://doi.org/10.1016/j.childyouth.2020.105248

Haim, O., & Tannenbaum, M. (2022). Teaching English to multilingual immigrant students: Understanding teachers' beliefs and practices. *Teachers and Teaching, 28*(4), 420–439. https://doi.org/10.1080/13540602.2022.2062737

Häkli, J., & Kallio, K. P. (2021). Bodies and persons: The politics of embodied encounters in asylum seeking. *Progress in Human Geography, 45*(4), 682–703. https://doi.org/10.1177/0309132520938449

Hamann, E. T., & Zúñiga, V. (2011). Schooling and the everyday ruptures transnational children encounter in the United States and Mexico. *International Journal of Educational Development, 31*(6), 544–553. https://doi.org/10.1016/j.ijedudev.2010.03.003

Hamman, L. (2018). Translanguaging and positioning in two-way dual language classrooms: A case for criticality. *Language and Education, 32*(1), 21–42. https://doi.org/10.1080/09500782.2017.1384006

Hamman-Ortiz, L. (2020). Becoming bilingual in two-way immersion: Patterns of investment in a second-grade classroom. *International Journal of Bilingual Education and Bilingualism, 26*(1), 69–83. https://doi.org/10.1080/13670050.2020.1783637

Hammersley, M. (2017). Childhood studies: A sustainable paradigm?. *Childhood, 24*(1), 113–127. https://doi.org/10.1177/0907568216631399

Handel, G. (Ed.). (2011). *Childhood socialization*. Transaction Publishers.

Hardman, C. (1973). Can there be an anthropology of children?. *Childhood, 8*(4), 501–517. https://doi.org/10.1177/0907568201008004004

Heidbrink, L. (2014). *Migrant youth, transnational families, and the state: Care and contested interests*. University of Pennsylvania Press.

Heidbrink, L. (2017). Assessing parental fitness and care for unaccompanied children. *RSF: The Russell Sage Foundation Journal of the Social Sciences, 3*(4), 37–52. https://doi.org/10.7758/RSF.2017.3.4.03

Heidbrink, L. (2020). *Migranthood: Youth in a new era of deportation*. Stanford University Press.

Held, V. (2006). *The ethics of care: Personal, political, and global*. Oxford University Press.

Hernández, C. C. G. (2023). *Migrating to prison: America's obsession with locking up immigrants*. The New Press.

Hersi, A. A., & Watkinson, J. S. (2012). Supporting immigrant students in a newcomer high school: A case study. *Bilingual Research Journal, 35*(1), 98–111. https://doi.org/10.1080/15235882.2012.668868

Hessom, T. (2020). U.S. has begun sending Brazilian migrants to Mexico to await U.S. court hearings. Reuters, January 29. https://www.reuters.com/article/world/us/us-has-begun-sending-brazilian-migrants-to-mexico-to-await-us-court-hearings-idUSKBN1ZS35V/

Heyman, J. (1995). Putting power in the anthropology of bureaucracy: The immigration and naturalization service at the Mexico-United States border. *Current Anthropology, 36*(2), 261–287. https://doi.org/10.1086/204354

Hirsch, J. (2003). *A courtship after marriage: Sexuality and love in Mexican transnational families*. University of California Press.

Hondagneu-Sotelo, P. (1994). *Gendered transitions: Mexican experiences of immigration*. University of California Press.

Hondagneu-Sotelo, P. (Ed.). (2003). *Gender and US immigration: Contemporary trends*. University of California Press.

Hondagneu-Sotelo, P., & Avila, E. (1997). "I'm here, but I'm there": The meanings of Latina transnational motherhood. *Gender & Society, 11*(5), 548–571. https://doi.org/10.1177/089124397011005003

Hopkins, M., Lowenhaupt, R., & Sweet, T. M. (2015). Organizing English learner instruction in new immigrant destinations: District infrastructure and subject-specific school practice. *American Educational Research Journal, 52*(3), 408–439. https://doi.org/10.3102/0002831215575383.

Horton, S. (2008). Consuming childhood: "Lost" and "ideal" childhoods as a motivation for migration. *Anthropological Quarterly, 81*(4), 925–943. https://doi.org/10.1353/anq.0.0033

Hos, R. (2016). Caring is not enough: Teachers' enactment of ethical care for adolescent students with limited or interrupted formal education (SLIFE) in a newcomer classroom. *Education and Urban Society, 48*(5), 479–503. https://doi.org/10.1177/00 13124514536440

Hu, S. (2017). "It's for our education": Perception of parental migration and resilience among left-behind children in rural China. *Social Indicators Research, 145*: 641–661. https://doi.org/10.1007/s11205-017-1823-y

Hurie, A. H., & Callahan, R. M. (2019). Integration as perpetuation: Learning from race evasive approaches to ESL program reform. *Teachers College Record, 121*(9), 1–38. https://doi.org/10.1177/016146811912100904

Ignatiev, N. (1995). *How the Irish became white*. Routledge.

Instituto de Pesquisa Econômica Aplicada (2021, September). Policy Brief: Em Questão: Evidências para políticas públicas. Number 8.

Instituto Nacional de Estadística Guatemala (2015). *República de Guatemala: Encuesta Nacional de Condiciones de Vida 2014: Principales resultados*.

Jaffee, A. T. (2016). Social studies pedagogy for Latino/a newcomer youth: Toward a theory of culturally and linguistically relevant citizenship education. *Theory & Research in Social Education, 44*(2), 147–183. https://doi.org/10.1080/00933104.2016.1170644

Jaffe-Walter, R., & Lee, S. J. (2018). Engaging the transnational lives of immigrant youth in public schooling: Toward a culturally sustaining pedagogy for newcomer immigrant youth. *American Journal of Education, 124*(3), 329–355. https://doi.org/10.1086/697215

Kaldor, N. (1970). The case for regional policies. *Scottish Journal of Political Economy, 17*(3), 337–348. https://doi.org/10.1111/j.1467-9485.1970.tb00496.x

Kang, H., & Raffaelli, M. (2016). Personalizing immigrant sacrifices: Internalization of sense of indebtedness toward parents among Korean American young adults. *Journal of Family Issues, 37*(10): 1331–1354. https://doi.org/10.1177/0192513X14560638

Keat, J. B., Strickland, M. J., & Marinak, B. A. (2009). Child voice: How immigrant children enlightened their teachers with a camera. *Early Childhood Education Journal, 37*, 13–21. https://doi.org/10.1007/s10643-009-0322-1

Kids in cages: Inhumane treatment at the border. (2025, March 24). https://www.congress.gov/event/116th-congress/house-event/LC64156/text

Kinsey, E. W., Kinsey, D., & Rundle, A. G. (2020). COVID-19 and food insecurity: An uneven patchwork of responses. *Journal of Urban Health, 97*, 332–335. https://doi.org/10.1007/s11524-020-00455-5

Kiramba, L. K., Kumi-Yeboah, A., Smith, P., & Sallar, A. M. (2021). Cultural and linguistic experiences of immigrant youth: Voices of African immigrant youth in United States urban schools. *Multicultural Education Review, 13*(1), 43–63. https://doi.org/10.1080/2005615X.2021.1886304

Kirksey, J. J., Sattin-Bajaj, C., Gottfried, M. A., Freeman, J., & Ozuna, C. S. (2020). Deportations near the schoolyard: Examining immigration enforcement and racial/ethnic gaps in educational outcomes. *Aera Open*, *6*(1). https://doi.org/10.1177/2332858419899074

Kittay, E. F. (2011). The ethics of care, dependence, and disability. *Ratio Juris*, *24*(1), 49–58. https://doi.org/10.1111/j.1467-9337.2010.00472.x

Knight, M. G. (2011). "It's already happening": Learning from civically engaged transnational immigrant youth. *Teachers College Record*, *113*(6), 1275–1292.

Lancy, D. F. (2012). Why anthropology of childhood? A brief history of an emerging discipline. *AnthropoChildren*, (2). http://popups.uliege.be/2034-8517/index.php?id=1629

Lancy, D. F. (2014). *The anthropology of childhood: Cherubs, chattel, changelings*. Cambridge University Press.

Lareau, A. (2003). *Unequal childhoods: Class, race, and family life*. University of California Press.

Lee, E. (2002). *At America's gates: Chinese immigration during the exclusion era, 1882–1943*. University of North Carolina Press.

Lee, E. (2015). *The making of Asian America: A history*. Simon & Schuster.

Lee, S. J., Park, E., & Wong, J.-H. S. (2017). Racialization, schooling, and becoming American: Asian American experiences. *Educational Studies: Journal of the American Educational Studies Association*, *53*(5), 492–510. https://doi.org/10.1080/00131946.2016.1258360

Lee, J., & Zhou, M. (2015). *The Asian American achievement paradox*. Russell Sage Foundation.

Levinson, B. A., & Holland, D. (1996). The cultural production of the educated person: An introduction. In B. A. Levinson, D. E. Foley, & D. C. Holland (Eds.), *The cultural production of the educated person: Critical ethnographies of schooling and local practice* (pp. 1–54). State University of New York Press.

Levitt, P. (2001). *The transnational villagers*. University of California Press.

Levitt, P. (2012). What's wrong with migration scholarship? A critique and a way forward. *Identities*, *19*(4), 493–500. https://doi.org/10.1080/1070289X.2012.676257

Li, S. S., Liddell, B. J., & Nickerson, A. (2016). The relationship between post-migration stress and psychological disorders in refugees and asylum seekers. *Current Psychiatry Reports*, *18*, 82. https://doi.org/10.1007/s11920-016-0723-0

Louie, V. (2012). *Keeping the immigrant bargain: The costs and rewards of success in America*. Russell Sage Foundation.

Lundberg, O. (2020). Defining and implementing social integration: A case study of school leaders' and practitioners' work with newly arrived im/migrant and refugee students. *International Journal of Qualitative Studies on Health and Well-Being*, *15*(sup2), 1783859. https://doi.org/10.1080/17482631.2020.1783859

Lupion, B. (2021). Por que a migração brasileira para os EUA explodium. *Made for Minds*. https://www.dw.com/pt-br/porque-amigra%C3%A7%C3%A3o-de-brasileiros-para-os-e ua-explodiu/a-60084542

Mahler, S. J. (1995). *American dreaming: Immigrant life on the margins*. Princeton University Press.

Mangual Figueroa, A. (2024). *Knowing silence: How children talk about immigration status in school*. University of Minnesota Press.

Mantoan E., Centeno V., & Feijo C. (2021). Financialization and Development Study Group (FINDE/UFF). Why has the Brazilian economy stagnated in the 2010s? A Minskyan analysis of the behavior of non-financial companies in a financialized economy. *Review of Evolutionary Political Economy, 2*(3), 529–550. doi: 10.1007/s43253-021-00051-6

Marsh, K. (2012). "The beat will make you be courage": The role of a secondary school music program in supporting young refugees and newly arrived immigrants in Australia. *Research Studies in Music Education, 34*(2), 93–111. https://doi.org/10.1177/1321103X12466138

Martin, D. A. (2005). Immigration policy and the post-9/11 world. *Transatlantic Trends: Immigration*.

Martin, P. (2006). The mounting costs of securing the "undefended" border. *Policy Options, 27*(3), 16–21.

Mason, J., & Hood, S. (2011). Exploring issues of children as actors in social research. *Children and Youth Services Review, 33*(4), 490–495. https://doi.org/10.1016/j.childyouth.2010.05.011

Masonbrink, A. R., & Hurley, E. (2020). Advocating for children during the COVID-19 school closures. *Pediatrics, 146*(3). https://doi.org/10.1542/peds.2020-1440

Massey, D. S., Durand, J., & Malone, N. J. (2002). *Beyond smoke and mirrors: Mexican immigration in an era of economic integration*. Russell Sage Foundation.

Massey, D. S., & Pren, K. A. (2012). Unintended consequences of US immigration policy: Explaining the post-1965 surge from Latin America. *Population and Development Review, 38*(1), 1–29. https://doi.org/10.1111/j.1728-4457.2012.00470.x

Mauss, M. (1925). *The gift: Forms and functions of exchange in archaic societies*. (I. Cunnison, trans.). Cohen & West (1966 English edition).

Mayall, B. (2002). Understanding childhoods: A London study. In *Conceptualising child-adult relations* (pp. 128–142). Routledge. https://doi.org/10.4324/9780203464872

McDevitt, S. E. (2021a). Teaching immigrant children: Learning from the experiences of immigrant early childhood teachers. *Journal of Early Childhood Teacher Education, 42*(2), 123–142. https://doi.org/10.1080/10901027.2020.1724167

McDevitt, S. E. (2021b). Through the lens of a Latino Jewish teacher: Uncovering funds of identity in teaching and advocating for newcomer immigrant children.

Journal of Latinos and Education, 22(4), 1–15. http://dx.doi.org/10.1080/15348431.2021.1974864

Mehta, S. N., Burger, Z. C., Meyers-Pantele, S. A., Garfein, R. S., Ortiz, D. O., Mudhar, P. K., . . . & Rodwell, T. (2022). Knowledge, attitude, practices, and vaccine hesitancy among the Latinx community in Southern California early in the COVID-19 pandemic: Cross-sectional survey. *JMIR Formative Research, 6*(8). https://doi.org/10.2196/38351

Menjívar, C. (2000). *Fragmented ties: Salvadoran immigrant networks in America*. University of California Press.

Menjívar, C., & Perreira, K. M. (2019). Undocumented and unaccompanied: Children of migration in the European Union and the United States. *Journal of Ethnic and Migration Studies, 45*(2), 197–217. https://doi.org/10.1080/1369183X.2018.1433025

Meyer, M., & Boggs, C. (2016). U.S. support for migration enforcement in Mexico: A humanitarian perspective. *Georgetown Journal of International Affairs, 17*(1), 28–37. https://doi.org/10.1353/gia.2016.0007

Migration Policy Institute [MPI]. (2023). Data Hub: State Immigration Data Profiles. https://www.migrationpolicy.org/data/state-profiles/state/demographics/MA

Migration Policy Institute [MPI]. (2024). Massachusetts: Demographics & social. https://www.migrationpolicy.org/data/state-profiles/state/demographics/MA

Miranda, C. P. (2017). Checks, balances, and resistance: The impact of an anti-immigrant federal administration on a school for immigrant teenagers. *Anthropology & Education Quarterly, 48*(4), 376–385. https://doi.org/10.1111/aeq.12215.

Mirra, N., & Garcia, A. (2020). "I hesitate but I do have hope": Youth speculative civic literacies for troubled times. *Harvard Educational Review, 90*(2), 295–321. https://doi.org/10.17763/1943-5045-90.2.295.

Montalvo, P. (2019). Resultados preliminares 2019: Barómetro de las Américas en Honduras. LAPOP. https://www.vanderbilt.edu/lapop/honduras/AB2018-19_Honduras_RRR_W_09.25.19.pdf

Moody, Z., & Darbellay, F. (2019). Studying childhood, children, and their rights: The challenge of interdisciplinarity. *Childhood, 26*(1), 8–21. https://doi.org/10.1177/0907568218798016

Ms. L v. Immigration and Customs Enforcement, 3:18-cv-00428 (2018). https://clearinghouse.net/case/16620/#:~:text=On%20September%204%2C%202019%2C%20Judge,the%20request%20to%2018%20parents

Murillo, M. A., Quartz, K. H., Garcia, L. W., & Liboon, C. A. (2021). Nested contexts of reception and K–12 schools: Addressing immigration status. *AERA Open, 7*(1), 1–13.

Nadasen, P. (2017). Rethinking care: Arlie Hochschild and the global care chain. *Women's Studies Quarterly, 45*(3/4), 124–128.

Nadasen, P. (2021). Rethinking care work: (Dis)affection and the politics of caring. *Feminist Formations, 33*(1), 165–188.

Nagasawa, M. K., & Swadener, B. B. (2017). Be/longing: Reciprocal mentoring, pedagogies of place, and critical childhood studies in the time of Trump. *Global Studies of Childhood*, 7(2), 207–221.

Ngai, M. M. (2004). *Impossible subjects: Illegal aliens and the making of modern America*. Princeton University Press.

Niles, M. T., Bertmann, F., Belarmino, E. H., Wentworth, T., Biehl, E., & Neff, R. (2020). The early food insecurity impacts of COVID-19. *Nutrients*, 12(7). https://doi.org/10.3390/nu12072096

Oliveira, G. (2018). *Motherhood across borders: Immigrants and their children in Mexico and in New York City*. New York University Press.

Oliveira, G. (2021a). Im/migrant children's stories in elementary school: Caring and making space in the classroom. *Diaspora, Indigenous, and Minority Education*, 15(4), 224–232.

Oliveira, G. (2021b). Im/migrant children's stories in elementary school: Caring and making space in the classroom. *Diaspora, Indigenous, and Minority Education*, 15(4), 224–232. https://doi.org/10.1080/15595692.2021.1944089

Oliveira, G. (2022, September 1). School is for hope. *The New York Times*. https://www.nytimes.com/2022/09/01/opinion/us-school-immigrant-children.html

Oliveira, G., & Gallo, S. (2021). "I have a story for you": Engaging with im/migrant children's politicized funds of knowledge in qualitative research. *International Journal of Qualitative Studies in Education*, 36(10), 1966–1980. https://doi.org/10.1080/09518398.2021.1956627

Oliveira, G., & Kentor, C. (2023). "It's part of me": Brazilian immigrant teachers' work in a global pandemic. *Gender, Work & Organization*, 30(2), 710–723.

Oliveira, G., & Segel, M. (2022). Im/migrant children's education experiences and families' sacrifices in a global pandemic. *Aera Open*, 8, https://doi.org/10.1177/23328584221092305

Orellana, M. F. (2009). *Translating childhoods: Immigrant youth, language, and culture*. Rutgers University Press.

Orellana, M. F., Thorne, B., Chee, A., & Lam, W. S. E. (2001). Transnational childhoods: The participation of children in processes of family migration. *Social Problems*, 48(4), 572–591. https://doi.org/10.1525/sp.2001.48.4.572

Ortner, S. B. (2006). *Anthropology and social theory: Culture, power, and the acting subject*. Duke University Press.

Page, K. R., & Flores-Miller, A. (2021). Lessons we've learned—Covid-19 and the undocumented Latinx community. *New England Journal of Medicine*, 384(1), 5–7. https://doi.org/10.1056/NEJMp2024897

Page, K. R., Venkataramani, M., Beyrer, C., & Polk, S. (2020). Undocumented US immigrants and Covid-19. *New England Journal of Medicine*, 382(21), e62. https://doi.org/10.1056/NEJMp2005953

Palmer, D. K., Martínez, R. A., Mateus, S. G., & Henderson, K. (2014). Reframing the debate on language separation: Toward a vision for translanguaging pedagogies in the dual language classroom. *The Modern Language Journal, 98*(3), 757–772. https://doi.org/10.1111/j.1540-4781.2014.12121.x

Panda, P. K., Gupta, J., Chowdhury, S. R., Kumar, R., Meena, A. K., Madaan, P., ... & Gulati, S. (2021). Psychological and behavioral impact of lockdown and quarantine measures for COVID-19 pandemic on children, adolescents and caregivers: A systematic review and meta-analysis. *Journal of Tropical Pediatrics, 67*(1). https://doi.org/10.1093/tropej/fmaa122

Park, J. Y. (2021). Contexts of reception as figured worlds: Recent-arrival immigrant youth in high school ESL and content-area classrooms. *Anthropology & Education Quarterly, 52*(3), 254–273. https://doi.org/10.1111/aeq.12364

Parreñas, R. S. (2005). *Children of global migration: Transnational families and gendered woes*. Stanford University Press.

Parreñas, R. S. (2021). *Unfree: Migrant domestic work in Arab States*. Stanford University Press.

Patchen, T. (2005). Prioritizing participation: Five things that every teacher needs to know to prepare recent immigrant adolescents for classroom participation. *Multicultural Education, 12*(4), 43.

Patel, L. (2016). *Decolonizing educational research: From ownership to answerability*. Routledge.

Paz, O. (1961). *The labyrinth of solitude: Life and thought in Mexico* (L. Kemp, Y. Milosz, & H. P. Alurista, trans.). Grove Press. (Original work published 1960)

Pelto, D. J., Ocampo, A., Garduño-Ortega, O., Barraza López, C. T., Macaluso, F., Ramirez, J., ... & Gany, F. (2020). The nutrition benefits participation gap: Barriers to uptake of SNAP and WIC among Latinx American immigrant families. *Journal of Community Health, 45*, 488–491. https://doi.org/10.1007/s10900-019-00765-z

Pier, L., Christian, M., Tymeson, H., & Meyer, R. H. (2021). COVID-19 impacts on student learning: Evidence from interim assessments in California. *Policy Analysis for California Education (PACE)*. https://edpolicyinca.org/publications/covid-19-impacts-student-learning

Plessner, H. (1975). *Die Stufen des Organischen und der Mensch. Einleitung in die philosophische Anthropologie, Gesammelte Schriften*, (The Levels of the organic and man: Introduction to philosophical anthropology, collected writings), Vol. 5. Suhrkamp.

Portes, A., & Rumbaut, R. G. (2014). *Immigrant America: A portrait*. University of California Press.

Prout, A., & James, A. (2015). A new paradigm for the sociology of childhood?: Provenance, promise and problems. In A. James & A. Prout (Eds.), *Constructing and reconstructing childhood* (pp. 6–28). Routledge. https://doi.org/10.4324/9780203362600-8

Quandt, S. A., LaMonto, N. J., Mora, D. C., Talton, J. W., Laurienti, P. J., & Arcury, T.

A. (2020). COVID-19 pandemic among Latinx farmworker and nonfarmworker families in North Carolina: Knowledge, risk perceptions, and preventive behaviors. *International Journal of Environmental Research and Public Health, 17*(16). https://doi.org/10.3390/ijerph17165786

Raghuram, P. (2016). Locating care ethics beyond the global north. *ACME: An International Journal for Critical Geographies, 15*(3), 511–533. https://acme-journal.org/index.php/acme/article/view/1353

Ramsay, G., & Askland, H. H. (2020). Displacement as condition: A refugee, a farmer and the teleology of life. *Ethnos, 87*(3), 600–621. https://doi.org/10.1080/00141844.2020.1804971

Reichman, D. R. (2022). Putting climate-induced migration in context: The case of Honduran migration to the USA. *Regional Environmental Change, 22*(3), 91. https://doi.org/10.1007/s10113-022-01946-8

Reynolds, J. F., & Orellana, M. F. (2009). New immigrant youth interpreting in white public space. *American Anthropologist, 111*(2), 211–223. https://doi.org/10.1111/j.1548-1433.2009.01114.x

Rios Casas, F., Ryan, D., Perez, G., Maurer, S., Tran, A. N., Rao, D., & Ornelas, I. J. (2020). "Se vale llorar y se vale reír": Latina immigrants' coping strategies for maintaining mental health in the face of immigration-related stressors. *Journal of Racial and Ethnic Health Disparities, 7*, 937–948. https://doi.org/10.1007/s40615-020-00746-0

Robertson, L. H., Drury, R., & Cable, C. (2014). Silencing bilingualism: A day in a life of a bilingual practitioner. *International Journal of Bilingual Education and Bilingualism, 17*(5), 610–623. https://doi.org/10.1080/13670050.2013.835978

Rodriguez, G. M. (2013). Power and agency in education: Exploring the pedagogical dimensions of funds of knowledge. *Review of Research in Education, 37*(1), 87–120. https://doi.org/10.3102/0091732X12462686

Rodriguez, S. (2015). The dangers of compassion: The positioning of refugee students in policy and education research and implications for teacher education. *Knowledge Cultures, 3*(2), 111–126.

Rodriguez, S. (2019). "We're building the community; it's a hub for democracy": Lessons learned from a library-based, school-district partnership and program to increase belonging for newcomer immigrant and refugee youth. *Children and Youth Services Review, 102*, 135–144. https://doi.org/10.1016/j.childyouth.2019.04.025

Rodriguez, S., Monreal, T., & Howard, J. (2020). "It's about hearing and understanding their stories": Teacher empathy and socio-political awareness toward newcomer undocumented students in the New Latino South. *Journal of Latinos and Education, 19*(2), 181–198. https://doi.org/10.1080/15348431.2018.1489812

Rodriguez, S., Roth, B. J., & Villarreal Sosa, L. (2022). "Immigration enforcement is a daily part of our students' lives": School social workers' perceptions of racialized nested contexts of reception for immigrant students. *Aera Open, 8*, https://doi.org/10.1177/23328584211073170

Rodriguez Kerr, K., Newhouse, K., & Vasudevan, L. (2020). Participatory, multimodal ethnography with youth. In A. Ibrahim & S. R. Steinberg (Eds.), *Critical youth research in education* (1st ed.). Routledge.

Rodriguez Vega, S. (2023). *Drawing deportation: Art and resistance among immigrant children.* New York University Press.

Roksa, J., & Potter, D. (2011). Parenting and academic achievement: Intergenerational transmission of educational advantage. *Sociology of Education, 84*(4), 299–321. https://doi.org/10.1177/0038040711417013

Ross, J., Diaz, C. M., & Starrels, J. L. (2020). The disproportionate burden of COVID-19 for immigrants in the Bronx, New York. *JAMA Internal Medicine, 180*(8), 1043–1044. https://doi.org/10.1001/jamainternmed.2020.2131

Roy, L., & Roxas, K. (2011). Whose deficit is this anyhow? Exploring counter-stories of Somali Bantu refugees' experiences in" doing school." *Harvard Educational Review, 81*(3), 521–542. https://doi.org/10.17763/haer.81.3.n4011r167648u186

Rumbaut, R. G. (2005). Children of immigrants and their achievement: The roles of family, acculturation, social class, gender, ethnicity, and school context. In R. D. Taylor (Ed.), *Addressing the achievement gap: Theory informing practice* (pp. 23–59). Information Age Publishing.

Ryu, M. (2013). "But at school . . . I became a bit shy": Korean immigrant adolescents' discursive participation in science classrooms. *Cultural Studies of Science Education, 8*, 649–671. https://doi.org/10.1007/s11422-012-9455-3

Saavedra, D. R. (2021). Leveraging affection: Embedded tensions in a teacher's relationships with students. *Curriculum & Teaching Dialogue, 23*, 71–86.

Said, E. (1978). *Orientalism.* Pantheon Books.

Sánchez, P. (2007). Urban immigrant students: How transnationalism shapes their world learning. *The Urban Review, 39*, 489–517. https://doi.org/10.1007/s11256-007-0051-8

Schanzenbach, D., & Pitts, A. (2020). Estimates of food insecurity during the COVID-19 crisis: Results from the COVID impact survey, week 1 (April 20–26, 2020). Institute for Policy Research Rapid Research Report. https://www.ipr.northwestern.edu/documents/reports/food-insecurity-covid_week1_report-13-may-2020.pdf

Schultz, K., & Coleman-King, C. (2012). Becoming visible: Shifting teacher practice to actively engage new immigrant students in urban classrooms. *Urban Review, 44*, 487–509. https://doi.org/10.1007/s11256-012-0209-7

Sepúlveda III, E. (2011). Toward a pedagogy of acompañamiento: Mexican migrant youth writing from the underside of modernity. *Harvard Educational Review, 81*(3), 550–573. https://doi.org/10.17763/haer.81.3.k6j2304422v43464

Sharma, M. (2018). Seeping deficit thinking assumptions maintain the neoliberal education agenda: Exploring three conceptual frameworks of deficit thinking in inner-city schools. *Education and Urban Society, 50*(2), 136–154. https://doi.org/10.1177/0013124516688325

Shirazi, R. (2018). Decentering Americanness: Transnational youth experiences of recognition and belonging in two US high schools. *Anthropology & Education Quarterly, 49*(2), 111–128. https://doi.org/10.1111/aeq.12243

Silver, L. J. (2020). Transformative childhood studies—a remix in inquiry, justice, and love. *Children's Geographies, 18*(2), 176–190. https://doi.org/10.1080/14733285.2019.1652633

Simon, S. S., Brucki, S. M. D., Fonseca, L. M., Becker, J., Cappi, C., Marques, A. H., . . . & Rivera-Mindt, M. (2023). The (in)visible Brazilians: A perspective review on the need for brain health and dementia research with Brazilian immigrants in the United States. *Alzheimer's and Dementia, 9*(3). doi: 10.1002/trc2.12425

Slavin, R. E., & Storey, N. (2020). The US educational response to the COVID-19 pandemic. *Best Evidence in Chinese Education, 5*(2), 617–633. https://eric.ed.gov/?id=EJ1288109

Small, M. L. (2009). *Unanticipated gains: Origins of network inequality in everyday life*. Oxford University Press.

Small, M. L., & Calarco, J. M. (2022). *Qualitative literacy: A guide to evaluating ethnographic and interview research*. University of California Press.

Smith, R. C. (2006). *Mexican New York: Transnational lives of new immigrants* (1st ed.). University of California Press. https://www.jstor.org/stable/10.1525/j.ctt1ppp41

Smith, L. T., Tuck, E., & Yang, K. W. (Eds.). (2018). *Indigenous and decolonizing studies in education: Mapping the long view*, 1st ed. Routledge. https://doi.org/10.4324/9780429505010

Smith-Morris, C. (2018). Care as virtue, care as critical frame: A discussion of four recent ethnographies. *Medical Anthropology, 37*(5), 426–432. https://doi.org/10.1080/01459740.2017.1416603

Soboroff, J. (2020). *Separated: Inside an American tragedy*. Custom House.

Socol, A. R. (2022). NAEP results show dismal learning loss due to pandemic. What can be done? The Education Trust. https://edtrust.org/the-equity-line/naep-results-show-dismal-learning-loss-due-to-pandemic-what-can-be-done/

Somerville, J., & Faltis, C. (2019). Dual languaging as strategy and translanguaging as tactic in two-way dual language programs. *Theory Into Practice, 58*(2), 164–175. https://doi.org/10.1080/00405841.2019.1569404

Southern Poverty Law Center. (2022, March 23). Family separation: A timeline. Southern Poverty Law Center. https://www.splcenter.org/resources/stories/family-separation-timeline/

Stargardter, G. (2021). A Brazilian town empties as migration to U.S. accelerates. Reuters. https://www.reuters.com/world/americas/brazilian-town-empties-migration-us-accelerates-2021-11-30/

Steimle, S., Gassman-Pines, A., Johnson, A. D., Hines, C. T., & Ryan, R. M. (2021).

Understanding patterns of food insecurity and family well-being amid the COVID-19 pandemic using daily surveys. *Child Development, 92*(5), e781–e797. https://doi.org/10.1111/cdev.13678

Straut-Eppsteiner, H. FY2024 EOIR Immigration Court Data: Caseloads and the pending cases backlog. (2025, April 20). https://www.congress.gov/crs-product/IN12492.

Suárez-Orozco, C., & Suárez-Orozco, M. M. (1995). *Transformations: Immigration, family life, and achievement motivation among Latino adolescents.* Stanford University Press.

Suárez-Orozco, C., & Suárez-Orozco, M. M. (2004). *Globalization: Culture and education in the new millennium.* University of California Press

Suárez-Orozco, C., Suárez-Orozco, M. M., & Todorova, I. (2008). *Learning a new land: Immigrant students in American society.* Harvard University Press.

Suárez-Orozco, C., Yoshikawa, H., Teranishi, R., & Suárez-Orozco, M. (2011). Growing up in the shadows: The developmental implications of unauthorized status. *Harvard Educational Review, 81*(3), 438–473. https://doi.org/10.17763/haer.81.3.g23x203763783m75

Sullivan, Stacy. (2018). No, the government did not make the deadline to reunify children with their parents. ACLU News and Commentary, July 27, 2018. https://www.aclu.org/news/immigrants-rights/no-government-did-not-make-deadline-reunify.

Takeuchi, M. (2015). The situated multiliteracies approach to classroom participation: English language learners' participation in classroom mathematics practices. *Journal of Language, Identity & Education, 14*(3), 159–178. https://doi.org/10.1080/15348458.2015.1030651

Talleyrand, R., Bailey, C. G., Saldana, M., Tran, J. T., & Li, Z. (2022). Exploring migration experiences of undocumented Latinx youth through a qualitative lens: Implications for mental health provide. *American Journal of Qualitative Research, 6*(3), 269–286. https://doi.org/10.29333/ajqr/12654

Telles, E. E., Ortiz, V., & Telles, E. M. (2008). *Generations of exclusion.* Russell Sage Foundation.

Terriquez, V. (2012). Civic inequalities? Immigrant incorporation and Latina mothers' participation in their children's schools. *Sociological Perspectives, 55*(4), 663–682. https://doi.org/10.1525/sop.2012.55.4.663

Thelen, T. (2021). Care as belonging, difference, and inequality. In *Oxford Research Encyclopedia of Anthropology.* https://doi.org/10.1093/acrefore/9780190225773.013.1399

Thibeault, M. A., Mendez, J. L., Nelson-Gray, R. O., & Stein, G. L. (2017). Impact of trauma exposure and acculturative stress on internalizing symptoms for recently arrived migrant-origin youth: Results from a community-based partnership. *Journal of Community Psychology, 45*(8), 984–998. https://doi.org/10.1002/jcop.21905

Tichenor, D. J. (2009). *Dividing lines: The politics of immigration control in America*. Princeton University Press.

Ticktin, M. I. (2011). *Casualties of care: Immigration and the politics of humanitarianism in France*. University of California Press.

Toppelberg, E. S., & Collins, B. A. (2010). Language, culture, and adaptation in immigrant children. *Child and Adolescent Psychiatric Clinics of North America, 19*(4), 697–717. https://doi.org/10.1016/j.chc.2010.07.003

Tronto, J. (1993). *Moral boundaries: A political argument for an ethic of care*. Routledge.

Tronto, J. C., & Fisher, B. (1990). Toward a feminist theory of caring. In E. Abel & M. Nelson (Eds.), *Circles of care* (pp. 36–54). State University of New York Press.

Trumbull, E., Greenfield, P. M., Rothstein-Fisch, C., Maynard, A. E., Quiroz, B., & Yuan, Q. (2020). From altered perceptions to altered practice: Teachers bridge cultures in the classroom. *School Community Journal, 30*(1), 243–266. http://www.schoolcommunitynetwork.org/SCJ.aspx

Turner, E. O. (2015). Districts' responses to demographic change: Making sense of race, class, and immigration in political and organizational context. *American Educational Research Journal, 52*(1), 4–39. https://doi.org/10.3102/0002831214560185

Turner, E. O., & Mangual Figueroa, A. (2019). Immigration policy and education in lived reality: A framework for researchers and educators. *Educational Researcher, 48*(8), 549–557. https://doi.org/10.3102/0013189X19879607

Turner, V. (1969). *The ritual process: Structure and anti-structure*. Aldine Publishing.

Twamley, K., Rosen, R., & Mayall, B. (2017). The (im) possibilities of dialogue across feminism and childhood scholarship and activism. *Children's Geographies, 15*(2), 249–255. https://doi.org/10.1080/14733285.2017.1282322

United Nations. (1998). Recommendations on statistics of international migration: Revision 1. unstats.un.org/unsd/publication/seriesm/seriesm_58rev1e.pdf

U.S. Customs and Border Protection. (n.d.). Migrant protection protocols FY2020. https://www.cbp.gov/newsroom/stats/migrant-protection-protocols

U.S. Immigration and Customs Enforcement. (2011). 2011 Operations Manual ICE Performance-Based National Detention Standards, Hold Rooms in Detention Facilities. https://www.ice.gov/doclib/detention-standards/2011/2-6.pdf

Valenzuela, A. (1999). *Subtractive schooling: U.S. Mexican youth and the politics of caring*. State University of New York Press.

Wallace, D. O. (2023). *The culture trap: Ethnic expectations and unequal schooling for Black youth*. Oxford University Press.

Ward, N., & Batalova, J. (2023). Frequently requested statistics on immigrants and immigration in the United States. *Migration Policy Institute, 14*. www.migrationpolicy.org/sites/default/files/publications/frs-print-2023.pdf

Waters, J., & Batalova, J. (2022). Brazilian immigrants in the United States. Migration Policy Institute. https://www.migrationpolicy.org/article/brazilian-immigrants-united-states

Watson, V. W., & Knight-Manuel, M. G. (2020). Humanizing the Black immigrant body: Envisioning diaspora literacies of youth and young adults from West African countries. *Teachers College Record, 122*(13), 1–28.

Weddle, H., & Oliveira, G. (2024). Imagining new possibilities through participatory qualitative methods. *International Journal of Qualitative Methods, 23.* https://doi.org/10.1177/16094069241301983

Wells, K. (2021). *Childhood in a global perspective.* Wiley.

Wilf, S., Maker Castro, E., Gupta, K. G., & Wray-Lake, L. (2022). Shifting culture and minds: Immigrant-origin youth building critical consciousness on social media. *Youth & Society,* https://doi.org/10.1177/0044118X221103890

Wilson, F. A., & Stimpson, J. P. (2020). US Policies increase vulnerability of immigrant communities to the COVID-19 pandemic. *Annals of Global Health, 86*(1), 57. https://doi.org/10.5334/aogh.2897

Wimmer, A., & Glick Schiller, N. (2002). Methodological nationalism and beyond: Nation-state building, migration and the social sciences. *Global Networks, 2*(4), 301–334. https://doi.org/10.1111/1471-0374.00043

Wolfson, J. A., & Leung, C. W. (2020). Food insecurity during COVID-19: An acute crisis with long-term health implications. *American Journal of Public Health, 110*(12), 1763–1765. https://doi.org/10.2105/AJPH.2020.305998

World Bank. (2020, April). *Poverty and equity brief: Latin America and the Caribbean: Brazil. April 2020.* https://databankfiles.worldbank.org/public/ddpext_download/poverty/33EF03BB-9722-4AE2-ABC7-AA2972D68AFE/Global_POVEQ_BRA.pdf

World Bank Group. (2023). *Tax revenue (% of GDP): Guatemala. World Bank Group Data.* https://data.worldbank.org/indicator/GC.TAX.TOTL.GD.ZS?locations=GT

World Economic Outlook Database. (2022). *Brazil: Gross domestic product, current prices and gross domestic product per capita, constant prices.* https://www.imf.org/en/Publications/WEO/weo-database/2022/April/weo-report?c=223,&s=NGDPD,NGDPRPC,&sy=2020&ey=2027&ssm=0&scsm=1&scc=0&ssd=1&ssc=0&sic=0&sort=country&ds=.&br=1

World Food Programme (2019). *Erratic weather patterns in the Central American dry corridor leave 1.4 million people in urgent need of food assistance.* https://www.wfpusa.org/news-release/erratic-weather-patterns-in-the-central-american-dry-corridor-leave-1-4-million-people-in-urgent-need-of-food-assistance/

Yarris, K. E. (2017). *Care across generations: Solidarity and sacrifice in transnational families.* Stanford University Press.

Yeates, N. (2012). Global care chains: A state-of-the-art review and future directions in care transnationalization research. *Global Networks, 12*(2), 135–154. https://doi.org/10.1111/j.1471-0374.2012.00345.x

Yoshikawa, H. (2011). *Immigrants raising citizens: Undocumented parents and their children*. Russell Sage Foundation.

Yoshino, K. (2007). *Covering: The hidden assault on our civil rights*. Random House.

Zatz, M. S., & Rodriguez, N. (2015). *Dreams and nightmares: Immigration policy, youth, and families*. University of California Press.

Zhou, M., & Bankston III, C. L. (1994). Social capital and the adaptation of the second generation: The case of Vietnamese youth in New Orleans. *International Migration Review, 28*(4), 821–845.

Zolberg, A. R. (2006). *A nation by design: Immigration policy in the fashioning of America*. Russell Sage Foundation.

INDEX

Page numbers in italics denote tables and figures. Endnotes are indicated by "n" followed by the endnote number.

9/11 attacks, 12, 191

Abrego, L. J., 39
Abu-Lughod, Lila, 15
activism, 105–10
Adichie, Chimamanda, 180
Adriana (youth from Brazil), 1, 75–76, 80, 143–44, 177
agency: children as agentive participants, 57, 59–60, 82, 184–85; classroom engagement and, 104–5; embodied political agency, 79–80
Alegría, Margarita, 70, 103
Allard, E. C., 116
alternate personhood, 61
Álvarez, K., 103
Anabelle (child from Brazil), 166
Andrade, Ms. (educator), 87, 89–90, 116–17, 152–53
Andrea (mother from Honduras), 52–54, 70, 71–73, 122, 139, 170
anthropology: author's ethnographic approach, 20–27, 24, 195–202; childhood studies, 59–62; of education, 15; spatial and temporal dimensions, 46–47. *See also* migration studies
anti-communism, 14
Askland, H. H., 79, 81
asset-based approaches to pedagogy, 113
asylum seekers, author's terminology, xi
Augusto (child from Guatemala), 150–51
Avila, E., 46

Barker, C., 82
Bartlett, L., 112
Beatriz (mother from Honduras), 133–34, 146–48
Bejarano, Alonso, 21
Bellino, M. J., 14
Bhabha, J., 184
Biden, Joseph: immigration policy under, 10–11, 14, 76, 193; migrant perspectives on, 155–56

229

230 Index

Black communities, family separation policy and, 14
Blitzer, Jonathan, 7
the body, refugee agency and, 79
Bolsonaro, Jair, 10

Brazil: children's migration narratives, 75–80, 77; migration trends and motivations, 5–7, 6, 9–11; parental migration narratives, 36–39, 47–50, 75. *See also* children's narratives of migration; COVID-19 pandemic; lost and found; parental narratives of migration; pedagogies of silence; reflections and recommendations
Briggs, Laura, 13–14
Brito, Ms. (educator), 91–92, 117, 152–53

cai-cai (migration strategy), 37, 76, 80
Calarco, J. M., 195, 197
care: constrained care, 85, 116–17; contested care spaces, 181–83; education and, 140–43; effects of COVID-19 on structures of, 118–19; meanings of sacrifice, 39–40; migration as form of, 19–20, 67; mobility as cultural elaboration of, 68; as responsibility, 185–87
Carlos (migrant youth), 167
Carly (child from Brazil), 175
Carpio, Glenda, 177–78
Cesar (child from El Salvador), 171–73
childhood studies, 59–62
children's narratives of migration: centering children's perspectives, 57–58, 81–82, 184–85; childhood studies, 59–62; embodiment of migration policy, 75–80, 77; Felipa, Daphne, and Francisco, 68–75, 74; Luz, 62–67; migration and childhood, 67–68
child standpoint theory, 60–61
China, migration trends, 11

Chinese Exclusion Act (1882), 12, 190
choices vs. decisions, 175–76
Cintia (mother from Brazil), 36–39, 121
climate migration, 9
Cohen, Elizabeth, 184
Cold War policy, 7, 14
Coll, Cynthia García, 181
Collins, B. A, 108–9
compounded trauma and loss, 17, 70
constructivism, childhood studies and, 59
COVID-19 pandemic: anxiety and hopefulness, 120–22, 143–48; author's approach during, 84, 199–200; care and education, 140–43; exacerbating inequities, 118–20, 122–28, 154–55; insights gained, 151–54; mental health impacts, 168–71; migrant apprehensions during, 5–7, 6; political context, 155–56; remote learning challenges, 136–39, 148–51; schooling and education, 128–36, 135; Title 42, invocation of, 14–15
cruel optimism, 112, 116
Cruz (child from El Salvador), 78–79, 80–81, 140–41, 155
culture: in migration studies, 18; pushing back against, 15–16; "socialization" in childhood studies, 59
cumulative causation, 11
Cusicanqui, Silvia, 201
Customs and Border Protection (CBP): migrant holding facilities, 147; migration trends (2017-2023), 5–7, 6, 37–38; zero-tolerance policy implementation, 12–13

Daiany (child from Brazil), 174–75
Daisy (mother from El Salvador), 132–33, 140–42
Daniel (youth from Guatemala), 105–7, 109, 159–64
Daniels, R., 11

Daphne (child from Honduras), 68–75, 76–78, 185
Davi (child from Brazil), 91–92, 121, 150
Dawson, Mrs. (educator), 107
decisions vs. choices, 175–76
Decolonizing Educational Research (Patel), 25
Decolonizing Ethnography (Bejarano et al.), 21
Deferred Action for Childhood Arrivals (DACA), 12, 192
De León, Jason, 7
Department of Homeland Security (DHS), 12–13, 191–92
determinism, childhood studies and, 59
Diana (mother from Guatemala), 96–97, 98, 99–103, 187
Diaz, Mrs. (educator), 94–95, 152–53
Diego (youth from Brazil), 75, 166–67
DiMarzio, K., 103
Displaced Persons Act (1948), 192
displacement, 79–80, 81
Drawing Deportation (Rodriguez Vega), 58
Dreby, Joanna, 39
Dryden-Peterson, Sarah, 181–82
Dylan (father from Guatemala), 93, 94–95, 121, 143, 168–69

Edgar (father from Guatemala), 42–45, 176
education: contested care spaces, 181–83; as currency of love and care, 15–17, 131–34, 140–43, 148; emphasis on English language learning, 105–10, 114–15; extant migrant studies scholarship, 17–18, 178–79; hope and, 157–58, 171–75; immigration in school curricula, 85, 107–8; inequitable effects of COVID-19, 118–20, 128–31, 154–55; as key motivator of migration, 2–3, 31–32, 55; "pedagogies of silence," 83–84; post-pandemic challenges, 168–71; remote learning challenges, 136–39; schooling vs., 133; topical constraints in the classroom, 92–93. *See also* COVID-19 pandemic; pedagogies of silence; reflections and recommendations
Electronic Benefits Transfer (P-EBT), 134–35, 135
El Salvador: children's migration narratives, 78–79, 80–81; migration trends (2017-2023), 5–8, 6. *See also* children's narratives of migration; COVID-19 pandemic; lost and found; parental narratives of migration; pedagogies of silence; reflections and recommendations
embodiment, of migration policy, 75–80, 77
Emily (mother from Brazil), 120
enculturation, 59
English language instruction, 105–10, 114–15
ethnography, author's approach and, 20–27, 24, 195–202
Everyone Who Is Gone Is Here (Blitzer), 7

family migration: author's approach, xi, 1–4, 20–27, 24, 195–202; education as currency of love, 15–17, 131–34, 148; extant scholarship, 17–19; as form of care, 19–20, 67; immigration policy overview, 11–15, 189–93; mental health and, 103–4, 141–42, 168–71; migration trends, 4–11, 6; text overview, 27–30. *See also* children's narratives of migration; COVID-19 pandemic; lost and found; parental narratives of migration; pedagogies of silence; reflections and recommendations

family separation: adoption of zero-tolerance policy, 12–13, 36; *cai-cai* (migration strategy), 37, 76, 80; children's narratives (William), 93; historical antecedents, 13–14; parental narratives (Beatriz), 146–48; parental narratives (Edgar), 43–45; parental narratives (Julio), 32–36, 50–51; parental narratives (Melanie), 40–43; parental narratives (Melissa), 48–49
Fatima (mother from Guatemala), 132, 157–58, 159–65
Felipa (youth from Honduras), 68–75, 74, 170–71
feminist theory, 20, 60–61
Ferguson, J., 200
Fernando (father from Guatemala), 105–6, 159–65
Flavia (migrant youth), 167
Flor (child from Brazil), 87–89, 121
Flor (mother from Guatemala), 105–6, 108
Flores, Andrea, 179, 181
Flores v. Reno (1985), 191
Francisco (child from Honduras), 71–74, 74, 185
Freire, Paulo, 96
functionalism, childhood studies and, 59

Gabriel (father from Brazil), 150
Gallo, Sarah, 88, 113
gang violence, 7–8, 10, 52, 96, 100, 105–6, 124
García, M.A.M., 21
gender: gender-based divisions in shelters, 34; in migrant studies, 18, 19; pressures faced by men, 44; problematic traditions in anthropology, 61–62; separation based on, 24, 40, 88, 126, 162
The Gift (Mauss), 16

gift-giving, 16
Giselly (youth from Brazil), 175
Gluckman, M., 14
Goldstein, D. M., 21
Gomez, Mrs. (educator), 98–99
gratitude, politics of, 110–13
Guatemala: children's migration narratives, 62–67, 79; migration trends and motivations, 5–9, 6; parental migration narratives, 32–36, 40–45. *See also* children's narratives of migration; COVID-19 pandemic; lost and found; parental narratives of migration; pedagogies of silence; reflections and recommendations
Gupta, A., 200
Gutierrez, Ms. (educator), 117, 150–52

Haddad, Fernando, 10
Häkli, J., 79
Heidbrink, L., 39, 67–68
Hernández, César Cuauhtémoc García, 184
Holland, D., 15
Homeland Security Act (2002), 191
Hondagneu-Sotelo, P., 46
Honduras: children's migration narratives, 68–75, 74, 76–78; migration trends and motivations, 5–8, 6; parental migration narratives, 52–54. *See also* children's narratives of migration; COVID-19 pandemic; lost and found; parental narratives of migration; pedagogies of silence; reflections and recommendations
Hopkins, Miss (educator), 112
Horst, Cindy, 181–82

Ian (father from Guatemala), 96–98, 99–100

identity: classroom engagement approaches and, 104–5; displacement and, 79–80
"illegal alien" category, 11–12, 189–90
Illegal Immigration Reform and Immigrant Responsibility Act (1996), 12, 191
"I'm Here but I'm There" (Avila and Hondagneu-Sotelo), 46
immigrants. *See* migrants
Immigrant Stories (Coll and Marks), 181
Immigration Act (1917), 12, 190
Immigration Act (1924), 12, 190
Immigration and Customs Enforcement (ICE), 34, 57, 79, 102, 192
Immigration and Nationality Act (1965), 12, 53, 190–91
Immigration and Naturalization Service (INS), 191–92
Immigration Reform and Control Act (1986), 12, 191
Indigenous peoples, 14, 21
inequity: in care and caregiving, 20; inequitable effects of COVID-19, 118–20, 122–28, 154–55; macro structures affecting migrants, 177–78; poverty as motivation for migration, 7–10; poverty in children's narratives, 66–67
International Schools network, 114

Jair (child from Honduras), 123–27
Javier (father from Honduras), 70, 71
Jonas, Miss (educator), 139
José (youth from Honduras), 123–27, 137–38
Juárez, L. L., 21
Juarez, Yazmin, 57
Juliana (migrant youth from Brazil), 75, 110–11

Julio (father from Guatemala), 32–36, 50–51, 121, 138, 185–86

Kallio, K. P., 79
Karina (mother from Brazil), 173–75, 179, 202
"Kids in Cages: Inhumane Treatment at the Border" (2019), 57
KIND (Kids in Need of Defense), 58

Lareau, Annette, 195
Latin America: as common place of origin, 11; family separation policies, Cold War-era, 14; in migration studies, 17–19; U.S. contributions to instability in, 7
learning lag, 154
Levinson, B. A., 15
liminality, 26
Link, H., 113
listening re-alignments, 88
"Lived Civics" curriculum, 113
loss, compounded, 17, 70
lost and found: decisions vs. choices, 175–76; family narratives, 159–65; hope and education, 157–58, 171–75; "lives lived in relief," 159; mental health, 168–71; the right to feel, 166–68
Lucas (youth from Guatemala), 111
Luz (child from Guatemala), 32–36, 62–67, 138, 145, 185–86

Machado, Ms. (educator), 112
Manning, Mrs. (educator), 112
Maria Clara (child from Brazil), 121, 145, 148
Marks, Amy Kerivan, 181
Massachusetts: author's methodology and, 23; migration trends, 11

Matos, Mrs. (educator), 152–54
Maurer, S., 103
Mauss, Maurice, 16
Melanie (mother from Guatemala), 40–43, 45, 111, 176
Melissa (mother from Brazil), 47–50, 75, 111
mental health, 103–4, 141–42, 168–71
methodological nationalism, 4
Mexico: 2014 southern border strategy, 182; Migrant Protection Protocols implementation, 14; migration trends (2017-2023), 5–7, 6, 10; notions of sacrifice, 39; parental narratives of migration through, 49, 53. *See also* Migrant Protection Protocols (MPP); U.S.-Mexico border
Migrant Aesthetics (Carpio), 177–78
Migranthood (Heidbrink), 67–68
Migrant Protection Protocols (MPP): children's embodiment of, 75–80, 77; historical antecedents, 190; implementation of, 14; parental experiences of, 52, 53–54. *See also* U.S.-Mexico border
migrants: author's terminology, xi–xii; immigration and mental health, 103–4, 141–42, 168–71; immigration in school curricula, 85, 107–8; inequitable effects of COVID-19 on, 118–20, 122–28; macro structures affecting, 177–78; misconceptions about, 100; nonlinear narratives of, 68, 164–65; paradoxical feelings of, 110–12, 158, 166–68; reflections on political contexts, 155–56; single-story stereotypes, 179–81; spatial and temporal experiences of, 46–47, 63, 65, 142–43, 181. *See also* children's narratives of migration; COVID-19 pandemic; lost and found; parental narratives of migration; pedagogies of silence; reflections and recommendations
Migrating to Prison (Hernández), 184
migration policy: children's embodiment of, 75–80, 77; focus on detention and deportation, 183–84; importance of educator training on, 182–83; strategic use of confusion, 50–51; US history of, 11–15, 189–93. *See also* Migrant Protection Protocols (MPP)
migration studies: author's ethnographic approach, 20–27, 24, 195–202; centering children's perspectives, 184–85; education outcomes and, 178–79; extant scholarship, 17–19; resisting linear narratives within, 164–65; spatial and temporal dimensions, 46–47, 181
Mila (mother from Guatemala), 142–43
Monroe, James, 7
Monroe Doctrine, 7
Motherhood Across Borders (Oliveira), 39
Muslim communities, 12

Natalia (mother from El Salvador), 131–32, 171–73
Naturalization Act (1790), 11–12, 189
Ngai, Mae, 11, 189–90
"Not a Sack of Potatoes" (Bhabha), 184

Obama, Barack: *cai-cai* (migration strategy) and, 37, 76, 80; deportations under, 12, 192; refugee policy under, 14
obligation, in scholarship, 20
Office of Refugee Resettlement (ORR), 58
Oliveira, G., 39, 112
Operation Gatekeeper (1994), 191

Operation Hold the Line (1993), 191
organized crime, 7–8, 10, 52, 96, 100, 105–6, 159
Ornelas, I. J., 103
Ortner, S. B., 20–21

Page Act (1875), 12, 190
Paloma (child from Honduras), 146–48
parental narratives of migration: centrality of education, 31–32, 55; Cintia and Ricardo, 36–39; complexities in, 32, 55–56; COVID-19 and, 47–50; Edgar, 43–45; (un)fulfilled promises, 50–54; Julio, 32–36; Melanie, 40–43; narratives of sacrifice, 39–40; spatial and temporal dimensions, 46–47
Patel, Leigh, 25
pedagogies of silence: authentic engagement, 113–15; characterized, 83–84; classroom constraints, 87–93, 182; constrained care, 85, 116–17; family narratives, 96–105; past as concern, 93–96, 116; promises and lies, 110–12; remote learning, 148–51; role of educators, 85–86; youth and activism, 105–10
Pedagogy of the Oppressed (Freire), 96
Pedro (father from Guatemala), 142–43
Peixoto, Mrs. (school psychologist), 112
Perez, G., 103
Plessner, H., 79
Plyler v. Doe (1982), 191
politics of encounters, 79
Portes, Alejandro, 108
poverty: in children's narratives of migration, 66–67; as motivation for migration, 7–10
power, knowledge production and, 21
prison-industrial complex, 183–84

race, in immigration legislation, 11–12, 190
Ramsay, G., 79, 81
Rao, D., 103
Reagan, Ronald, 12, 191
Real ID Act (2005), 192
reciprocity, 16–17, 201
reflections and recommendations: centering children's perspectives, 184–85; changing narratives around migrants, 177–79; contested care spaces, 181–83; political landscapes, 183–84; responsibility of care, 185–87; single-story stereotypes, 179–81
refugee policy, 14, 81, 192–93
relationality, in ethnographic research, 25
"remain in Mexico policy." *See* Migrant Protection Protocols (MPP)
Ricardo (father from Brazil), 36–39
Rios Casas, F., 103
Rita (migrant youth), 167–68
Rodriguez Vega, Silvia, 58
Rosa (youth from Guatemala), 105–9, 159–64
Ryan, D., 103

sacrifice, meanings of, 39–40
Said, Edward, 21
Santana, Mrs. (educator), 112
Santo (child from Guatemala), 96–99, 145
Secure Fence Act (2006), 192
Separated (Soboroff), 36
September 11th attacks, 12, 191
Sessions, Jeff, 23, 93
Shire, Warsan, 55
Small, M. L., 25, 195, 197
Smith, L. T., 21
Soboroff, Jacob, 36

social embodiment, 79
socialization, 59
social networks, migration patterns and, 11
Soldiers and Kings (De León), 7
Souza, Mrs. (educator), 153–54

Taking Children (Briggs), 13–14
Title 42 expulsion, 14–15, 193
Toppelberg, E. S., 108–9
Tran, A. N., 103
transborder thinking, 113–14
trauma: compounded, 17, 70, 141–42, 168–71; in educational settings, 93–96, 116; family narratives, 96–105. *See also* pedagogies of silence
Trump, Donald: 2024 re-election, 183; first-term immigration policy, 12–13, 14–15, 76; migrant perspectives on, 155–56; termination of MPP program, 93
Trump v. Hawaii (2018), 12
Tuck, E., 21
Turner, Victor, 26

Ungemah, L., 112
UNICEF, 58
United Nations, xi
United Nations Refugee Convention (1951), 192
United States: destabilizing influence of, 7; immigration policy overview, 11–15, 189–93; migration trends, 4–11, 6. *See also* children's narratives of migration; COVID-19 pandemic; lost and found; parental narratives of migration; pedagogies of silence; reflections and recommendations
USA Patriot Act (2001), 12, 191

U.S. Citizenship and Immigration Services (USCIS), 192
U.S.-Mexico border: 2006 Secure Fence Act, 192; *cai-cai* (migration strategy) and, 80; children's experiences of, 70–72, 76–78, 81–82; Migrant Protection Protocols implementation, 14; migration trends (2017-2023), 5–7, 6, 10, 37–38; parents' experiences of, 97, 100–102, 160–63, 171–74; zero-tolerance policy implementation, 12–13, 36. *See also* Migrant Protection Protocols (MPP)

Vinny (child from Brazil), 87, 88–91, 121, 150
violence, as motivation for migration, 7–9, 33–34, 52, 100, 105–6, 159
Vivi (child from Guatemala), 105–6, 108–9, 159–64

Wallace, Derron, 195
War on Terror, 12, 191
William (child from Guatemala), 79, 93–95, 145, 168–69
women: immigration-related stressors, 103; problematic traditions in anthropology, 61–62

Yanet (mother from Honduras), 26, 120, 123–27, 136–38, 184
Yang, K. W., 21
Yarris, K. E., 19
youth activism, 105–10

zero-tolerance policy: adoption of, 12–13, 36; *cai-cai* (migration strategy) and, 80. *See also* family separation; Migrant Protection Protocols (MPP)
Zolberg, A. R., 11